T0135775

Technisch-Naturwissenschaftliche
Fakultät

Extending BPMN with Deontic Logic

DISSERTATION

zur Erlangung des akademischen Grades

Doktorin

im Doktoratsstudium der

Technischen Wissenschaften

Eingereicht von:

DI (FH) Christine D. Natschläger-Carpella, MA

Angefertigt am:

Institut für Anwendungsorientierte Wissensverarbeitung

Beurteilung:

Prof. Dr. Klaus-Dieter Schewe (Betreuung)

Univ.-Prof. Dr. Gabriele Kotsis

Linz, Juni 2012

Bibliografische Information der Deutschen Nationalbibliothek

Die Deutsche Nationalbibliothek verzeichnet diese Publikation in der
Deutschen Nationalbibliografie; detaillierte bibliografische Daten sind
im Internet über http://dnb.d-nb.de abrufbar.

ISBN 978-3-8325-3225-3

Logos Verlag Berlin GmbH
Comeniushof, Gubener Str. 47,
10243 Berlin
Tel.: +49 (0)30 42 85 10 90
Fax: +49 (0)30 42 85 10 92
INTERNET: http://www.logos-verlag.de

Danksagung

Mein größter Dank gilt meinem Betreuer, Prof. Dr. Klaus-Dieter Schewe, welcher meine Forschung in den letzten Jahren betreut und somit die Erstellung dieser Dissertation ermöglicht hat. Mit seinem umfangreichen Wissen und seiner großen Erfahrung unterstützte er mich bei vielen schwierigen Aufgaben wie der Themenfindung oder Abgrenzung dieser Arbeit, und half mir, auf dem richtigen "Pfad" zu bleiben.

Bedanken möchte ich mich auch bei Univ.-Prof. Dr. Gabriele Kotsis, welche mich seit Beginn des Doktoratsstudiums betreute und in mehreren Dissertantenseminaren eine wissenschaftliche Vorgehensweise lehrte. Ihr verdanke ich außerdem viele wertvolle Ratschläge sowie eine kompetente Unterstützung bei der Erstellung dieser Arbeit.

Besonderer Dank gilt auch meinem Arbeitgeber, dem Software Competence Center Hagenberg (SCCH), welcher mir die Möglichkeit zur Durchführung dieser Dissertation bot. Die Forschung wurde im Rahmen des Projekts *Vertical Model Integration* (VMI) durch das Programm "Regionale Wettbewerbsfähigkeit OÖ 2007-2013" aus Mitteln des Europäischen Fonds für Regionale Entwicklung sowie aus Mitteln des Landes Oberösterreich gefördert. Ich möchte mich außerdem bei allen Kollegen für ihre vielen Vorschläge und Anmerkungen bedanken.

Zuletzt möchte ich mich noch bei meiner Familie bedanken: bei meinem Mann, Martin Carpella, für die vielen Diskussionen und das Interesse an meiner Arbeit, bei meinen Eltern, Edith und Franz Natschläger, für die ermöglichte Ausbildung und die von ihnen geweckte naturwissenschaftliche Begeisterung, sowie bei meinem Bruder, Andreas Natschläger, für seine moralische Unterstützung.

Kurzfassung

Die *Business Process Model and Notation* (BPMN) ist ein weitverbreiteter Standard zur Geschäftsprozessmodellierung und wird von der *Object Management Group* (OMG) verwaltet. Nachteile von BPMN sind jedoch die eingeschränkten Organisationsmodellierungskonzepte sowie die ausschließlich implizite Darstellung der Modalitäten durch die Struktur des Prozessflusses. Zusätzlich sind die syntaktischen Definitionen der BPMN Spezifikation in mehreren Fällen unpräzise, unvollständig, oder widersprüchlich. Die vorliegende Dissertation greift diese Probleme auf und präsentiert eine formale syntaktische Definition sowie eine Erweiterung von BPMN mit deontischen Konzepten zur expliziten Darstellung der Modalitäten und Unterstützung bei der Akteursmodellierung.

Der erste Teil dieser Arbeit umfasst die formale Definition der BPMN Syntax im Rahmen einer Ontologie. Diese Ontologie basiert auf der finalen Version von BPMN 2.0 und wird *BPMN 2.0 Ontology* genannt. Die *BPMN 2.0 Ontology* enthält die syntaktischen Definitionen aus dem BPMN Metamodell sowie den textuellen Abschnitten der Spezifikation und deckt mehrere Widersprüche im Standard auf. Die Ontologie kann sowohl als Wissensbasis für BPMN Elemente sowie zur syntaktischen Überprüfung von konkreten BPMN Modellen verwendet werden. Ein Vorteil der ontologie-basierten syntaktischen Überprüfung ist die mögliche Ableitung von zusätzlichem Wissen.

Im zweiten Teil dieser Arbeit werden Geschäftsprozessmodellierungssprachen (business process modeling languages, BPMLs) im Allgemeinen, und im Speziellen BPMN, mit deontischer Logik erweitert, um die Modalitäten explizit darzustellen. Dies ermöglicht eine präzise Spezifikation der von Verpflichtungen und Rechten abgeleiteten Konzepte. Nach einer Einführung in verschiedene deontische Klassifikationen enthält dieser Teil der Dissertation eine Diskussion von benutzerbestimmten oder bedingten Entscheidungen. Die Anwendung der deontischen Konzepte kann in unterschiedlichen Ausprägungsstufen erfolgen. Ein weiterer wesentlicher Bestandteil ist die deontische Klassifikation aller *Workflow Patterns*, die den Kontrollfluss betreffen. Da die *Workflow Patterns* unabhängig von konkreten BPMLs definiert wurden, kann die deontische Erweiterung mit geringem Aufwand an konkrete BPMLs, wie z.b. BPMN, angepasst werden. Das Ergebnis der Erweiterung von BPMN mit deontischen Konzepten wird *Deontic BPMN* genannt. Die deontische Klassifikation wird durch Pfadanalysen unterstützt und die Vorteile von *Deontic BPMN* werden anhand einer Fallstudie und einer Umfrage demonstriert. Des Weiteren wird ein neuer Ansatz zur Modellierung von Akteuren basierend auf deontischer Logik und *Speech Act Theory* vorgestellt und anhand der Ressourcen-bezogenen *Workflow Patterns* evaluiert.

Der dritte und letzte Teil dieser Dissertation zeigt die Definition eines Graphentransformationssystems namens *DeonticBpmnGTS*, welches Modelle einer Teilmenge von BPMN nach *Deontic BPMN* transformiert. *DeonticBpmnGTS* basiert auf dem algebraischen Graphentransformationsansatz und definiert einen attribuierten Typgraph mit Vererbungsbeziehungen sowie mehrere Transformationsregeln mit positiven und negativen Anwendungsbedingungen. Die Transformation von BPMN nach *Deontic BPMN* ist global deterministisch, wie durch den Nachweis der strengen AC-Konfluenz und der Terminierung bewiesen wird. Der Terminierungsbeweis erfordert jedoch eine Auflösung der Vererbungsbeziehungen (Flattening) in *DeonticBpmnGTS*. Zu diesem Zweck wird ein entsprechender Flattening Algorithmus definiert und als Prototyp implementiert.

Abstract

The *Business Process Model and Notation* (BPMN) is a widely-used standard for business process modeling and is maintained by the *Object Management Group* (OMG). However, major drawbacks of BPMN are the limited support for organizational modeling and the only implicit expression of modalities through the structure of the process flow. In addition, the syntactical definitions of the BPMN specification are in several cases inaccurate, incomplete, or inconsistent. The current work addresses these issues and provides a formal definition of the BPMN syntax as well as an extension of BPMN with deontic concepts to highlight modalities and support actor modeling.

The first contribution of this thesis is the definition of an ontology that formally represents the syntactical definitions of BPMN. This ontology is based on the final release of BPMN 2.0 and is called the *BPMN 2.0 Ontology*. The *BPMN 2.0 Ontology* comprises the syntactical definitions from the BPMN metamodel and the natural text of the specification and reveals several contradictions in the standard. The ontology can be used as a knowledge base to investigate the BPMN elements and for syntax checking of concrete BPMN models. A major advantage of the ontology-based syntax checker is the possibility to also infer additional knowledge.

The second contribution is an extension of business process modeling languages (BPMLs) in general and BPMN in particular with deontic logic to highlight modalities and provide a precise specification of concepts adapted from obligations and permissions. This contribution comprises an introduction to possible deontic classifications, a discussion of user and conditional choices, and several gradations concerning the extent to which deontic logic can be used in process flows. Furthermore, the control-flow perspective of the *Workflow Patterns* is extended with deontic concepts. Since the *Workflow Patterns* are independent of concrete BPMLs, the deontic extension can be easily adapted for most concrete BPMLs including BPMN. The result of the extension of BPMN with deontic concepts is called *Deontic BPMN*. The

deontic analysis is supported by a path exploration approach and the benefits of *Deontic BPMN* are demonstrated by a case study and a preliminary
survey. Another issue addressed in this work is the limited support for actor
modeling in BPMN. A new approach including deontic logic and speech act
theory is proposed and evaluated based on the resource perspective of the
Workflow Patterns.

Finally, the third contribution of this thesis is the definition of *DeonticBpmn-
GTS*, a graph transformation system that transforms models from a subset
of BPMN to *Deontic BPMN*. *DeonticBpmnGTS* is based on the algebraic
graph transformation approach and consists of an attributed type graph with
inheritance and several transformation rules with positive and negative application conditions. In order to show that the transformation from BPMN to
Deontic BPMN is globally deterministic, it is proven that *DeonticBpmnGTS*
is strictly AC-confluent and terminating. Due to inheritance relationships
in the type graph, the termination proof requires a flattening of *Deontic-
BpmnGTS*, so a flattening algorithm is proposed and a flattening prototype
developed.

Contents

List of Figures

Chapter 1

Introduction

The goal of this thesis is to extend the *Business Process Model and Notation* (BPMN) with deontic concepts to highlight modalities and support actor modeling. The first section starts with an overview of the research domain and provides the motivation. Subsequently, the objectives of the current work as well as three hypotheses are presented. The final section concludes with an outline of subsequent chapters.

1.1 Motivation

Efficient business processes are a key factor for a company's success and are addressed by the discipline *Business Process Management* (BPM), which comprises the definition, implementation, control, and improvement of business processes. BPM is supported by a number of technologies and disciplines, whose maturity is described once a year within Gartner's BPM Hype Cycle (see [29] for the BPM Hype Cycle 2011). Important concepts of BPM are the modeling and execution of business processes, which are summarized under the term *BPM standards*. According to Gartner's BPM Hype Cycle, BPM standards are currently in the *Trough of Disillusionment* phase and it is assumed that they will reach productivity in approximately five to ten years. Thus, BPM standards are still a demanding research area and issues like process design reuse and process implementation portability must be addressed. However, it is also mentioned that the user acceptance of key BPM standards like the *Business Process Model and Notation* (BPMN) contributes positively to the overall rating (cf. for this paragraph [29]).

BPMN is a popular and successful standard for business process modeling and is maintained by the *Object Management Group* (OMG). The current version, BPMN 2.0, was published in January 2011. BPMN addresses business analysts and technical developers and has already reached a high maturity level (cf. [29], [105]); however, major drawbacks of BPMN consist in the following issues:

1. contradictions in the syntactical definitions,

2. limited support for organizational modeling, and

3. only implicit expression of modality (obligation, permission) through the structure of the process flow.

The first issue are contradictions in the syntactical definitions of the BPMN specification. The BPMN specification only provides a semi-formal definition of the BPMN metamodel in form of class diagrams, corresponding tables specifying the attributes and model associations, as well as XML schemas (see Fig. 1.1 for an extract of the BPMN metamodel). However, the definition of an element in the class diagram is partly overlapping with the refined specification in the corresponding table and redundant to the XML schema. Thus, the description of the metamodel is in several cases inconsistent and contradictory. For example, considering the *Transaction* element, the class diagram specifies two attributes, *protocol* and *method*, both of type string (see Fig. 1.1(a)), but in the corresponding table only *method* is mentioned and defined to be of type *TransactionMethod* (see Fig. 1.1(b)). Moreover, the XML schema defines the default value "Compensate" (see Fig. 1.1(c)), which is missing in the attribute description of the table. For a full definition of an element, it is further necessary to consider the specification of all superclasses (cf. for this paragraph [99]).

So the BPMN metamodel describes the structure of the elements including their attributes and relationships, however, further syntactical rules are defined within the natural text of the BPMN specification, for example: "The Start Event trigger (EventDefinition) MUST be from the following types: Message, Error, Escalation, Compensation, Conditional, Signal, and Multiple [...]" [99, p. 177]. The natural language definitions are informal and, thus, sometimes inaccurate (e.g., the *Timer* trigger is missing) or again contradictory with each other or with the BPMN metamodel. The identification of contradictions is complicated by the distribution of the natural language definitions across various sections (e.g., *StartEvents* are described several times within the chapter *Overview* (see [99, p. 40, 57, 61f]), in chapters *Process*

([99, p. 238ff]), *Choreography* ([99, p. 339f]) and *BPMN Execution Seman-tics* ([99, p. 439f]), as well as in sections describing other elements that can comprise or connect to *StartEvents*, e.g., *EventSubProcesses* ([99, p. 177]]). Furthermore, the BPMN 2.0 specification is quite comprehensive and spans more than 500 pages. A detailed list of contradictions in the BPMN specification is provided in appendix A.2. So, the missing formal definition of BPMN leads to several problems including inaccuracy and inconsistency (cf. for this paragraph [99]).

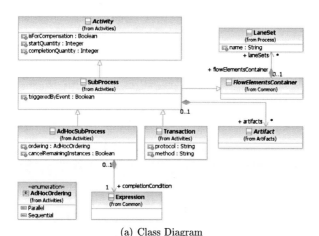

(a) Class Diagram

Attribute Name	Description/ Usage
method: Transac-tion-Method	The method is an attribute that defines the Transaction method used to commit or cancel a Transaction. For executable Processes, it SHOULD be set to a technology specific URI [...]. For compatibility with BPMN 1.1, it can also be set to "##compensate", "##store", or "##image".

(b) Corresponding Table

```xml
<xsd:element name="transaction"
  type="tTransaction"
  substitutionGroup="flowElement"/>
<xsd:complexType name="tTransaction">
    <xsd:complexContent>
        <xsd:extension base="tSubProcess">
            <xsd:attribute name="method"
              type="tTransactionMethod"
              default="Compensate"/>
        </xsd:extension>
    </xsd:complexContent>
</xsd:complexType>

<xsd:simpleType name="tTransactionMethod">
    <xsd:restriction base="xsd:string">
        <xsd:enumeration value="Compensate"/>
        <xsd:enumeration value="Image"/>
        <xsd:enumeration value="Store"/>
    </xsd:restriction>
</xsd:simpleType>
```

(c) XML schema

Figure 1.1: BPMN Metamodel: Element *Transaction* (Source: [99])

The second issue is the limited support for organizational modeling in BPMN. According to the BPMN specification (see [99, p. 22]), BPMN only supports those concepts of modeling that are applicable to business processes, whereas, for example, the definition of organizational models and resources is out of the scope of BPMN. However, one of the five basic categories of BPMN elements is called *Swimlanes* and provides two concepts, *Pools* and *Lanes*, which can be used to model participants (see Fig. 1.2) [99]. These two concepts reveal the need for organizational modeling and are frequently used by BPMN modelers (see [65]), but are also repeatedly criticized for their restrictive support for organizational modeling [105, 106, 139]. The modeling of participants (i.e., entities and roles (cf. [99, p. 502])) is limited by the fact that an activity can only be located in at most one lane. This leads to the following issues:

1. Expressiveness: BPMN does not provide the possibility to express that an activity (e.g., a sub-process) can be executed by two or more roles in collaboration.

2. Inaccuracy: Lanes may comprise all types of elements including those that are automatically executed, like business rules and scripts (see activity *Script* in Fig. 1.2).

3. Redundancy: An activity that is executed by two or more roles on parallel or alternative paths must be duplicated for every additional lane (see activity *B* in Fig. 1.2).

So organizational modeling is out of the scope of BPMN, but, nevertheless, the pool and lane concepts are defined. However, these concepts are specified in a restrictive manner, which not only limits the expressiveness, but also leads to further problems like inaccuracy and redundancy.

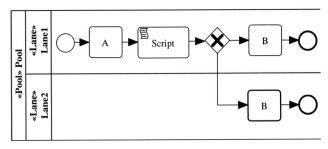

Figure 1.2: Organizational Modeling in BPMN

The third issue is constituted by the solely implicit expression of modality through the structure of the process flow. In BPMN, all activities are implicitly obligatory (mandatory), and whenever something should be permissible (optional), the process flow is split to offer the possibility to execute the activity or to do nothing. This implies that the decision whether to execute an activity is described within another element, e.g. a gateway. The separation of decision and execution requires additional modeling elements to split and merge the process flow and a comprehensive understanding of the entire process to identify obligatory and permissible activities.

Four examples of BPMN process flows are shown in Fig. 1.3. In the first case, activity A must be executed in every process instance and is, thus, obligatory (see Fig. 1.3(a)). In the second case, the process flow is split to express that activity B is permissible (see Fig. 1.3(b)). In addition, the modality also depends on the type of the split (free vs. conditional choice, parallel/exclusive/inclusive split) and on alternative elements. For example, the process flow shown in Fig. 1.3(c) has the same structure, but comprises a conditional choice. In this case, the activity is obligatory if the condition evaluates to true (conditional obligation). In the last case shown in Fig. 1.3(d), activities D and E are alternatives. However, if an additional empty path is inserted between the split and merge, then both activities are permissible. So the modality of an activity depends on several structural aspects like preceding splits of the process flow, the splitting types, and alternative elements. This is imprecise and requires additional modeling elements as well as a comprehensive understanding of the entire process to identify the modalities.

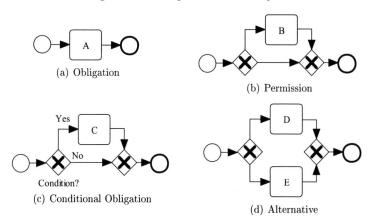

(a) Obligation

(b) Permission

(c) Conditional Obligation

(d) Alternative

Figure 1.3: Implicit Expression of Modality through Process Flow Structure

1.2   Objectives

The issues mentioned in section 1.1 are addressed by the *Vertical Model Integration* (VMI) research project executed at the *Software Competence Center Hagenberg GmbH* (SCCH). The main goals of VMI are to formally define the syntax and semantics of BPMN, to suggest adaptations of conflicting or unclear BPMN elements, and to provide a holistic modeling framework by extending BPMN with:

- a typed approach to support user interaction (see [42]),

- deontic logic to define modality (obligation, permission) and support actor modeling (current work), and

- aspects of database constraints to support data modeling (future goal).

Further goals of the VMI project are to formally define the semantics of the control flow, event-based communication, user interaction, data handling, and exception handling. The semantics of BPMN and of all extensions are defined based on *Abstract State Machines* (ASMs) to provide a formal basis. Further important aspects of the VMI project are the validation and verification of the results in order to ensure consistency and correctness.

The goals of the VMI project are addressed within various research groups and by several PhD theses. The realization of all these goals will result in a new approach for business process modeling called $BPMN_-^+$. $BPMN_-^+$ will comprise several extensions of BPMN to address open issue (e.g., asynchronous sub-processes and optional activities), but also restrictions in case of redundant, unnecessary, or imprecise functionalities.

In this thesis, three major goals of the VMI project are addressed. The goals of the current work are:

1. to provide a formal definition of the BPMN syntax,

2. to extend BPMN with deontic concepts (called *Deontic BPMN*)

   (a) to highlight modalities and

   (b) support actor modeling, and

3. to define a graph transformation from BPMN to Deontic BPMN.

The first goal of this thesis is to provide a formal definition of the BPMN syntax. This goal is addressed by formally defining the syntactical restrictions of the BPMN metamodel and the natural text within an ontology based on description logic. The motivation is to provide a precise definition and to identify and resolve contradictions in the BPMN specification. The ontology is called the *BPMN 2.0 Ontology* and can further be used as a knowledge base to familiarize with the BPMN elements as well as for syntax checking of concrete BPMN models.

The second goal of this thesis is sub-divided into two subgoals. The first subgoal is to also explicitly express the modality within the corresponding activity. This goal is addressed by extending business process modeling languages (BPMLs) in general and BPMN in particular with the deontic concepts of obligation, permission, and prohibition. The extension of BPMN with deontic concepts is called *Deontic BPMN*. An explicit definition of modality will reduce the structural complexity and increase the understandability of the process flow. The second subgoal is to extend the support for organizational modeling in BPMN. This goal is addressed by a task-based approach for actor modeling based on deontic logic and speech act theory. This approach will increase the expressiveness and avoid inaccuracy and redundancy.

The third goal of this thesis is to automatically transform BPMN diagrams to Deontic BPMN diagrams. This goal is addressed by defining a graph transformation based on the algebraic approach. The graph transformation system is called *DeonticBpmnGTS* and defines a type graph and several transformation rules with positive and negative application conditions. In order to show that DeonticBpmnGTS is globally deterministic, it is proven that the graph transformation system is strictly AC-confluent and terminating. Due to inheritance relationships in the type graph, the termination proof requires a flattening of DeonticBpmnGTS, so a flattening algorithm is proposed and a flattening prototype developed.

In summary, the main idea of this thesis is to support optional activities in business process modeling languages like BPMN. An explicitly optional activity is deemed to be more intuitive and also positively affects the structural complexity and the understandability of the process flow. In the current work, optional activities are expressed based on deontic logic to provide a formal basis and support further concepts like pre- and postconditions. However, alternative representations may be used for concrete BPMLs, e.g., an optional marker can be defined for BPMN activities.

1.3   Hypotheses

In the following, three hypotheses regarding *Deontic BPMN* and *Deontic-BpmnGTS* are presented, which are proven in subsequent chapters. The first hypothesis concerns Deontic BPMN and suggests that the structural complexity of a process flow in Deontic BPMN is equal to or lower than the BPMN equivalent, since an explicit definition of modalities may provide the possibility to remove surrounding gateways and alternative sequence flows, thereby simplifying the structure of the process flow.

Hypothesis 1 (Structural Complexity in Deontic BPMN):
The structural complexity of a process flow expressed in BPMN and Deontic BPMN is either the same or lower in the deontic extension.

The second hypothesis concerns the extension of Deontic BPMN with actor modeling and suggests that this approach is more expressive than the current *Pool* and *Lane* concepts provided by BPMN.

Hypothesis 2 (Expressiveness of Deontic BPMN with Actors):
The extension of Deontic BPMN with actor modeling is more expressive than the Swimlane concept provided by standard BPMN.

Finally, the third hypothesis concerns DeonticBpmnGTS and states that the transformation from BPMN to Deontic BPMN is globally deterministic (i.e. determinate), which means that, for each pair of terminating graph transformations with the same source graph, the target graphs are equal [31].

Hypothesis 3 (Global Determinism of DeonticBpmnGTS):
The transformation from BPMN to Deontic BPMN defined by the graph transformation system DeonticBpmnGTS is globally deterministic.

1.4 Outline

This chapter started with the motivation for this thesis and presented three major drawbacks of BPMN, these being contradictions in the BPMN specification, limited support for organizational modeling, and only implicit expression of modality through the structure of the process flow. The objectives of this thesis address these issues and suggest a formal definition of the BPMN syntax within an ontology, an extension of BPMLs in general and BPMN in particular with deontic logic to highlight modalities and support actor modeling, and a graph transformation from BPMN to Deontic BPMN. The chapter concluded with three hypotheses concerning the suggested contributions.

The second chapter provides background information and an overview of related work concerning the three main parts of this thesis: BPMN, deontic logic, and graph transformation. Regarding BPMN, the main elements used in subsequent chapters are introduced and a literature review of suggested extensions, formal definitions of the syntax and semantics, previous ontologies, and identified issues is provided. The introduction to deontic logic comprises a description of so-called *Standard Deontic Logic* (SDL), several extensions, and a summary of the most important paradoxes. In addition, related work regarding the application of deontic logic in process modeling is presented. The final part provides an overview of graph transformation with focus on the algebraic approach.

The third chapter presents the first contribution of this thesis: a formal representation of the syntactical definitions of BPMN within an ontology called the *BPMN 2.0 Ontology*. The *BPMN 2.0 Ontology* comprises the syntactical definitions from the BPMN metamodel and the natural text of the specification and can be used as a knowledge base and for syntax checking of concrete BPMN models. A major advantage of the ontology-based syntax checker is the possibility to also infer additional knowledge.

The fourth chapter presents the second contribution of this thesis and comprises an extension of BPMLs in general and BPMN in particular with deontic logic to highlight modalities. This chapter introduces possible deontic classifications of an activity, provides a discussion of user and conditional choices, and an overview on the extent to which deontic concepts can be used in process flows. Then the control-flow perspective of the *Workflow Patterns* is extended with deontic concepts. Since the *Workflow Patterns* are independent of concrete BPMLs, the deontic extension can be easily adapted to BPMN and the result is called *Deontic BPMN*. The deontic analysis is supported by a path exploration approach and the benefits of Deontic BPMN are demonstrated by a case study and a preliminary survey. Another issue addressed in this chapter is the limited support for actor modeling in BPMN. A new approach including deontic logic and speech act theory is proposed and evaluated based on the resource perspective of the *Workflow Patterns*.

The fifth chapter provides the third contribution of this thesis: a graph transformation from a subset of BPMN to Deontic BPMN called *Deontic-BpmnGTS*. After an introduction to the basic definitions of algebraic graph transformation, DeonticBpmnGTS is defined and comprises a type graph with inheritance as well as several transformation rules. Furthermore, it is proven that DeonticBpmnGTS is strictly AC-confluent and terminating, which implies that the transformation is globally deterministic. Due to inheritance relationships in the type graph, the termination proof requires a flattening of DeonticBpmnGTS, so a flattening algorithm is proposed and a prototype developed. The chapter concludes with a discussion of the results.

Finally, the last chapter provides the conclusion and is sub-divided into a summary of the results, a final discussion of the three hypotheses and optional activities, as well as a description of future work.

Chapter 2

Background and Related Work

This chapter provides background information and an overview of related work concerning the three main parts of this thesis: BPMN, deontic logic, and graph transformation.

2.1 BPMN

The first section starts with an overview of BPMN including possible extensions suggested by related work. Afterwards, several approaches to formally define the syntax and semantics of BPMN are presented. One approach is to specify the syntax of BPMN based on description logic as shown by two BPMN ontologies. Finally, the section concludes with a description of BPMN issues identified by formal analyses and surveys.

2.1.1 Overview

The *Business Process Model and Notation* (BPMN), formerly called *Business Process Modeling Notation*, is a standard maintained by the Object Management Group (OMG) and addresses business analysts and technical developers (see [99]). BPMN was first published by the Business Process Management Initiative in 2004 and is maintained by OMG since 2005. The current version, BPMN 2.0, was published in January 2011. BPMN provides a graphical notation for business process modeling and supports three diagram types: process, choreography, and collaboration. All diagram types are considered in the formal definition of the BPMN syntax and may be extended with deontic logic, but the focus of this thesis is on process diagrams. Furthermore, BPMN 2.0 provides five basic categories of elements: *Flow Objects, Data, Connecting Objects, Swimlanes* and *Artifacts* [99]. The main elements used in subsequent chapters are presented in the following.

Flow Objects

Flow Objects are the main graphical elements of a business process and subdivided into *Activities, Gateways,* and *Events*. Flow objects are identified by an *id* and an optional *label* and may have incoming and/or outgoing sequence flows (cf. for this paragraph [99]).

Activities: *Activities* denote work that has to be performed within a business process and are further divided into *Tasks, Sub-Processes,* and *Call Activities* [99]. In the deontic extension, all activities are deontically classified.

A *Task* is an atomic activity in a process flow and shown in Fig. 2.1(a). BPMN distinguishes between different task types (*Abstract, Service, Business Rule, Send, Receive, Human, Manual,* and *Script*) and specifies three possible marker types (compensation, loop, and multi-instance) [99].

A *Sub-Process* is a compound activity (see Fig. 2.1(b)) and comprises further activities, gateways, events, and sequence flows. BPMN distinguishes between an *Embedded Sub-Process* (standard sub-process), *Event Sub-Process* (used within a process or sub-process, no incoming/outgoing sequence flows), *Transaction* (controlled through a transaction protocol), and *Ad-Hoc Sub-Process* (activities have no required sequence relationships). Besides the collapsed marker shown in Fig. 2.1(b), four further marker types may be used (compensation, loop, multi-instance, and ad-hoc) (cf. for this paragraph [99]).

A *Call Activity* calls a global process or task and thereby supports reusability within a business process (see Fig. 2.1(c)). The call activity shares the same shape and markers as the called activity but has a bold border line [99].

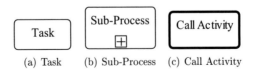

(a) Task   (b) Sub-Process   (c) Call Activity

Figure 2.1: BPMN Activities (based on [99])

Gateways: *Gateways* provide a mechanism to split and merge the process flow and are classified based on the number of incoming and outgoing sequence flows into *converging, diverging, mixed,* or *unspecified.* BPMN further defines five different gateway types: *Parallel, Exclusive, Inclusive, Complex,* and *Event-Based* (cf. for this paragraph [99]).

The *Parallel Gateway* (see Fig. 2.2(a)) creates and synchronizes parallel flows, so all incoming sequence flows must provide a token and all outgoing sequence flows receive a token [99].

In contrast, an *Exclusive Gateway* (see Fig. 2.2(b)) sends a token on exactly one outgoing path (alternative paths) and also waits for exactly one token on any incoming sequence flow (no synchronization mechanism) [99].

More complex is an *Inclusive Gateway* (see Fig. 2.2(c)), since it may create alternative and parallel paths. All paths are considered to be independent and, thus, zero to all paths may be taken after a diverging inclusive gateway. Similarly, a converging inclusive gateway is used to synchronize a combination of alternative and parallel paths. Both, exclusive and inclusive gateways can optionally define a default path marked by a diagonal slash (see Fig. 2.4(c)) (cf. for this paragraph [99]).

The fourth gateway type is called a *Complex Gateway* and used to model complex synchronization behavior defined by an expression [99]. The complex gateway is not relevant for the deontic extension, since the split behavior and the synchronization semantics are the same as for the inclusive gateway [99] and, thus, also the deontic classification is the same.

The last gateway type is the *Event-Based Gateway*, which provides a branching point in the process where the selection of a path is based on the occurrence of events. Event-based gateways are further sub-divided into exclusive and parallel event-based gateways, depending on whether only one event (further events are disabled) or all events must be triggered (cf. for this paragraph [99]). Since the splitting behavior of the exclusive/parallel event-based gateway resembles that of an exclusive/parallel gateway, the deontic classification is again the same.

(a) Parallel   (b) Exclusive   (c) Inclusive

Figure 2.2: BPMN Gateways (based on [99])

Events: *Events* describe things that happen in a business process. BPMN distinguishes between events that start a process (*Start Events*, Fig. 2.3(a)), events that end a process (*End Events*, Fig. 2.3(c)), and events that may happen in between (*Intermediate Events*, Fig. 2.3(b)). Events are further classified based on whether they catch or throw an event. *Catch Events* have an unfilled trigger as shown in Fig. 2.3(d) and can only be used for start events and some intermediate events. In contrast, *Throw Events* have a filled trigger as shown in Fig. 2.3(e) and can only be used for end events and some intermediate events. Intermediate events can either be placed in the normal flow or on the boundary of an activity. If an intermediate event is placed on the boundary of an activity, then it must be a catch event. In addition, every event has a trigger (also called event marker), which is placed within the circle. Possible triggers are *None, Message, Timer, Error, Escalation, Cancel, Compensation, Conditional, Link, Signal, Terminate, Multiple*, and *Parallel Multiple*. The most important triggers are shown in Fig. 2.3. However, the BPMN diagrams provided in this thesis only use events without a visible trigger (e.g. Fig. 2.3(a)), which are said to have the trigger *None* and do not define an *EventDefinition* (see [99, p. 233ff] for a description of the other triggers). Moreover, events can either be interrupting resulting in alternative paths or non-interrupting resulting in parallel paths. Interrupting events are marked by a solid line whereas non-interrupting events have a dotted line and can only be used for start events of an event sub-process as well as for intermediate boundary events. Finally, several restrictions define which events (catch/throw, triggers, interrupting/non-interrupting) may be used under which circumstances, e.g., a start event must not have the trigger *Terminate* (cf. for this paragraph [99]).

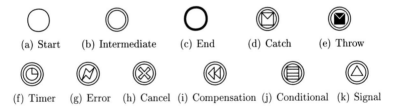

Figure 2.3: BPMN Events (based on [99])

In summary, events can influence the process flow and may lead to alternative or parallel paths. Thus, also events affect the deontic classification. However, the possible splits of the process flow are similar to that of gateways and so the deontic classification must only be defined once for all possible split patterns.

Connecting Objects

Connecting Objects are used to connect *Flow Objects* with each other or with further information thereby representing dependencies in the process flow. Connecting objects are further sub-divided into *Sequence Flows, Message Flows, Associations*, and *Data Associations. Message Flows* are used to show the flow of messages between two participants whereas *Data Associations* move data between flow objects and data elements. In addition, *Associations* are used to connect flow objects with artifacts. These three connecting objects are not used in subsequent chapters and, thus, not described in more detail. Since *Sequence Flows* are the only connecting objects that can pass through tokens, thereby defining the order of the process flow, only sequence flows are relevant for the deontic extension and described in more detail in the following (cf. for this paragraph [99]).

Sequence Flows: *Sequence Flows* define the order of flow objects in the process flow and connect exactly one source object to exactly one target object (see Fig. 2.4(a)). A sequence flow can further define a condition, in which case a token is only passed down the sequence flow if the expression evaluates to true. A conditional sequence flow is either shown with a diamond marker if it has an activity as its source (see Fig. 2.4(b)), or like the standard sequence flow in case of a preceding exclusive, inclusive, or complex gateway (see Fig. 2.4(a)). In addition, if several conditional sequence flows have the same source, then one sequence flow can be defined as the default flow marked by a diagonal slash (see Fig. 2.4(c)). The default sequence flow is only taken if the conditions of all alternative sequence flows evaluate to false. Moreover, if several sequence flows reference the same target activity, then the paths are not synchronized and the activity is instantiated whenever a token arrives (cf. for this paragraph [99]).

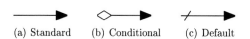

(a) Standard   (b) Conditional   (c) Default

Figure 2.4: BPMN Sequence Flows (based on [99])

So several sequence flows with the same source activity can split the process flow and thereby affect the deontic classification. The process flow can be split into parallel paths in case of unconditional sequence flows or in exclusive/inclusive alternatives in case of conditional sequence flows. Again the deontic classification must only be defined once for all possible split patterns.

Swimlanes

Swimlanes provide a graphical container for partitioning a set of activities from other activities and are sub-divided into *Pools* and *Lanes* (see Fig. 2.5) [99]. A goal of the deontic extension is to extend the support for actor modeling.

Pools: A *Pool* is a graphical representation of a participant (i.e. a business entity like a company or a role like buyer/seller (cf. [99, p. 502])) and can either be defined as a black box with all details hidden or as a white box that contains exactly one business process. Only message flows can cross the boundary of a pool to show the interaction with other business processes. BPMN further defines a multi-instance marker to support multiple instances of participants (cf. for this paragraph [99]).

Lanes: A *Lane* partitions a process (often within a pool) and is used to organize and categorize activities. Lanes may represent internal roles, systems, or internal departments and can be nested (cf. for this paragraph [99]).

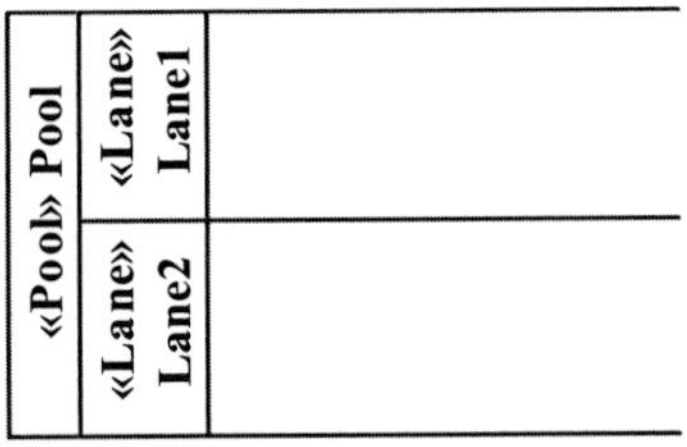

Figure 2.5: BPMN Swimlanes (based on [99])

In summary, the main BPMN elements used in this thesis are *Flow Objects* (*Activities, Gateways,* and *Events*), *Connecting Objects* (*Sequence Flows*), and *Swimlanes* (*Pools* and *Lanes*). In the extension of BPMN with deontic concepts, all *Activities* (*Tasks, Sub-Processes,* and *Call Activities*) are deontically classified.

A further advantage of BPMN is that it considers process execution and provides the execution semantics for BPMN elements. This supports the use of languages designed for the execution of business processes such as the *Web Services Business Process Execution Language* (WS-BPEL) (see [96]) (cf. for this paragraph [99]).

In addition to the BPMN 2.0 specification, several books provide an overview of BPMN. Well-known is, e.g., the "BPMN Modeling and Reference Guide" by White and Miers (see [137]). White, who is working group chair and specification editor of BPMN, has a lot of experience with business process modeling in general and BPMN in particular. Although the book is based on BPMN 1.1, it nevertheless provides a good overview of the main BPMN elements with several examples and a detailed description of the token concept. Another very good description of BPMN is provided by Silver, also an active member of the BPMN 2.0 working group, in his book "BPMN Method & Style" (see [118]). The author describes the BPMN notation and suggests a modeling method based on a top-down approach as well as several guidelines. Although this book is already based on BPMN 2.0, a more current version (second edition) was published recently. In addition, a detailed description of BPMN 2.0 is provided by Allweyer in [7]. This book not only describes the notation and the token concept with several examples, but also considers more complex issues like instantiation in case of parallel incoming sequence flows or several start events. Finally, the book "Praxishandbuch BPMN" (see [40]) by Freund et al. provides a short comparison with other notations (*UML Activity Diagrams* (UML ADs), *Event-Driven Process Chains* (EPCs)) and suggests a BPMN framework consisting of four levels (strategic, operative, technical, and implementation). Together, the BPMN specification and the books impart sufficient knowledge to understand and define BPMN models.

However, although BPMN defines a large number of different elements, some application domains nevertheless require further functionality. Thus, the BPMN specification explicitly permits extensions, e.g., by using new markers, various colors or other line styles, or by defining new shapes of type *Artifact*. Several BPMN extensions have then been suggested in related work. For example, iBPMN extends BPMN with interaction modeling [25], rBPMN weaves the metamodel of BPMN with the REWERSE Rule Markup Language (R2ML) to integrate business rules [85], and Time-BPMN considers temporal constraints and dependencies [41]. Other approaches extend BPMN with data representation [76] (partly integrated in BPMN 2.0), cost calculation [75], or goals and performance measures [62]. In addition, considering actor modeling, support for task-based authorization constraints is provided in [140], security requirements like access control and privacy are considered in [108], and an approach for task-based human resource allocation based on an extension of the BPMN metamodel with the *Object Constraint Language* (OCL) is suggested in [11]. Finally, within our research project, we extended BPMN with a form-based approach based on the submit/response-style interaction paradigm to support user interaction (see [42]).

2.1.2   Formal Specifications

Another aspect of BPMN is the formal definition of its syntax and semantics. According to Recker, BPMN is already used in over thirty countries and it seems that the influence of BPMN will further increase [105]. However, BPMN is repeatedly criticized for its lack of formal semantics, e.g., concerning the OR-join [17]. Thus, several current research projects investigate approaches to formally define BPMN, e.g., based on *Abstract State Machines* (ASM), *Communicating Sequential Processes* (CSP), or *Petri Nets*.

For example, Dijkman et al. state that the static analysis of BPMN models is complicated by ambiguities in the specification and the complexity of the language [28]. The lack of formal semantics further hinders the development of tool support for checking the correctness of BPMN models from a semantic perspective. Thus, Dijkman et al. provide a formal semantics of BPMN defined in terms of a mapping to Petri Nets (cf. for this paragraph [28]).

Furthermore, according to Wong and Gibbons, the BPMN specification does not include formal semantics [141]. Hence, the authors describe the abstract syntax for a subset of BPMN using Z schemas and the behavioral semantics in CSP. Such semantics allow developers to formally analyze and compare BPMN models (cf. for this paragraph [141]).

A further approach by Börger and Sörensen defines the dynamic semantics of the core process modeling concepts of BPMN (gateways, activities, and events) in terms of ASMs [14]. The resulting model can be used to test reference implementations (cf. for this paragraph [14]).

In addition, an approach that supports syntax-based user assistance in diagram editors based the syntax of the visual language being defined by a graph grammar has been applied to business process models by Mazanek and Minas (cf. for this paragraph [77]).

Moreover, the BPMN 2.0 specification itself (see [99]) provides a metamodel for BPMN elements in the form of UML class diagrams and XML schemas. BPMN 2.0 is the first release to provide such a formal definition.

2.1.3   BPMN Ontologies

The syntax of BPMN can also formally be defined within an ontology based on description logic. Up to now, two BPMN ontologies have been published and are described below.

The first BPMN ontology is called the sBPMN ontology and specifies a semantically enhanced BPMN [1]. The ontology is developed within the SUPER project[1] and based on the final release of BPMN 1.0. The classes correspond to the elements of BPMN and are divided in categories like *Flow Objects, Connecting Objects, Swimlanes, Artifacts*, and *Processes*. The entire ontology consists of 95 classes and about 50 axioms (cf. for this paragraph [1]).

The second BPMN ontology is based on BPMN 1.1 and presented in [44]. Again, the specification is based on the BPMN elements resulting in 95 classes, 108 object properties, 70 data properties, and 439 class axioms. The elements are divided into two categories representing *Supporting Elements* and *Graphical Elements*, with the latter further detailed into *Flow Object, Connecting Object, Swimlane*, and *Artifact*. In subsequent publications, for example [39], this ontology is called BPMNO. However, the ontology does not contain a description of all properties documented in the BPMN specification, since some describe the execution behavior of the process and others cannot be defined based on the well-known limitations in the expressiveness of OWL (e.g., default values) (cf. for this paragraph [44]). BPMNO is also not intended to model the dynamic behavior of diagrams (how the flow proceeds within a process) [39]. These limitations also apply to the *BPMN 2.0 Ontology* presented in this thesis. BPMNO has been adapted to BPMN 1.2 by Michael zur Muehlen et al. as described in [144].

Both ontologies, sBPMN and BPMNO, are based on former releases of the BPMN specification and classes are mainly defined for concrete BPMN elements. Thus, a current ontology, the *BPMN 2.0 Ontology*, is developed and presented in chapter 3. This ontology is based on the BPMN metamodel leading to a different and more extensive structure, which better reflects the BPMN specification.

2.1.4 BPMN Issues

Besides the formal specification of the BPMN syntax and semantics, several other issues have been identified by related work. For example, Recker presented a global survey with 590 BPMN users in [105]. The survey is based on BPMN 1.0, but nevertheless provides interesting information about BPMN users (who uses BPMN where, how, and why). For example, BPMN is used for business (51%) and technical purposes (49%), 60% of the respondents work in the private sector, and more than 40% work in large organizations

---

[1]SUPER project: www.ip-super.org

with more than 1000 employees. Furthermore, 36% of the respondents only use a core BPMN set, 37% an extended set of BPMN symbols, and 27% all the functionality BPMN 1.0 has to offer. In addition, five major issues were identified in the survey including limited support for business rule specification, process decomposition, and organizational modeling as well as unnecessary elements (off-page connectors and groups), and the large number of event types (cf. for this paragraph [105]). The problem of process decomposition and reuse has also been studied in our research project and several solutions were suggested (see [91]).

Recker et al. also presented an evaluation of BPMN based on the Bunge-Wand-Weber (BWW) ontology and on interviews in [106]. The ontological evaluation revealed construct deficits (state, history, and system structure), construct redundancies (pool and lane concept, transformations, and events), construct excess (off-page connectors, groups), and construct overload (pool and lane concept). During the following interview, the missing state, unnecessary elements (off-page connectors, groups) and the pool and lane concept were voted in the highest problem category (cf. for this paragraph [106]). Concerning the unnecessary elements, a more recent analysis is provided by Kunze et al. in [65]. The authors studied the use of elements in 1210 BPMN models. The most popular elements, which are used in more than 50% of the BPMN models, are sequence flows, tasks, start/end events, and the pool and lane concept. However, more than 20 elements are used in less than 10% of the BPMN models, e.g., the intermediate error event, inclusive gateway, or event sub-process (not used at all) (cf. for this paragraph [65]).

Furthermore, Wohed et al. studied the suitability of BPMN for business process modeling and used the *Workflow Patterns* as an evaluation framework (see [139]). According to this evaluation, BPMN provides good support for the control-flow perspective, medium support for the data perspective, but only low support for the resource perspective. Concerning the resource perspective, extensions to BPEL have been proposed (e.g., BPEL4People), but in BPMN the pool and lane concepts are specified in a restrictive manner and, thus, only a minimal set of resource patterns is supported. Further issues identified in the evaluation are the partial mapping from BPMN to BPEL, which does not consider unstructured models or OR-joins, the missing support for pre- and postconditions, and the ambiguities in the BPMN specification due to the lack of formalization (cf. for this paragraph [139]).

Since all publications mentioned limited support for organizational modeling and problems with the pool and lane concept, the issue of actor modeling will be addressed in section 4.4. Furthermore, another frequently mentioned problem are unstructured BPMN diagrams, which complicate, e.g., process decomposition and the interpretation of OR-joins (see [17]). In our research project, we studied the problems of unstructuredness and suggested some approaches to nevertheless support process decomposition (see [91]). In addition, also the extension of BPMN with deontic logic must support unstructured models, e.g., by using multiple deontic classifications (see section 4.1.3).

Furthermore, Indulska et al. studied current issues and future challenges in business process modeling within a survey [58]. The survey was executed based on the Delphi technique (multiple-round approach) and answered by 62 respondents from three key stakeholder groups (academics, practitioners, and tool vendors). The result of the survey were two top 10 lists, one with current issues and the other with future challenges. The most important current issue in the first list is standardization, followed by the value of process modeling, model-driven process execution, and model management. The extension of BPMN with deontic logic and actor modeling described in chapter 4 has to cope with problems concerning the modeling method, e.g., multi-perspective modeling, modeling views, and view integration. The most important future challenge in the second list is the value of process modeling, followed by model-driven process execution, standardization, and Business-IT-alignment. Concerning the future challenges, the tool vendors further mention the development of ontologies (addressed in chapter 3). In addition, both lists comprise the problem of model management, i.e., managing of model variants, versions, and releases (cf. for this paragraph [58]). The problem of model management and versioning was also identified by France and Rumpe in [38] and can be confirmed based on our research project. This problem is, for example, addressed by SMoVer (Semantically enhanced Model Version Control System), an optimistic graph-based version control system that also considers the semantics of modeling languages (see [8]).

Besides model management, France and Rumpe identified two further categories with challenges in model-driven engineering: modeling language and separation of concerns challenges (see [38]). The first category comprises the abstraction (problem-level abstraction) and the formality challenge (formal specification of semantics to rigorously analyze models). The formality challenge is addressed by the *BPMN 2.0 Ontology* presented in chapter 3. The second category describes challenges that arise if modeling systems use multiple, overlapping viewpoints especially in case of heterogeneous languages (cf. for this paragraph [38]). The last issue is addressed by an integration of the control-flow and resource perspective in section 4.4 and by an integrated framework that supports seamless transition between four models (process, dialog, technical, and data) defined in different languages (see [42]).

2.2   Deontic Logic

This section provides an overview of deontic logic in general and its application in process modeling.

2.2.1   Overview

Deontic logic is the logical study of the normative use of language and its subject matter is a variety of normative concepts including obligation (O), prohibition (F), permission (P), and commitment (e.g., conditional obligation) [104, p. 148]. These concepts can be linked with the logical connectives for negation ($\neg$), conjunction ($\wedge$), disjunction ($\vee$), material implication ($\rightarrow$), and material equivalence ($\leftrightarrow$) [104, p. 162]. In addition, the logical truth can be symbolized by $\top$ and the logical falsehood by $\bot$ [104, p. 163].

The term 'deontic' is derived from the Greek word '$\delta\varepsilon\acute{o}\nu\tau\omega\varsigma$', which means 'as it should be' or 'duly', and was first used by the Austrian philosopher Mally in 1926 to refer to the logical study of the normative use of language [37]. Mally presented an axiomatic system for the notion of *ought*; however, a major issue of Mally's deontic logic is the consequence that x is obligatory if and only if x is the case, which is unacceptable for any reasonable deontic logic [72]. Thus, most of the current interest in deontic logic is based on von Wright's renowned paper 'Deontic Logic' published in 1951 (see [131]). Von Wright divided modal concepts into three main groups: (i) alethic modes or modes of truth (necessary, possible, and contingent), (ii) epistemic modes or modes of knowing (verified, undecided, and falsified), and (iii) deontic modes or modes of obligation (obligatory, permitted, and forbidden) [131]. So von Wright's approach to deontic logic is based on modal logic and on similarities between the deontic concepts of obligation and permission and the alethic notions of necessity and possibility [37]. A detailed comparison of alethic and deontic modalities is provided by von Wright in [133].

So-called *Standard Deontic Logic* (SDL) is based on a propositional modal logic that comprises the systems K and D. System K specifies the axiom $O(x \rightarrow y) \rightarrow (O(x) \rightarrow O(y))$, so whenever it is obligatory that x implies y and x is obligatory then also y is obligatory. In addition, system D extends system K with the axiom $\neg(O(x) \wedge O(\neg x))$, which states that it is not allowed that x and $\neg x$ are obligatory (or x is obligatory and forbidden). Thus, whenever x is obligatory, it must also be permissible. SDL is further closed under the inference rules of modus ponens ($x, x \rightarrow y \vdash y$) and necessitation (*if* $\vdash x$ *then* $\vdash O(x)$). The normative concept of obligation can then be used to express prohibition ($F(x) = O(\neg x)$) and permission ($P(x) = \neg O(\neg x)$). Furthermore, due to its modal logical basis, SDL can be easily extended with modal accounts of actions (cf. for this paragraph [52]).

In his article 'Deontic Logic' published in 1951, von Wright suggested to apply deontic operators to "propositions [...] about [...] deontic characters of acts" [131]. However, the variables represented types of actions instead of propositions (i.e. sentences or states of affairs) [57]. Since actions cannot be true or false, several researchers suggested to conform to the usual style of modal syntax by using propositions [57] and, thus, also SDL is based on propositional modal logic. According to Broersen and van der Torre, this is a major problem of SDL, since, in contrast to other modalities that usually pertain to static situations or states, deontic modalities concern in most cases the application of actions [18]. Furthermore, Horty criticizes the concept of "ought to be" (propositional) and claims that it has been taken only as a technical convenience to ease working with formalisms and that it is just more general than what an agent "ought to do" (action) [57]. Finally, von Wright also insisted in later work on reading propositions in SDL as actions [18].

The use of propositions in SDL instead of actions further leads to a paradox known as Ross' paradox. The paradox occurs if the sentence "it is obliged to post the letter" (action) is represented by the proposition "post" ($O(post)$). Since SDL is closed under the logical implications of propositions, it can further be concluded that $O(post \lor burn)$. The obligation is then also satisfied if the letter is burned instead of posted. So the main reasons for the Ross paradox to emerge are that actions are interpreted as propositions and logical connectives as action connectives. The paradox can be resolved by defining the deontic language on top of an action language (cf. for this paragraph [18]). In this thesis, a similar approach is applied and a deontic logic of actions is used.

Another frequently mentioned paradox is Chisholm's (or contrary-to-duty imperative) paradox, which emerges if an obligation is not satisfied. Consider the following four sentences (based on [37, 52]):

1. It ought to be that a certain man goes to the assistance of his neighbors.

2. It ought to be that if he does go, he tells them he is coming.

3. If he does not go, then he ought not to tell them he is coming.

4. He does not go.

The first sentence describes the primary obligation, whereas the third sentence provides the contrary-to-duty obligation. Although these sentences seem to be consistent and non-redundant, every formalization of the sentences is either inconsistent or one formula is a logical consequence of another formula. For example, the formalization (1. $O(x)$, 2. $O(x \rightarrow y)$, 3. $\neg x \rightarrow O(\neg y)$, 4. $\neg x$) is inconsistent, because the first and second sentence imply $O(y)$ (based on the axiom of system K and modus ponens) which, according to the axiom of system D, contradicts with $O(\neg y)$ (concluded from sentences three and four with modus ponens) (cf. for this paragraph [52] and [104, p. 190ff]). Chisholm's paradox can be addressed by the concept of conditional commitment as provided in dyadic deontic logic (described in a subsequent paragraph) [104, p. 192f].

Further paradoxes and dilemmas are, e.g., the Free Choice Permission paradox ($\nvdash P(A \vee B) \rightarrow (P(A) \wedge P(B))$), Prior's paradox of derived obligation ($(O(\neg A) \rightarrow O(A \rightarrow B))$), the Good Samaritan paradox ($\vdash O(A \wedge B) \rightarrow O(B)$), and Jørgensen's dilemma (norms cannot be true or false) [20, 51, 52]. In addition, Broersen and van der Torre identified ten problems of deontic logic and normative reasoning in computer science [18]. The problems include the Jørgensen's dilemma, the Chisholm's paradox, temporal aspects, actions in deontic reasoning, the use of norms in games, interaction of norms with beliefs and intentions, permissive norms with free choice permissions, constitutive norms, and norm compliance [18]. Some of the mentioned problems are also relevant for Deontic BPMN, e.g., Jørgensen's dilemma, an action logic, and the distinction of user (free) and conditional choice (see section 4.1.5). Jørgensen's dilemma is, for example, addressed by claiming that normative statements (i.e. descriptions of normative situations) can be true or false [52].

Several extensions to SDL have then been suggested in related work. For example, Åqvist presented ten systems of monadic (i.e. unconditional) deontic logic in [104, p. 207] (partly based on Hanson [53] and Smiley [119]). The system OK corresponds to SDL (without system D), system OM additionally specifies the axiom $O(O(A) \rightarrow A)$, which roughly states that obligations must be fulfilled [79], and system OS4 further defines the axiom $O(A) \rightarrow O(O(A))$. Moreover, system OB extends system OM with the axiom $O(P(O(A)) \rightarrow A)$ and system OS5 extends system OS4 with the axiom $P(O(A)) \rightarrow O(A)$. Each of the five systems can then be extended with the axiom $O(A) \rightarrow P(A)$ (corresponds to system D), which defines that whenever something is obligatory then it is also permissible (the corresponding systems are called OK$^+$, OM$^+$, OS4$^+$, OB$^+$, OS5$^+$). Since the last axiom is also useful for the current work, the deontic logic of this thesis is based on the system OK$^+$ (SDL) (cf. for this paragraph [104, p. 207]).

A further extension of SDL supports conditional commitments and thereby addresses the paradoxes of Prior and Chisholm [104, p. 148, 192f]. While monadic deontic logic considers unconditional normative concepts, conditional commitments are part of dyadic deontic logic (compare [68]) in which obligations and permissions are conditional on certain circumstances. The concept of conditional commitment was introduced by von Wright in 1956 (see [132]) with the definition of a new primitive symbol $P(p|c)$, which states that p is permitted if the preconditions c are fulfilled. The idea of using binary (i.e. two-place) primitives together with the definition of two axioms resulted in the first known system of dyadic deontic logic (cf. for this paragraph [104, p. 185]). A more detailed description of dyadic deontic logic is provided by Lewis in [68].

Furthermore, Castro and Maibaum introduce a propositional deontic logic that is applied to actions (ought-to-do) and extended with further operators (*done* operator, relative complement of actions (with respect to the other actions), and two versions of permissions (strong and weak)) as well as temporal aspects [21]. In addition, Dignum and Weigand use a dynamic deontic logic extended with speech acts for modeling communication between cooperative systems [27]. The dynamic deontic logic is based on the propositional deontic logic PD_eL presented by Meyer in [84], which is a variant of dynamic logic that can deal with several paradoxes like the Chisholm or the Free Choice Permission paradox. Meyer et al. further refer to the importance of distinguishing between ought-to-be and ought-to-do constraints [83]. For the ought-to-do variant dynamic deontic logic can be used, but for the ought-to-be variant the authors suggest a multi-modal extension (multiple O-operators) to also address the Chisholm paradox (see [83]).

In addition, another important aspect of this thesis is to represent and reason about what agents ought to do based on deontic logic (ought-to-do variant). Several approaches address this issue and suggest different notations. For example, Dignum and Weigand [27] write $O_{ij}(\alpha(i))$ to denote that agent i is obliged to agent j to perform action $\alpha(i)$. This notation (definition of two roles) is similar to that of speech act theory (definition of speaker and hearer). Speech act theory is also used by the authors to extend dynamic deontic logic (see [27]). Another approach for agency in deontic logic is provided by Horty in [57]. The author argues that what an agent ought to do is not the same as what it ought to be that the agent does and proposes an analysis of the notion of what an agent ought to do based on a parallel between action in indeterministic time and choice under uncertainty. Horty further suggests to define actions based on *stit* semantics (α *stit* : A: agent α sees to it that action A) with the goal to provide a precise semantics within the setting of indeterministic time (cf. for this paragraph [57]). Moreover, Hilpinen states that the definition of actions or actors can be expressed by an action description of the form $Do(r, p)$, where Do is a modal operator for action or agency, r stands for an agent (or role) and p describes a propositional expression (e.g., an action A) [55]. The action description can then be extended with a deontic operator (e.g., $O\ do(r, A)$). In this thesis the last notation is used, since the modal operator do highlights that it is an ought-to-do constraint and the specification of one role (executing role) is sufficient for an activity in a Deontic BPMN model.

An overview of the main applications of deontic logic in computer science is then given by Wieringa and Meyer [138]. According to the authors, deontic logic is primarily used for the specification of fault-tolerant computer systems, normative user behavior, normative behavior in and of organizations, and normative behavior of general object systems (e.g., definition of law, legal thinking, integrity constraints, or scheduling problems) (see [138]). The second and third application area is also addressed by the extension of BPMN with deontic logic and actor modeling.

Further information concerning deontic logic is provided in the following articles. First of all, the article "Deontic Logic" by Åqvist presents the history of deontic logic, the most important paradoxes and dilemmas, ten systems of monadic deontic logic, ten systems of alethic modal logic, and an overview of dyadic deontic logic (see [104]). Similarly, the article "Deontic Logic" by McNamara provides the background of deontic logic, an introduction to most standard monadic deontic systems, and an overview of challenges including several dilemmas and paradoxes (see [79]). Furthermore, a more detailed description of the history of deontic logic is provided by Føllesdal and Hilpinen in [37] and Hilpinen considers actions and agency in deontic logic in [55].

In summary, the deontic logic used in this thesis is based on SDL (applied to actions) and will be extended with an additional logical connective for contravalence ($\dot{\vee}$), conditional commitments defined in dyadic deontic logic, and support for actor modeling (see section 4.1).

2.2.2   Deontic Logic in Process Modeling

According to Goedertier and Vanthienen [47], most process modeling languages like BPMN, BPEL, and UML ADs are procedural and only implicitly keep track of why design choices have been made. Thus, this publication presents a vocabulary for declarative process modeling that supports business concerns, execution scenarios, execution mechanisms, modality, rule enforcement, and communication. Concerning modality, procedural modeling only specifies what *must* be the case, while declarative process modeling supports *must, ought,* and *can* based on deontic logic (cf. [47]). In [46], the same authors introduce a language to express temporal rules about obligations and permissions in business interactions called *Penelope.* The publications provide a good foundation for the current research, but the focus of the normative concepts is more on agents and temporal constraints, whereas deontic analysis, transformation, or optimization capabilities are not presented at all.

Furthermore, Schewe and Thalheim present a modeling approach for *Web Information Systems* (WISs) called *Storyboarding* that is analog to business process modeling (see [115]). Storyboards are used for high-level modeling and consist of three parts. The first part is the story space, which comprises all paths (or stories) that users may follow while navigating through the WIS. The second part describes the actors, i.e. groups of users with the same user profile, and the third part consists of tasks that link the activities of actors with the story space. The story space can then be expressed by an edge-labeled directed multi-graph and described by a suitable story algebra based on the storyboarding language *SiteLang.* The story algebra can further be used to reason about story spaces thereby enabling personalization at a high level of abstraction. The personalization of story spaces is already achievable at the level of storyboarding by exploiting the axioms of Kleene algebra with tests (KAT). This allows to define a role model in which the role of an actor usually has obligations and rights which are expressed with a deontic action logic. The deontic action logic was introduced by Schewe et al. in [117] and allows to specify the conditions under which actions by a particular role are obligatory, permissible, or forbidden, and conditions for their actual execution (cf. for this paragraph [115, 116, 117]).

In addition, other approaches assure business process compliance based on deontic logic. According to Sadiq et al. [111], process and control modeling are two distinct specifications, but convergence is necessary to achieve business practices that are compliant with control objectives. The authors propose a *Formal Contract Language* (FCL) as formalism to express normative specifications. This language is a combination of defeasible logic and a deontic logic of violations. Ghose and Koliadis further present an approach to enhance business process modeling notations with the capability to detect and resolve compliance related issues [45]. They define a framework for auditing BPMN process models and suggest that activity-, event-, and decision inclusion may be defined with deontic modalities.

Furthermore, as already mentioned, Broersen and van der Torre identified ten problems of deontic logic and normative reasoning in computer science. One problem is how to combine legal ontologies, normative systems, business process notations, and compliance checking tools (cf. problem 10 in [18]). Regarding this issue, the authors recommend the *Semantics of Business Vocabulary and Business Rules* (SBVR) for interaction between norms and business processes. SBVR is a standard of OMG and expresses modality with alethic or deontic logic [98]; however, it does not consider the influence on the process flow (e.g., readability or reduction of structural complexity). Considering constitutive norms, the authors refer to speech acts, which will be part of the extension of Deontic BPMN with actor modeling (see section 4.4).

Further publications focus on the formal model of normative reasoning and deontic logic in combination with business rules and process modeling. Padmanabhan et al. consider process modeling and deontic logic in [102]. They develop a logical framework based on multi-modal logic to capture the normative positions among agents in an organizational setting. Furthermore, Governatori et al. present a language for expressing contract conditions in terms of deontic concepts called *Business Contract Language* (BCL) [49]. However, these publications do not provide a detailed study of modality, but rather focus on agents and their contractual relationships.

Regarding the use of deontic logic for actor modeling, Dignum and Weigand provide a logical foundation for modeling communication processes in cooperative systems that is based on dynamic deontic logic and speech act theory (see [26, 27]). Weigand et al. further present an approach that provides a bridge between interoperable transactions (consist of communicating agents and describe the behavior of cooperative information systems) and business process models based on deontic logic [135]. In addition, Grossi et al. propose a semantic framework based on dynamic logic with deontic operators to formally define organizational structures and responsibilities between groups of agents (see [50]). Furthermore, Meyer studies the use of dynamic logic for reasoning about actions and agents and suggests an extension with deontic logic to also consider the deontics of actions (see [82]).

In summary, deontic logic in process modeling is mainly used for compliance checking and actor modeling. Since none of the presented publications studies the influence on the process flow (e.g., readability and optimization capabilities) or provides a deontic analysis or transformation, these issues will be addressed by the extension of BPMN with deontic concepts described in chapter 4. Finally, considering deontic logic for actor modeling, a more detailed description of related work is provided in section 4.4.1.

2.3 Graph Transformation

This section provides an overview of graph transformation with focus on the algebraic approach.

"Graph transformation" is a generic term and comprises the concepts of graph grammar and graph rewriting. Graph rewriting describes the application of rules to a given graph, while graph grammars additionally provide an initial graph [87, p. 194]. Thus, graph rewriting is mainly used for transformation processes, whereas graph grammars focus on building up models or programs.

Research on graph transformation started around the 1970s; the main idea is the rule-based modification of a graph, where each application of a rule leads to a graph transformation step [31, p. 5f]. Fig. 2.6 shows the transformation of a graph L (left-hand side) to a graph R (right-hand side) based on a rule r (also called *production*). Applying the rule $r = (L, R)$ means finding a match of L in the source graph and replacing L by R, leading to the target graph of the graph transformation [31, p. 6].

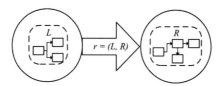

Figure 2.6: Rule-based Modification of Graphs (Source: [31, p. 6], modified)

The roots of graph transformations are (cf. [31, p. 6]):

- from Chomsky grammars on strings to graph grammars;

- from term rewriting to graph rewriting;

- from textual description to visual modeling.

Noam Chomsky developed the Chomsky grammars in the 1950s in order to describe the structure of sentences in natural language as derivation tree. A Chomsky grammar consists of a set of terminal T and nonterminal N symbols, a starting symbol Z and several rules that define a transformation from $L \rightarrow R$. In a concrete sentence, the syntactical term *noun* is a nonterminal symbol, whereas a word like "house" is a terminal symbol.

Chomsky grammars are classified based on the form of the rules in unrestricted, context-sensitive, context-free, and regular grammars (cf. for this paragraph [48, p. 33-36]).

A term rewriting system consists of terms and rewrite (or reduction) rules. The rewrite rules describe a *pair*(L, R) of terms and every occurrence of L is substituted by R within an atomic reduction step. Two restrictions on the reduction rules ensure that L is not a variable and that every variable in R also occurs in L (cf. for this paragraph [60, p. 34f]).

The last mentioned aspect is the progress from textual description to visual modeling. Regarding this issue, visual modeling is used especially within the design phase of the software life cycle. The range of modeling languages is widespread and includes, among others, business process modeling languages like BPMN.

The transformation from BPMN to Deontic BPMN describes a model transformation; one of the application areas of graph transformations. Further application areas are provided in [31, p. 19]:

- model and program transformation;

- syntax and semantics of visual languages;

- visual modeling of behavior and programming;

- modeling, metamodeling, and model-driven architecture;

- software architectures and evolution;

- refactoring of programs and software systems;

- security policies.

Furthermore, different graph transformation approaches are available and listed below (cf. [31, p. 10]):

- Node label replacement approach

- Hyperedge replacement approach

- Algebraic approach

- Logical approach

- Theory of 2-structures

- Programmed graph replacement approach

DeonticBpmnGTS uses the algebraic graph transformation approach, which was initiated by H. Ehrig, M. Pfender (both TU Berlin) and H.J. Schneider (University of Erlangen) in 1973 (see [34]). The Technical University of Berlin (TU Berlin) is also playing a central role in further research on graph transformations and the development of a tool for attributed graph grammar systems (AGG). Graph transformations have also been studied by research groups at the Universities of Bremen, Pisa, Rome, Leiden, Paderborn, Porto Allegre and others [31, p. 3].

The tool AGG is used to define the graph transformation from BPMN to Deontic BPMN. AGG was introduced by Löwe and Beyer in 1993 (see [74]) and later redesigned and extended by Taentzer (see [121], [122]). In December 2010, AGG was updated to version 2.0 [4]. AGG is implemented in Java [31, p. 305]; it can be extended with new Java classes and graphs can be attributed by using Java objects and types [3]. AGG provides a graphical editor and can be used for specifying graph grammars with a start graph or for typed attributed graph transformations like DeonticBpmnGTS. Furthermore, AGG offers analysis techniques such as consistency checking, critical pair analysis, and termination evaluation. More information on AGG can be found on the AGG Homepage [4], in the User Manual [3], and the algebraic graph transformation book [31, chapter 15].

The algebraic graph transformation approach is based on pushout (PO) constructions (see definition in section 5.1), which are used to model the gluing of graphs. The double-pushout approach (DPO) was introduced in 1973 (see [34]) and uses two gluing constructions as shown in Fig. 2.7. A rule is given by $r = (L, K, R)$, where K is the intersection of L and R and must exist in order to apply the rule. $L \backslash K$ then describes the part which has to be deleted, whereas $R \backslash K$ will be created. In addition, for a graph transformation $G \Rightarrow H$, a graph morphism $m : L \to G$, called match, must exist such that m is structure-preserving. Rule r and match m have to satisfy a gluing condition, so that no edges are left dangling. r and m satisfy the gluing condition if all identification points (different nodes or edges in L that are mapped to the same image in G by m) and all dangling points (nodes in L whose images under m are the source or target of an edge in G that does not belong to $m(L)$) are also gluing points (nodes and edges in L that are not deleted by r). The gluing condition would be violated, e.g., if a node is deleted within a rule r and the node has incoming or outgoing edges in G

which are not part of L. The resulting graph morphism $R \to H$ is called the comatch of the graph transformation $G \Rightarrow H$ (cf. for this paragraph [31, p. 10ff, 44]).

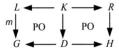

Figure 2.7: Double-Pushout Approach (Source: [31, p. 12])

The single-pushout approach (SPO) was initiated by Raoult in 1984 (see [103]) and fully worked out by Löwe in 1990 (see [73]). The SPO approach is shown in Fig. 2.8; the horizontal morphisms are partial (total graph morphism between subgraphs or morphism between partial functions of vertices and edges [107]) and only the vertical ones are total graph morphism (see definition in section 5.1). Rule r is considered as partial graph morphism $r : L \to R$ with domain $dom(r) = K$ and the partial graph morphism $s : G \to H$ uses the domain $dom(s) = D$. The main difference compared to the DPO approach concerns the deletion of graph elements. If the gluing condition is not satisfied in the DPO approach, then the rule is not applicable. However, in the SPO approach dangling edges might occur after the deletion of $L\backslash K$ from G and are as well deleted, leading to a well-defined graph H (cf. for this paragraph [31, p. 13f]).

Figure 2.8: Single-Pushout Approach (based on [31, p. 13f])

Since no edges should be removed automatically and maybe unintentionally, the DPO approach is used for DeonticBpmnGTS as shown in the example in Fig. 2.9. The rule is in fact a combination of several rules defined within DeonticBpmnGTS but allows to demonstrate the DPO approach.

In summary, the main steps of an algebraic graph transformation from G to H based on the DPO approach are (cf. [31, p. 9]):

1. *Choose* a rule $r : L \Rightarrow R$ with an occurrence of L in G.

2. *Check* the application conditions of the rule.

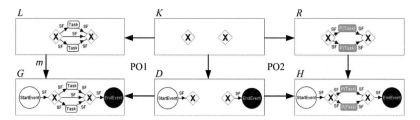

Figure 2.9: Double-Pushout Example

3. *Remove* from G that part of L which is not part of R. If dangling edges would occur after the deletion, then the rule cannot be applied. The resulting graph is called D.

4. *Glue* R to the graph D at the part of L which still has an image in D. The part of R not coming from L is added disjointly to D. The resulting graph is called E.

5. If the rule contains an additional embedding relation, then embed R further into the graph E according to this embedding relation. The resulting graph is called H.

For DeonticBpmnGTS only the first four steps are relevant, since no embedding relations are defined.

The algebraic approach to graph transformation has been generalized to further graph types and high-level structures such as typed graphs, labeled graphs, hypergraphs, attributed graphs, and algebraic specifications. This extension to high-level structures is called high-level replacement (HLR) and was introduced in 1991 (see [32, 33]) (cf. for this paragraph [31, p. 14ff]). The graph transformation from BPMN to Deontic BPMN is defined as typed attributed graph transformation system that includes labels (see chapter 5).

.

Chapter 3

BPMN Syntax Validation

This chapter provides a formal representation of the syntactical definitions of the *Business Process Model and Notation* (BPMN) within an ontology called the *BPMN 2.0 Ontology*. After describing the motivation for the ontology and the used language, the *BPMN 2.0 Ontology* is presented. The *BPMN 2.0 Ontology* comprises the syntactical definitions from the BPMN metamodel and the natural text of the specification and serves as a knowledge base. Consistency and correctness of the *BPMN 2.0 Ontology* are evaluated based on reasoners and on syntax validation.

The *BPMN 2.0 Ontology* was first presented in [90]. The ontology is available under the creative commons license (CC BY-NC-SA 3.0) (see `http://creativecommons.org/licenses/by-nc-sa/3.0`) and can be downloaded from: `http://www.scch.at/en/zugang-download-ontologie`

Note that throughout this chapter, all BPMN elements and relationships are named according to the BPMN metamodel and the *BPMN 2.0 Ontology* (e.g., *SubProcess* instead of *Sub-Process*) and have an italic font.

3.1 Motivation

The *Business Process Model and Notation* (BPMN) is a widely-used standard for business process modeling and maintained by the OMG. The final release of the current version (BPMN 2.0) was published in January 2011. However, the BPMN 2.0 specification is quite comprehensive and spans more than 500 pages. The definitions of elements are distributed across various sections (e.g., *StartEvents* are described several times within the chapter

Overview (see [99, p. 40, 57, 61f]), in chapters *Process* ([99, p. 238ff]), *Choreography* ([99, p. 339f]), and *BPMN Execution Semantics* ([99, p. 439f]), as well as in sections describing other elements that can comprise or connect to *StartEvents*, for example, *EventSubProcesses* ([99, p. 177])). The BPMN metamodel describes the structure of the elements, their attributes and relationships, however, further syntactical rules are defined within the natural text of the BPMN specification, for example: "A Start Event MUST NOT be a target for Sequence Flows; it MUST NOT have incoming Sequence Flows." [99, p. 245]. For a full definition of an element, it is further necessary to consider the specification of all superclasses. In addition, the BPMN specification is in several cases inaccurate or contradictory. In the metamodel, for example, the *Transaction* element specifies two attributes, *protocol* and *method*, both of type string [99, p. 176], but in the corresponding description only *method* is mentioned and defined to be of type *TransactionMethod* [99, p. 180]. All these issues not only make the understanding of BPMN difficult and time-consuming, but also complicate the development of syntax checkers.

An ontology is a formal representation of knowledge and consists of statements that define concepts, roles, individuals, and axioms. It is analogous to an object-oriented class diagram and forms an information domain model [54, p. 11]. Furthermore, an ontology allows a shared common understanding and the reuse and analysis of domain knowledge [95]. Thus, an ontology is suited to represent the BPMN metamodel.

Therefore, I developed an ontology that provides a formal definition of the BPMN syntax and is based on the final release of BPMN 2.0 (see [99]). The main goals of the *BPMN 2.0 Ontology* are as follows:

- Knowledge Base: The primary goal of the ontology is to provide a knowledge base that can be used to familiarize with BPMN. The syntactical rules are combined within the corresponding element and all inherited restrictions are listed below. In addition, every restriction provides the full text of the BPMN specification in an annotation. This allows a much faster understanding of BPMN.

- Contradiction Identification: During the definition of the ontology, several contradictions within the BPMN specification were identified. The most important issues have been reported to the OMG.

- Syntax Checker: The ontology can be used as a syntax checker to validate concrete BPMN models as described in section 3.4.2. The syntax checker can detect correct, incorrect, and incomplete models. A major advantage of the ontology is the possibility to draw conclusions.

3.2 Web Ontology Language (OWL)

The *Web Ontology Language* (OWL) is a knowledge representation language provided by the World Wide Web Consortium (W3C). OWL allows to define the knowledge of a domain of interest and to reason about it. The first version of OWL was derived from the language DAML+OIL and published in 2004 [9]. The current version is called OWL 2 and was published in 2009. Three sublanguages were distinguished in the first version of OWL: OWL Full (unrestricted OWL, undecidable), OWL DL (restrictions based on description logic, decidable), and OWL Lite (minimal subset of language elements). However, OWL Lite eliminated too many useful features without providing sufficient computational benefit. Thus, in OWL 2 only two alternatives to specify the semantics are distinguished. The first is called the direct model-theoretic semantics (or OWL 2 DL) and provides the semantics of OWL in a description logic style. The second is called RDF-based semantics (or OWL 2 Full) and allows unrestricted use of Resource Description Framework (RDF) constructs. Since OWL 2 Full is undecidable, OWL 2 DL is used for the definition of the *BPMN 2.0 Ontology* (cf. for this paragraph [54] and [134]).

OWL 2 DL is, as already mentioned, based on description logics (DLs). DLs are a decidable subset of first-order logic with a formal semantics. This formal semantics allows a precise specification of knowledge without ambiguity and the inference of additional information. However, the reasoning algorithms can be very complex, thus it is necessary to find the balance between the expressiveness of the language and the complexity of reasoning. In order to model relationships between entities of a given domain, DLs further consist of three types of entities (concepts, roles, and individual names) and of a set of statements (or axioms). New concepts and roles can be defined using constructors like basic boolean constructors (with operations like intersection, union, and complement), role restrictions (e.g., existential, universal, or number restrictions), or nominals in case of concepts and universal or inverse role in case of roles. In addition, axioms are distinguished based on their type in terminological *(TBox)*, assertional *(ABox)*, and relational axioms *(RBox)* (cf. for this paragraph [64]).

The expressiveness of OWL 2 DL largely corresponds to the description logic $\mathcal{SROIQ}$ (some minor differences are described in a subsequent paragraph). $\mathcal{SROIQ}$ is one of the most expressive description logics and includes many features as can be seen by the respective letters. For example, the letter $\mathcal{S}$ indicates that the description logic $\mathcal{ALC}$ (consisting of the concept constructors intersection, union, complement, existential and universal restriction) is extended with transitive roles. The letter $\mathcal{R}$ further refers to the features role inclusion (role hierarchy), local reflexivity, universal role and additional role characteristics like transitivity, symmetry, asymmetry, role disjointness, reflexivity and irreflexivity. Role inclusion without composition is, e.g., described by the letter $\mathcal{H}$. Furthermore, the letter $\mathcal{O}$ refers to nominals, $\mathcal{I}$ to inverse roles and $\mathcal{Q}$ to qualified number restrictions (cf. for this paragraph [64]).

In summary, $\mathcal{SROIQ}$ consists of the following concept expressions: atomic concept (A), intersection ($C \sqcap D$), union ($C \sqcup D$), complement ($\neg C$), top concept ($\top$), bottom concept ($\bot$), existential restriction ($\exists R.C$), universal restriction ($\forall R.C$), at-least restriction ($\geq n\ R.C$), at-most restriction ($\leq n\ R.C$), local reflexivity ($\exists R.Self$), and nominal ($\{a\}$); of the following role expressions: atomic role (R), inverse role (R^-), and universal role (U); and of individual names (a) [64]. Furthermore, axioms in the *TBox* are defined by concept inclusion ($C \sqsubseteq D$) and concept equivalence ($C \equiv D$); axioms in the *ABox* by concept assertion ($C(a)$), role assertion ($R(a, b)$), individual equality ($a \approx b$), and individual inequality ($a \not\approx b$); and axioms in the *RBox* by role inclusion ($R \sqsubseteq S$), role equivalence ($R \equiv S$), complex role inclusion ($R_1 \circ R_2 \sqsubseteq S$), and role disjointness ($Disjoint(R, S)$) (based on [64]). A complete and terminating reasoning algorithm for $\mathcal{SROIQ}$ then exists if $\mathcal{SROIQ}$ is restricted to simplicity (no complex role inclusion axiom implies instances of a role) and regularity (limitation of cyclic dependencies) [64].

A comparison of the syntax of OWL 2 DL and the description logic $\mathcal{SROIQ}$ shows many similarities. However, OWL uses a prefix notation (*Functional-Style Syntax*) and concepts and roles are called classes and properties. Furthermore, OWL provides some additional operators that are logically redundant. The expressiveness of OWL is, however, increased by supporting data types and keys (similar to key constraints in databases). In addition, OWL supports further aspects like naming an ontology, defining annotations or importing from other ontologies (cf. for this paragraph [64]).

The *BPMN 2.0 Ontology* presented in the following section does not require transitive roles (ALC instead of S), role composition (H instead of R), or nominals (no O). However, in order to specify, e.g., the name of BPMN elements, data types are necessary (denoted by the letter ($\mathcal{D}$)). Thus, the ontology is based on the description logic $\mathcal{ALCHIQ}(\mathcal{D})$, which comprises the same concept expressions as $\mathcal{SROIQ}$ except local reflexivity ($\exists R.Self$) and nominals ($\{a\}$) and the same role expressions except the universal role (U). Furthermore, the syntax validation examples also include nominals and are, thus, based on the description logic $\mathcal{ALCHOIQ}(\mathcal{D})$.

3.3 BPMN 2.0 Ontology

This section presents the *BPMN 2.0 Ontology*, which is based on the BPMN
2.0 specification (final release) and developed using the Web Ontology Language (OWL 2 DL) and the open source ontology editor Protégé (see [120]).
The *BPMN 2.0 Ontology* is divided into two sub-ontologies; the first is called
bpmn20base and presented in section 3.3.1. This ontology only contains the
specifications taken from the BPMN metamodel including all class diagrams,
the tables specifying the attributes and model associations, as well as the
XML schemas. The second sub-ontology is called *bpmn20* and presented in
section 3.3.2. This ontology is derived from the *bpmn20base* ontology and
provides an extension. The *bpmn20* ontology contains further syntactical
requirements taken from the natural text of the BPMN specification. It may
refine inherited restrictions but does not change them. Furthermore, it contains some new classes (e.g., subclasses of *SubProcess*), which are justified
in section 3.3.2. Together, the two ontologies build the *BPMN 2.0 Ontology*
(see section 3.3.3 and appendix A). Finally, concluding remarks are provided
in section 3.3.4.

3.3.1 BPMN 2.0 Base Ontology (*bpmn20base*)

The *bpmn20base* ontology is based on the specification of the BPMN metamodel including all class diagrams, the tables specifying the attributes and
model associations, as well as the XML schemas. Considering, for example,
the BPMN element *Transaction*, the *bpmn20base* ontology contains the information from the class diagram [99, p. 176], from the table specifying the
attributes [99, p. 180], and from the corresponding XML schema definition
[99, p. 203]. Every BPMN element is inserted as a class; the full hierarchy is
shown in Fig. 3.4. Some elements are shown twice since multiple-inheritance
is used in the BPMN metamodel and, therefore, also in the ontology (e.g.,
SubProcess is derived from *Activity* and *FlowElementsContainer* (cf. [99,
p. 176])).

The definition of the hierarchy was difficult since some inheritances are not
explicitly described in the BPMN class diagram. The superclasses are sometimes only mentioned in the natural text of the specification, within the XML
schema or in the case of *InteractionNode* the superclass is not described at
all (assumed to be derived from *BaseElement*). Nevertheless, it was possible
to define a hierarchy that corresponds to the BPMN metamodel.

Different subclasses are specified to be disjoint to avoid that individuals can be an instance of several classes (e.g., *ExclusiveGateway* is disjoint from *EventBasedGateway, ComplexGateway, InclusiveGateway,* and *ParallelGateway*). Furthermore, the BPMN metamodel specifies the package of a class. However, this information is not inherited and subclasses may be contained in a different package. Therefore, this information cannot be stored within a restriction; instead an annotation must be used as shown in Fig. 3.1(a).

After describing a class in general, relationships are defined to restrict the class and specify the details. An ontology supports two types of relationships:

1. Object Property (see Fig. 3.5(a)): Describes the relationship between two individuals.

2. Data Property (see Fig. 3.5(b)): Describes the relationship between individuals and data values.

The properties of the class *SubProcess* are shown in Fig. 3.1(b). The object property *artifacts* defines a relationship between individuals of the class *SubProcess* and individuals of the class *Artifact*. In addition, the data property *triggeredByEvent* defines a relationship between individuals of the class *SubProcess* with boolean data values (cf. [99, p. 176]).

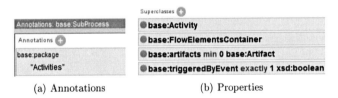

(a) Annotations   (b) Properties

Figure 3.1: Class *SubProcess*

Every restriction further defines the cardinality of allowed relationships. In the *bpmn20base* ontology the following cardinalities are used:

- Exactly x: Exactly the value x

- Min x: Cardinality $(x, *)$

- Max x: Cardinality $(0, x)$

In several cases the cardinality is strengthened in subclasses (e.g., the minimum boundary is increased or the maximum boundary is decreased). A cardinality of type (x, y) is not used within the *bpmn20base* ontology, but would require two restrictions.

The restriction of cardinalities to small numbers like 0 and 1 has special modeling utility [6]:

- Min 1: At least one value

- Max 1: Unique value (but need not exist)

- Min 0: Optional value, multiple allowed

- Max 0: No value allowed

All of the mentioned special cases are also used in the *bpmn20base* ontology, especially the last case (max 0), which forbids a relationship between two individuals.

The BPMN specification further defines instance attributes for some BPMN elements (e.g., *Process* has an instance attribute *state* (cf. [99, p. 149])). In an ontology it is difficult to distinguish attributes and instance attributes since the same object and data properties are used to define the relationship. Therefore, an annotation property named *instanceAttribute* has been created and is set to *yes* for every instance attribute as shown in Fig. 3.2.

The BPMN specification also provides for default values (e.g., the instance attribute *state* has the default value *None*). These default values are not definable within a monotonic OWL. Therefore, in the *bpmn20base* ontology, default values are specified by an annotation property *defaultValue* as shown in Fig. 3.2. An alternative approach for non-monotonic reasoning based on Reiter's default logic is provided by Kolovski et al. and supports default property values as well as an unspecified version of the closed world assumption [61].

The fourth and final annotation property is called *bpmnSpecification* and includes for every attribute and relationship the corresponding definition from the BPMN specification (see Fig. 3.2). In the *bpmn20base* ontology the text is taken from the description/usage column of the corresponding attributes and model associations table. In the *bpmn20* ontology further syntactical requirements are specified and the text for the annotation is taken from the natural text of the BPMN specification. In both cases, this annotation property is very important since it supports the usage of the *BPMN 2.0 Ontology* as a knowledge base. While the descriptions of a BPMN element are spread across the BPMN specification, the descriptions in the ontology are combined

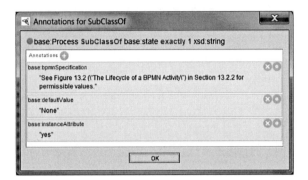

Figure 3.2: Annotations of Instance Attribute *state*

within one class and further explanations are provided in the annotations. This allows for a much faster understanding of the BPMN element.

All in all, the *bpmn20base* ontology consists of 171 classes, 167 object properties, 58 data properties, and 4 annotation properties. Furthermore, the ontology defines 528 necessary conditions (superclasses and restrictions), 9 sufficient conditions (equivalent classes), and 33 disjoint classes.

3.3.2   BPMN 2.0 Extended Ontology (*bpmn20*)

The *bpmn20* ontology is derived from the *bpmn20base* ontology and provides an extension to it. It contains further syntactical requirements taken from the natural text of the BPMN specification. Therefore, the *bpmn20* ontology adds new or refines existing classes and restrictions but does not alter or remove them. The overall goal is that the *BPMN 2.0 Ontology* serves as a knowledge base for almost all syntactical rules of the BPMN specification.

Additional Classes:

The following 85 classes are inserted in the *bpmn20* ontology based on the natural text of the BPMN specification:

- Collapsed/Expanded subclasses for *SubProcess*, *SubChoreography*, and *SubConversation* (detailed description follows),

- Subclasses of *SequenceFlow*: *SequenceFlowConditional*, *SequenceFlow-*

Default, and *SequenceFlowNormal*,

- *PublicProcess* and *PrivateProcess* (with subclasses *PrivateExecutable-Process* and *PrivateNonExecutableProcess*) as subclasses of *Process*,

- *EmbeddedSubProcess* and *EventSubProcess* as subclasses of *SubProcess* (detailed description follows),

- *AbstractTask* as subclass of *Task*, which is disjoint from the other subclasses (e.g., *ScriptTask*, *SendTask*, ...),

- Four subclasses of *Gateway* specifying the direction: *GatewayDirectionUnspecified*, *GatewayDirectionConverging*, *GatewayDirectionDiverging*, and *GatewayDirectionMixed*,

- *ExclusiveEventBasedGateway* and *ParallelEventBasedGateway* as subclasses of *EventBasedGateway*,

- Several subclasses of *Event* representing the markers (e.g., *CancelEvent*, *MessageEvent*, *ErrorEvent*, ...) with further subclasses for expressing interrupting/non-interrupting *Events* (e.g., *CancelEventInterrupting*, *MessageEventInterrupting*, *MessageEventNonInterrupting*, ...),

- Subclasses of *StartEvent*: *StartEventEventSubProcess* (*StartEvent* of an *EventSubProcess*) and *StartEventNotEventSubProcess* (*StartEvent* not of an *EventSubProcess*), and

- *EventMarkerEnumeration*, *TransactionResultEnumeration*, and *MarkerEnumeration* as further enumerations.

Collapsed/Expanded Classes: Three BPMN elements can be collapsed or expanded, namely *SubProcess*, *SubChoreography*, and *SubConversation*. The collapsed view shows a *CollapsedMarker*, whereas the expanded view shows the details but no *CollapsedMarker*. The two subclasses are defined to be disjoint from each other, but are not disjoint from any further subclasses (e.g., a concrete *SubProcess* can be simultaneously collapsed and a *Transaction*).

For example, the class *CollapsedSubProcess* has the following two necessary conditions:

```
base:SubProcess
hasMarker exactly 1 CollapsedMarker
```

The first restriction defines that the class *CollapsedSubProcess* is a subclass of *SubProcess*. The second restriction specifies that it must have exactly one *CollapsedMarker*. This restriction differs from that of an expanded class since expanded classes have no *CollapsedMarker*. The two restrictions together are defined to be sufficient. Since both classes, *CollapsedSubProcess* and *ExpandedSubProcess*, specify necessary and sufficient conditions, they are called *Defined Classes*.

There are three further classes (*CallActivity*, *CallChoreography*, and *Call-Conversation*) which are sometimes shown with a *CollapsedMarker*. However, these classes call other elements and only display the markers of the called element. If they call, for example, a *GlobalTask*, then collapsing or expanding is not possible at all.

SubProcess: Considering the subclasses of *SubProcess*, the BPMN meta-model only refers to two subclasses (*AdHocSubProcess* and *Transaction*) (cf. [99, p. 176]), whereas the natural text mentions five different types (*EmbeddedSubProcess*, *CallActivity*, *EventSubProcess*, *Transaction*, and *Ad-HocSubProcess*) (cf. [99, p. 173-183]). The *CallActivity* corresponds to the *Reusable SubProcess* in BPMN 1.2 and is now derived from *Activity* and, thus, a sibling of *SubProcess*. However, the question remains, why *Embed-dedSubProcess* and *EventSubProcess* have not been defined as subclasses in the BPMN metamodel and whether they should be or not.

The class *SubProcess* defines the following important restriction (cf. [99, p. 176]):

```
base:triggeredByEvent exactly 1 xsd:boolean
```

The data property *triggeredByEvent* serves as a flag. If set to true, the *Sub-Process* is an *EventSubProcess* otherwise it is a "normal" *SubProcess* (*Em-beddedSubProcess*).

The data property *triggeredByEvent* of *SubProcess* is inherited by the sub-classes *Transaction* and *AdHocSubProcess*; however, no restriction specifies that it must be set to false within a subclass. Therefore, the following com-binations are possible:

1. *AdHocSubProcess* and *EmbeddedSubProcess* (*triggeredByEvent*: false)

2. *Transaction* and *EmbeddedSubProcess* (*triggeredByEvent*: false)

3. *AdHocSubProcess* and *EventSubProcess* (*triggeredByEvent*: true)

4. *Transaction* and *EventSubProcess* (*triggeredByEvent*: true)

Since the *EmbeddedSubProcess* represents the "normal" *SubProcess*, the first two cases can be reduced to *AdHocSubProcess* and *Transaction*. However, the last two cases are problematic. A combination of *AdHocSubProcess* and *EventSubProcess* conflicts with the BPMN specification since an *AdHocSubProcess* may be part of the normal flow (cf. [99, p. 153]) whereas an *EventSubProcess* is not allowed to have incoming and outgoing *SequenceFlows* (cf. [99, p. 176f]). Moreover, an *AdHocSubProcess* is not allowed to have a *StartEvent* (cf. [99, p. 182]), whereas every *EventSubProcess* must have exactly one *StartEvent* (cf. [99, p. 177]). Therefore, the combination *AdHocSubProcess* and *EventSubProcess* should be forbidden. In addition, the combination of *Transaction* and *EventSubProcess* is contradictory as well. Again, the integration into the normal flow and the number of *StartEvents* is conflicting. Furthermore, only a *Transaction* is allowed to have a *BoundaryEvent* with a *Cancel* marker (cf. [99, p. 255]).

Therefore, it is suggested that *triggeredByEvent* must be false for *Transactions* and *AdHocSubProcesses*. In addition, the question remains whether *EmbeddedSubProcess* and *EventSubProcess* should be subclasses of *SubProcess*. Several reasons militate in favor of this suggestion:

- Explicit/Implicit Classes: In the BPMN metamodel only two classes are explicit whereas the others are implicit. However, the natural text of the BPMN specification explicitly describes all *SubProcess* types on the same level and as distinct elements. Therefore, all classes should be explicit.

- Disjoint: The four classes can be defined to be disjoint. This explicitly forbids combinations of different types.

- Restrictions: If explicit subclasses are used, further restrictions that only apply to *EventSubProcess* or *EmbeddedSubProcess* can be easily specified. For example, an *EmbeddedSubProcess* is only allowed to have *StartEvents* with marker *None* (cf. [99, p. 241f]), whereas an *EventSubProcess* must not have a *None* marker (cf. [99, p. 242]). If the two elements are expressed within one class and only distinguished by a data property, then the restrictions require implications and are more complex.

- Inherited Restrictions: Since restrictions are inherited, only *Transaction* and *AdHocSubProcess* (but not *EmbeddedSubProcess* or *EventSubProcess*) can refine a restriction. According to the BPMN specification, only a *Transaction* is allowed to have a *BoundaryEvent* with a *Cancel* marker (cf. [99, p. 255]). The structure of the metamodel allows to specify that an *AdHocSubProcess* must not have a *BoundaryEvent* with a *Cancel* marker, whereas a *Transaction* is allowed to have such a *BoundaryEvent*. However, it is not possible to specify that an *EmbeddedSubProcess* or an *EventSubProcess* must not have such a *BoundaryEvent* since both classes are described within the class *SubProcess*. If *Cancel* markers are forbidden in the superclass, then *Transaction* inherits this restriction and cannot have a *Cancel* marker itself.

Based on these arguments, we define *EventSubProcess* and *EmbeddedSubProcess* as subclasses of *SubProcess* and suggests an adaptation of the BPMN metamodel.

Additional Restrictions:

Besides the additional 85 classes, 11 further object properties and 1 data property are specified in the *bpmn20* ontology. In addition, 428 further necessary conditions (superclasses and restrictions), 70 sufficient conditions (equivalent classes), and 23 additional disjoint classes are defined according to the natural text of the BPMN specification. The restrictions of the class *MessageFlow* are shown in Fig. 3.3. Note that the restrictions defined in the *bpmn20* ontology have a bold font.

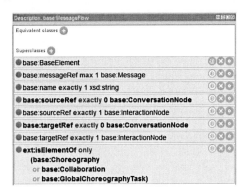

Figure 3.3: *MessageFlow* Restrictions

3.3.3 BPMN 2.0 Ontology (*bpmn20base* and *bpmn20*)

Together, the *bpmn20base* and *bpmn20* ontologies form the *BPMN 2.0 Ontology*. The hierarchy of the *BPMN 2.0 Ontology* with 256 classes is divided into three columns and shown in Fig. 3.4. Nearly all classes are expanded except the enumerations and some elements with multiple inheritance which are only expanded once. Note that the classes and properties defined in the *bpmn20base* ontology are shown with the "base:" prefix, whereas those defined in the *bpmn20* ontology have the prefix "ext:". Classes that have been created or extended in the *bpmn20* ontology have a bold font.

Figure 3.4: Class Hierarchy of *BPMN 2.0 Ontology*

Furthermore, Fig. 3.5(a) shows an extract of the 178 object properties and Fig. 3.5(b) an extract of the 59 data properties. In addition to the predefined annotation properties, four further properties (*bpmnSpecification, defaultValue, instanceAttribute,* and *package*) are defined in the *bpmn2Obase* ontology and shown in Fig. 3.5(c).

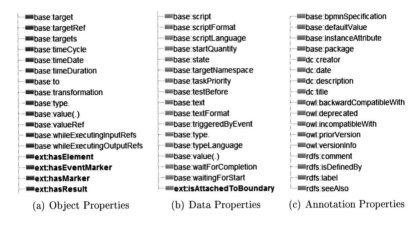

base:target	base:script	base:bpmnSpecification
base:targetRef	base:scriptFormat	base:defaultValue
base:targets	base:scriptLanguage	base:instanceAttribute
base:timeCycle	base:startQuantity	base:package
base:timeDate	base:state	dc:creator
base:timeDuration	base:targetNamespace	dc:date
base:to	base:taskPriority	dc:description
base:transformation	base:testBefore	dc:title
base:type.	base:text	owl:backwardCompatibleWith
base:value(.)	base:textFormat	owl:deprecated
base:valueRef	base:triggeredByEvent	owl:incompatibleWith
base:whileExecutingInputRefs	base:type.	owl:priorVersion
base:whileExecutingOutputRefs	base:typeLanguage	owl:versionInfo
ext:hasElement	base:value(.)	rdfs:comment
ext:hasEventMarker	base:waitForCompletion	rdfs:isDefinedBy
ext:hasMarker	base:waitingForStart	rdfs:label
ext:hasResult	**ext:isAttachedToBoundary**	rdfs:seeAlso
(a) Object Properties	(b) Data Properties	(c) Annotation Properties

Figure 3.5: Properties of *BPMN 2.0 Ontology*

3.3.4 Further Remarks

After introducing the ontology, further remarks are presented in this section.

Distinct Names and Keywords: In the BPMN metamodel relationships with the same name are used several times between different classes. However, the names of object and data properties in an ontology must be distinct. Therefore, object and data properties with the same name are reused in different restrictions and the domain and range of the property is extended to cover all classes. Also reused in different enumerations are classes representing values like *None* and *Both*. In addition, the class and property names "Import", "value" and "language" are keywords in the ontology. To distinguish these names from the keywords, a dot is appended (e.g., "Import."). Furthermore, the Pellet reasoner (see section 3.4.1) defines some own keywords and cannot classify an ontology with the names "type" and "value.". Therefore, a dot is appended to "type" ("type.") and "value." is further changed to "value(.)".

Association and Composition: The BPMN metamodel distinguishes between different types of relationships: associations and compositions. This distinction cannot be expressed in the ontology, although in most cases the different types also affect the cardinality (e.g., compositions tend to have a cardinality of (1, 1) or (0, 1) on the source side while associations often have a cardinality of (0, *) on both sides). An approach to express part-of relations in ontologies is provided in [5].

Implication: Some syntactical requirements include an implication (e.g., if a *SequenceFlow* originates from a *StartEvent*, then the *conditionExpression* must be set to *None* [99, p. 245]). OWL only provides constructs for intersection ($\sqcap$), union ($\sqcup$), and complement ($\neg$); however, an implication can be expressed with union and complement: $A \rightarrow B \equiv \neg A \sqcup B$. This alternative representation is used several times within the *BPMN 2.0 Ontology*.

Open Syntactical Restrictions: Almost all syntactical rules of BPMN are defined in the *BPMN 2.0 Ontology*. The only exceptions are syntactical rules with open questions as well as rules that depend on other elements in a complex way. For example, for the requirement "The Initiator of a Choreography Activity MUST have been involved [...] in the previous Choreography Activity." [99, p. 336] it is not sufficient to determine the source of the incoming *SequenceFlow*, since *Gateways* and *Events* can be defined in between. Instead a new object property *previousChoreographyActivity* can be defined; however, the value of the property cannot be determined automatically. Nevertheless, most rules that depend on other elements can be specified as, e.g., the rule "Target elements in an Event Gateway configuration MUST NOT have any additional incoming Sequence Flows [...]" [99, p. 298]. This rule can be expressed with the following restriction for an *EventBasedGateway*:

```
base:outgoing only (base:targetRef only
(base:incoming exactly 1 base:SequenceFlow)))
```

Contradictions in the BPMN Specification: During the definition of the ontology, several contradictions in the BPMN specification were identified. The most important 30 issues were reported to the OMG. Some examples are given below; further contradictions are provided in appendix A.2:

- According to the class diagram, *InteractionNode* has four subclasses: *Participant, ConversationNode, Task*, and *Event* (cf. [99, p. 122]). However, the natural text mentions the subclass *Activity* instead of *Task* (cf. [99, p. 123]) and the connection rules of *MessageFlow* allow to connect to a *SubProcess* (cf. [99, p. 44]) (a subclass of *Activity*). The open question is whether *Task* or *Activity* should be the subclass of *InteractionNode*.

- According to the class diagram, *StandardLoopCharacteristics* defines a relationship to *Expression* called *loopMaximum* (cf. [99, p. 189]). However, in the corresponding attribute description, *loopMaximum* is defined to be an attribute of type integer (cf. [99, p. 191]).

- According to the class diagram, *Collaboration* references exactly one *ConversationAssociation* [99, p. 109], but in the corresponding description of the model associations, the relationship is defined to have a cardinality of (0, *) (cf. [99, p. 110]).

3.4 Evaluation

The consistency and correctness of the ontologies are evaluated based on two different methods. First, several different reasoners are used to validate the *bpmn20base* and the *bpmn20* ontology and described in section 3.4.1. In addition, concrete BPMN models are checked against the ontology and presented in section 3.4.2. Considering the open questions and contradictions, proving the completeness of the ontologies is currently not possible. However, the entire BPMN specification was revised several times to ensure an almost complete *BPMN 2.0 Ontology*.

3.4.1 Reasoner

A reasoner is also known as a classifier and used for consistency checking as well as to compute the inferred class hierarchy. A class in an ontology is classified as consistent if it can have instances, otherwise it is inconsistent. The following three reasoners have been used to classify the *BPMN 2.0 Ontology*:

- *FaCT++* is an OWL-DL reasoner that is available under the GNU Public License (GPL) and implemented using C++ [125].

- *Pellet* is an open source OWL 2 reasoner that is based on Java [71]. Pellet also supports some forms of closed world reasoning, which is required for one of the examples described in section 3.4.2.

- *HermiT 1.3.5* is an OWL 2 reasoner that is compatible with Java. HermiT is released under the GNU Lesser General Public License (LGPL) and pre-installed in Protégé [126].

The ontologies are classified to be consistent by all three reasoners.

3.4.2 Syntax Validation

In addition to the validation through reasoners, the *BPMN 2.0 Ontology* is used as a syntax checker and concrete BPMN models are checked against the ontology. New ontologies are created for every example and derived from the *bpmn20* ontology as shown in Fig. 3.6. The presented examples show a correct, two incorrect, and an incomplete model. More complex examples are checked similarly, but the definition of the model requires more effort. Thus, the syntax checker may be extended with a graphical tool as described in section 3.5. A major advantage of the ontology is the possibility to draw conclusions as shown in the first example. If it can be concluded that an element of type *A* must in fact be an element of subtype *B*, then this conclusion allows to check whether the element fulfills the restrictions defined by the subtype.

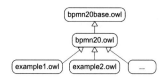

Figure 3.6: Derived Ontologies

Example 1:

The first example consists of one *StartEvent*, one *EndEvent*, two *Sequence-Flows*, and one *Task* as shown in Fig. 3.7(a). Instances of the same class (e.g., the *SequenceFlows*) are defined to represent different individuals. For all elements the data property *id* is defined, the *Activities* further specify a *name*, and the *isInterrupting* property of the *Events* is set to true.

Considering object properties, all *SequenceFlows* specify the *sourceRef* and *targetRef*, and the *Activities* define the *incoming* and *outgoing Sequence-Flows*. The model is then classified to be correct. Note that based on the open world assumption it is not necessary to specify all mandatory properties.

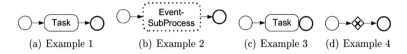

| (a) Example 1 | (b) Example 2 | (c) Example 3 | (d) Example 4 |

Figure 3.7: Syntax Checking Examples

Afterwards the example is adapted and the data property *isInterrupting* of *StartEvent* is set to false. Since only *EventSubProcesses* are allowed to have non-interrupting *StartEvents* (cf. [99, p. 242ff]), the reasoner automatically concludes that the *StartEvent* must be of type *StartEventEventSubProcess* as shown in Fig. 3.8. This conclusion allows to check further restrictions, for example, the marker type. Although a general *StartEvent* is allowed to have a marker of type *None*, the *StartEvent* of an *EventSubProcess* must not have this marker type. If, nevertheless, the marker is defined to be of type *None*, then an inconsistency is reported by all reasoners. An inconsistency is also reported if it is explicitly specified that the non-interrupting *StartEvent* is of type *StartEventNotEventSubProcess*.

Example 2:

The second example comprises an *EventSubProcess* as shown in Fig. 3.7(b). The *EventSubProcess* specifies the data properties *id*, *name*, and *triggered-ByEvent* with the last property set to true. In addition, the *incoming* and *outgoing SequenceFlows* are defined. The model is incorrect since an *EventSubProcess* is not allowed to have *incoming* or *outgoing SequenceFlows* (cf. [99, p. 176f]). The ontology is classified to be inconsistent by all reasoners.

Example 3:

In the third example, one *SequenceFlow* is omitted and the *Task* directly connects to the *EndEvent* as shown in Fig. 3.7(c). The BPMN model is incorrect since the range of the properties *incoming* and *outgoing* is *SequenceFlow*. This inconsistency can be detected if the classes are defined to be disjoint from each other (e.g., *SequenceFlow* is disjoint from *FlowNode*) and if the range of the object property is specified. In the *BPMN 2.0 Ontology*, the domain and range of every object property is specified and different classes are defined to be disjoint. Thus, the ontology is classified to be inconsistent by all reasoners.

(a) Class *owl:Thing*　(b) Negative Assertions

Figure 3.8: Inferred Individuals　　Figure 3.9: Closed World Reasoning

Example 4:

In the fourth example, a *Gateway* is inserted between the two *SequenceFlows* as shown in Fig. 3.7(d). This BPMN model is incomplete since the *Gateway* has only one *incoming* and one *outgoing SequenceFlow*, but is required to have at least two *incoming* or at least two *outgoing SequenceFlows* (cf. [99, p. 290]):

```
(base:incoming min 2 base:SequenceFlow)
or (base:outgoing min 2 base:SequenceFlow)
```

In a first step, the inconsistency cannot be detected based on the open world assumption since the *Gateway* might have further unspecified *incoming* or *outgoing SequenceFlows*. This problem is solvable by closed world reasoning as described for the Pellet reasoner in [71]. The class *owl:Thing* must be equivalent to the enumeration of all known individuals as shown in Fig. 3.9(a) and it is necessary to define negative assertions for things that are definitely not true as shown in Fig. 3.9(b). Afterwards, the ontology is classified to be inconsistent by all reasoners.

Further Examples:

- Violation of Range: If the range of a data property is violated (e.g., *id* is defined to be an integer ≤ 5, but one element has a value ≥ 6) then all reasoners detect an inconsistency.

- Wrong Data Type: If a wrong data type is specified (e.g., for an individual the data property *isInterrupting* is defined to be of type double, but the value is correct and set to true), then only the reasoners HermiT and Pellet report an error. However, this mistake is based on an incorrect specification of the model and can be avoided if a graphical modeling tool is used.

3.5   Summary

In this chapter, two ontologies that formally represent the BPMN 2.0 specification were presented. The *bpmn20base* ontology is based on the BPMN
metamodel and the *bpmn20* ontology contains further syntactical requirements taken from the natural text of the BPMN specification. Together, the
two ontologies form the *BPMN 2.0 Ontology*. This ontology can be used
as a knowledge base since the descriptions are combined within the corresponding class and further explanations are provided in annotations. This
allows a much faster understanding of BPMN. In addition, the ontology can
be used as a syntax checker, which detects correct, incorrect, and incomplete
models. A major advantage of the syntax checker is the possibility to draw
conclusions. Finally, three different reasoners proved the consistency of the
ontology.

A further goal is to automatically generate the basic structure of the *bpmn20-
base* ontology from the XML schema of the BPMN specification once the
XML schema corresponds to the UML class diagram. In addition, syntax
checking currently requires the manual definition of concrete models, so only
simple models have been defined up to now. Thus, another goal is to extend the syntax checker with a graphical tool (e.g., the BPMN Modeler for
Eclipse [30]), and to automatically check the model against the ontology. For
this purpose, the Jena Semantic Web framework can be used as suggested
in [54].

Chapter 4

Extending BPMLs with Deontic Logic

A drawback of many business process modeling languages (BPMLs) is that modalities are implicitly expressed through the structure of the process flow. All activities are implicitly obligatory (mandatory), and whenever something should be permissible (optional), a gateway is used to split the process flow to offer the possibility to execute the activity or to do nothing. This implies that the decision whether to execute one or more activities is described within another element, e.g. a gateway. The separation of decision and execution requires additional modeling elements and a comprehensive understanding of the entire process to identify obligatory and permissible activities (see [89]).

This chapter addresses the problem and presents an extension for BPMLs based on deontic logic to highlight modalities and specify the decisions within the corresponding activities. The first section introduces possible deontic classifications of an activity and provides a discussion of user and conditional choices and an overview to which extent deontic concepts can be used in process flows. Then the *Workflow Patterns* by van der Aalst et al. (see [129]) are presented, which describe the main constructs of BPMLs. Extended with deontic logic are the *Control-Flow Patterns*, which specify the process flow. In the third section, the deontic extension is applied to BPMN and called *Deontic BPMN* (see also [89]). The deontic analysis is supported by a path exploration approach and the benefits of Deontic BPMN are demonstrated by a case study and a preliminary survey. Another issue addressed in this chapter is the limited support for actor modeling in BPMN. A new approach including deontic logic is proposed and applied to the resource perspective of the Workflow Patterns. The last section summarizes the results.

4.1   Deontic Classification

An introduction to deontic logic and an overview of the corresponding literature is given in section 2.2. In this section, all deontic constructs used for the extension of BPMLs are presented. First of all, the monadic deontic operators for *obligation, permission,* and *prohibition* are provided. In addition, the derived operator *alternative* and the concept of an *empty activity* are specified. Afterwards, *preconditions* are defined to support the concept of dyadic deontic logic.

The deontic operators can then be combined using the logical connectives for negation ($\neg$), conjunction ($\wedge$), disjunction ($\vee$), material implication ($\rightarrow$), and material equivalence ($\leftrightarrow$) described in [104, p. 205]. In addition, a further connective for contravalence ($\veebar$) is used to define that either the first or the second term but not both must be true.

In case of unstructured diagrams, multiple deontic classifications might be necessary and are described in the third subsection. The fourth subsection then comprises the definition of actors within deontic logic. Moreover, for the deontic classification of choices (exclusive or multi-choice), user and conditional decisions must be distinguished. Finally, different gradations concerning the extent to which deontic logic affects the process flow are presented.

4.1.1   Monadic Deontic Logic

Monadic deontic logic comprises the unconditional or absolute normative concepts [104, p. 148]. The core concepts are *obligation* (O), *permission* (P), and *prohibition* (F). In addition, a derived operator for *alternative* (X) is defined. Furthermore, an empty (or *Phi*) activity is specified to highlight that nothing has to be done.

Empty Activity

First of all, an empty activity (*Phi* or Φ) is introduced to highlight that the user has the possibility to do nothing. This empty activity is inserted whenever a sequence flow directly connects a choice or split with the corresponding merge. In the deontic extension of BPMLs, an empty activity is highlighted with a gray background color and the text *Phi* as shown in Fig. 4.1. In addition, every path that comprises an empty activity is called a *Phi*-Path.

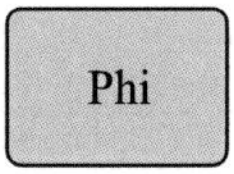

Figure 4.1: Empty Activity

However, in the following deontically classified diagrams, empty activities are rare, since the deontic extension allows to remove almost all *Phi*-Paths.

Obligation

The deontic concept for obligation (O) is expressed in natural language by the word "must" [104, p. 148]. In the deontic extension of BPMLs, an obligatory (or mandatory) activity is highlighted with a red background color and by surrounding the text with O() for obligatory as shown in Fig. 4.2. All obligatory activities must be executed within every process instance.

Figure 4.2: Obligatory Activity

Activities are obligatory if they are, for example, defined in the main flow ($Start; A; B; C; End \equiv Start; O(A); O(B); O(C); End$) or after a parallel split in the main flow ($Start; A \wedge B; End \equiv Start; O(A) \wedge O(B); End$).

Permission

The deontic concept for permission (P) is expressed in natural language by the word "may" [104, p. 148]. In the deontic extension of BPMLs, a permissible (or optional) activity is highlighted with a green background color and by surrounding the text with P() for permissible as shown in Fig. 4.3. The semantics of a permissible activity is that if a token reaches the activity it can either be executed or not.

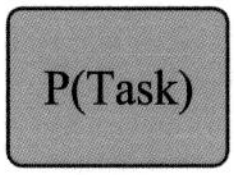

P(Task)

Figure 4.3: Permissible Activity

Activities are permissible if they are, for example, specified after an exclusive or multi-choice and if there is at least one alternative *Phi*-Path (*Start*; $A \lor B \lor Phi$; $End \equiv Start$; $P(A) \lor P(B)$; End). In the deontic extension, the *Phi*-Paths can be removed, since the optionality is directly expressed within the corresponding activity.

Prohibition

The deontic concept for prohibition (F) is expressed in natural language by the term "must not" [104, p. 148] and can alternatively be expressed with the concepts for obligation or permission ($F(Task) \equiv O(\neg Task) \equiv \neg P(Task)$). In the deontic extension of BPMLs, a forbidden (or prohibited) activity is highlighted with a blue background color and by surrounding the text with F() for forbidden as shown in Fig. 4.4. The semantics of a forbidden activity is that if a token reaches the activity, the token is passed on but the activity is not executed. So forbidden activities must not be executed within any process instance.

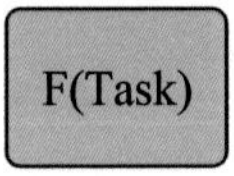

Figure 4.4: Forbidden Activity

Activities that are only forbidden (monadic concept) are rare, since the intention of process flows is to comprise activities that might be executed. However, more common is the use of activities that are forbidden under some circumstances (dyadic deontic logic), especially in case of multiple deontic classifications.

Alternative

The deontic concept for alternative (X) is expressed in natural language by the phrase "either ... or ...". This concept will be used in the work at hand to simplify the otherwise complex definition of contravalence. The concept of alternatives is also defined in [10]:

$$X(A, B) = (O(A) \lor O(B)) \land \neg(P(A) \land P(B))$$

In the deontic extension of BPMLs, an alternative activity is highlighted with a yellow background color and by surrounding the text with X() for alternative as shown in Fig. 4.5. If two activities are alternative, then either the first or the second activity must be executed within every process instance.

Figure 4.5: Alternative Activity

Activities are alternative if they are, for example, defined after an exclusive choice and if there is no alternative *Phi*-Path $(Start; A \dot{\lor} B; End \equiv Start; X(A) \dot{\lor} X(B); End)$.

4.1.2 Dyadic Deontic Logic

Dyadic deontic logic supports conditional or relative normative concepts and, thus, the concept of commitment [104, p. 148]. Every monadic deontic operator can be extended with a precondition, for example, a conditional obligation is expressed in natural language by the sentence "if ..., then it must be the case that" [104, p. 148].

Different notations have been proposed to specify conditions, e.g., a task A with a precondition B can be defined as AfB (A "fordert" (requires) B) [72], $A \Rightarrow O(B)$ (A implies that B is obligatory) [10], $O_B A$ (A is obligatory given B) [104, p. 151], or $O(A|B)$ (it is obligatory that A given B) [68]. Several conditions can then be concatenated with $\land$ or $\lor$. In our deontic extension of BPMLs, the last notation type $(O(A|B))$ is used due to its understandability (see Fig. 4.6). Furthermore, the extension of BPMLs with dyadic deontic logic allows additional definitions that have not been possible in the original language, e.g., it is criticized in [139] that BPMN does not directly support pre- and postconditions.

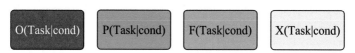

Figure 4.6: Conditional Normative Concepts

The semantics of a conditional activity is that the deontic expression must only be fulfilled in process instances where the condition evaluates to true. If, for example, an obligatory activity specifies as precondition the completion of the previous activity, then this activity must only be executed if the previous activity was executed before. However, if the previous activity was not executed, then the behavior is undefined. A complete formal definition would specify the behavior in case the condition is not fulfilled, e.g., define that the activity is forbidden. However, it can also be assumed that whenever the behavior is undefined, the execution is forbidden and the token is passed on. This approach provides a shorter and better understandable definition and will, thus, be used for the deontic extension of BPMLs. Note that the evaluation of a condition may also have a third state "undecided", e.g. in case of a deferred choice (see section 4.2). If the evaluation of the condition is in the state *undecided*, then the token is blocked until a decision is reached.

4.1.3   Multiple Deontic Classifications

The concept of multiple deontic classification is necessary in case of unstructured diagrams. According to Liu and Kumar [70], a structured workflow is one in which each split element is matched with a properly nested join element of the same type. The authors further identified four basic types of structured workflows (based on the definition of structured workflows by Kiepuszewski et al. in [59]): sequence, decision structure, parallel structure, and structured loop. Diagrams that are restricted to these types are well-structured. Furthermore, since each of the four workflow types has exactly one entry and one exit point, an activity is addressed by at most one splitting gateway. Thus, an expression with one deontic operator is sufficient.

On the contrary, unstructured constructs allow arbitrary connections between activities, so a construct may have multiple entry or exit points [23]. Hence, an activity may be addressed by different splitting gateways. For example, Fig. 4.7 shows an unstructured diagram, in which task B is on the one hand an alternative to task C if the splitting gateway after task A is taken into account and on the other hand permissible according to the splitting gateway after task D. Unstructured workflows are presented in more detail in [70] and the weaknesses of unstructured business process modeling languages are studied in particular in [23].

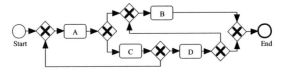

Figure 4.7: Unstructured Diagram

We also studied the consequences of unstructured diagrams in terms of decomposition and reusability in [91]. For example, considering Fig. 4.7, it is not possible to comprise two or three activities in a sub-process. Thus, we suggested some approaches to create structured from unstructured diagrams. However, since it is not the goal of the current work to transform unstructured to structured diagrams, multiple deontic classifications are necessary.

Multiple deontic classification means that several deontic expressions are concatenated, for example, with ∧ or ∨. The unstructured diagram in Fig. 4.8(a) can be extended with deontic concepts as shown in Fig. 4.8(b). Task A is classified as alternative and as permissible and the background color is a mixture of yellow and green. In addition, preconditions can be used to define which classification is applicable under which circumstances and to remove the *Phi*-Path as well as the surrounding gateways as shown in Fig. 4.8(c).

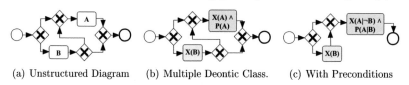

(a) Unstructured Diagram   (b) Multiple Deontic Class.   (c) With Preconditions

Figure 4.8: Multiple Deontic Classification in Unstructured Diagram

The semantics of an activity with multiple deontic classifications depends on the number of applicable expressions. The following cases are distinguished:

- If no expression evaluates to true, then the activity is forbidden as described in section 4.1.2 and the token is passed on.

- If one expression is applicable, for example task A in Fig. 4.8 is either alternative or permissible depending on the previous task, then only this expression must be considered.

- If several expressions are applicable at the same time, then all expressions must be fulfilled. For example, every activity after a multi-choice (inclusive gateway) without *Phi*-Path is permissible and obligatory if no alternative activity is executed $(P(A) \land O(A|\neg AlterActivity))$. When the precondition evaluates to true, the activity is simultaneously permissible and obligatory, so it must be executed. However, the applicable expressions can also be contradictory, e.g. an activity may be obligatory and forbidden at the same time as defined for incomplete decisions in section 4.2.3. Due to the contradiction, the activity is neither executed nor is the token passed on resulting in a runtime exception.

4.1.4   Deontic Logic with Agency

A further concept of deontic logic is the definition of actors. For example, an action description can have the form $Do(r, p)$, where Do is a modal operator for action or agency, r stands for an agent (or role) and p describes a propositional expression (e.g., an action A) [55]. Every deontic operator can then be extended with an action description, e.g., $O\ do(r, A)$, $P\ do(r, A)$, or $F\ do(r, A)$ (A user with role r is obliged/permitted/forbidden to perform action A). Since the deontic logic used in this thesis is based on actions (see section 2.2.1), the modal operator Do (expressed e.g. as "ought to do" or "permitted to do") can either be used implicitly or explicitly. In the following, the modal operator is only used explicitly if agents are defined.

4.1.5   User vs. Conditional Choice

According to the Workflow Patterns and most concrete BPMLs like BPMN and UML ADs, all exclusive and multi-choices must define conditions on the outgoing paths. The conditions depend on the outcome of a preceding task, on the evaluation of data or an expression, or on another programmatic selection mechanism. The only exception are default arcs, which have their own semantics and do not specify an explicit condition (cf. for this paragraph [128]).

However, an important aspect for the deontic classification is the differentiation of human (or user) and state-based (or conditional) decisions. The result of both decisions can be determined, e.g., within a preceding task, but in the first case the user can freely decide whereas in the second case the outgoing path is selected based on a state, data, or rule. For example, an exclusive choice with the decision "Choose Color" could describe a user choice, whereas the answer to the question "Credit Card Valid?" would be based on the verification of the credit card.

The reason for the differentiation of user and conditional choices is that the deontic extension is intended for a different level of abstraction than most BPMLs. For example, in BPMN the level of abstraction is such that the resulting models can be executed by a business process engine and every model is supposed to be deterministic. The deontic extension, however, takes the viewpoint of the user, who is not seen as a deterministically operating machine, but as an agent who is capable of autonomously taking decisions and also authorized to do so. Thus, the tasks following such a user choice are classified as permissible (cf. for this paragraph [93]).

To be able to compare standard models and their deontic extensions, the deontically classified models must be transformed to the same level of abstraction. In a standard model, every task must be seen as obligatory as soon as the firing conditions are met, e.g. by a token on the incoming path. In order to establish a relation between a permissible and a standard task, a permissible task can be considered to be a conditionally obligatory task, where the precondition is determined by the user input ("UserChoice"). The precondition "UserChoice" then has to be matched with the firing condition of the respective outgoing path of the choice which leads to the task in question. It should also be noted that due to the different layers addressed, the deontically extended models may show a certain redundancy where user-centric and process-engine-centric concepts overlap. This redundancy is assumed to be very helpful from the user's point of view (cf. for this paragraph [93]).

4.1.6 Gradation of Deontic Classification

Regarding the deontic classification of process flows, different gradations are possible concerning the extent to which deontic concepts affect the process flow, and they range from highlighting modalities to a detailed work list in which the process flow can be omitted. The following gradings of deontic classification can be distinguished:

1. Deontic logic is used to highlight the modality of activities by classifying them as obligatory, alternative, or permissible. However, the classification does not affect the process flow and, thus, the number of gateways and sequence flows remains the same.

2. The deontic classification affects the process flow and reduces the structural complexity:

   (a) The number of gateways and sequence flows can be reduced by removing the *Phi*-Paths and possible surrounding gateways in case only one further path is addressed.

   (b) The exclusive and inclusive choices are replaced by parallel splits resulting in only one gateway type without conditions and irrelevant order of the outgoing paths. This extension is presented in section 4.2.3.

3. The entire process flow is expressed with deontic logic, for example, by using preconditions or deontic rules to define the dependencies. The

activities can then be provided in a work list starting with those activities that have no defined precondition or where the precondition is already fulfilled. The process flow is no more required.

In general, it can be said that the lower gradings (1 and 2a) increase the human understandability. Modalities are highlighted and the structural complexity might be reduced, but the applied deontic constructs are easy to understand. However, the higher gradings (2b and 3) may comprise complex deontic expressions. The resulting expressions are hard to understand for humans, but simplify the execution by a process engine.

The goal of the current work is to increase the human understandability. Thus, the necessary deontic extensions for reaching grading 2a are presented. Furthermore, the required extension for reaching grading 2b is described for the Workflow Patterns in section 4.2.3 and for the graph transformation in section 5.3.3.

4.2 Workflow Patterns

This section considers the *Workflow Patterns* (WP) developed by research groups around Wil van der Aalst and Arthur ter Hofstede [128] and describes how the patterns of the control-flow perspective, the *Control-Flow Patterns*, can be extended with deontic concepts to highlight modalities. In addition, the suggested classification of exclusive and multi-choices can be extended and replaced by parallel splits as shown in the last section.

4.2.1 Overview

The *Workflow Patterns* define requirements for workflow and business process modeling languages by a collection of patterns divided into four perspectives (control-flow, resource, data, and exception handling) with the goal to provide a conceptual basis for process technology [128, 129]. The Workflow Patterns have been developed by research groups around Wil van der Aalst and Arthur ter Hofstede since 1999 and are presented on the Workflow Patterns Homepage (see [128]) or in corresponding publications (e.g., [110, 129] for Control-Flow Patterns). A major advantage of the Workflow Patterns is that they are independent of concrete BPMLs and, thus, an extension defined for the Workflow Patterns can be easily adapted for most concrete BPMLs including BPMN, UML ADs, and EPCs.

The first perspective comprises the *Control-Flow Patterns*, which specify the requirements for the process flow and include patterns for branching, synchronizing, multiple instances, cancellation, iteration, termination, and triggering. The original 20 patterns described in [129] have been extended in 2006 to 43 patterns presented in [110]. For each pattern a formal description is provided in form of a *Coloured Petri-Net* (CPN) (cf. for this paragraph [128]). The Control-Flow Patterns are extended with deontic logic in section 4.2.2.

The 43 *Workflow Resource Patterns* are used to capture the various ways in which resources are represented and utilized in workflows and business processes [109]. These patterns are described in more detail in section 4.4.4. Similarly, the 40 *Workflow Data Patterns* describe how data is represented in workflows and business processes [128]. For the last perspective, the *Exception Handling Patterns*, a classification framework for exception handling based on patterns has been developed [128]. Neither the Workflow Data Patterns nor the Exception Handling Patterns are extended with deontic logic.

The research groups further analyzed whether and how patterns are implemented in fourteen commercial offerings (Staffware, IBM WebSphere MQ, FLOWer, COSA, iPlanet, SAP Workflow, FileNet, BPEL, WebSphere Integration Developer, Oracle BPEL, BPMN 1.0, XPDL, UML ADs, and EPCs) [110]. Three further commercial offerings (jBPM, OpenWFE, and Enhydra Shark) are considered in a current analysis provided in [128]. White, one of the specification editors of BPMN, studied how BPMN and UML ADs can represent the Workflow Patterns [136]. A more comprehensive comparison of BPMN and the WPs also considering the resource and data perspective is presented in [139]. According to this analysis, BPMN provides good support for the Control-Flow Patterns, medium support for the Data Patterns, but only low support for the Resource Patterns. Thus, extending BPMN with actor modeling is important and addressed in section 4.4. Furthermore, an analysis of EPCs based on the Workflow Patterns is provided in [81].

Interesting is also the formal specification of the 43 Control-Flow Patterns in terms of *Abstract State Machines* (ASMs) by Börger (see [16]). Eight basic workflow patterns were identified, four for sequential (sequence, iteration, begin/termination, and selection) and four for parallel control flows (splitting, merging, interleaving, and trigger). Although this definition helps to structure the WPs, the refined patterns must be considered for the deontic analysis, since the deontic classification depends, e.g., on how many outgoing paths of a selection (or choice) may be taken. Börger further criticized the WPs for their ambiguous and incomplete description and the unsuitable comparison with other approaches (no consideration of *workarounds*) in [13].

However, although the WPs are widely used and often referenced as shown by the *Impact* section on the homepage (see [128]), no approach is available that extends the Workflow Patterns with deontic logic. Nevertheless, some publications focus on the organizational part of process modeling and either reference the Workflow Patterns or deontic logic as related work (e.g., [102]).

4.2.2   Control-Flow Patterns with Deontic Logic

In this section, the *Control-Flow Patterns* are studied and extended with deontic concepts. An overview of the 43 Control-Flow Patterns is given in Tab. 4.1. The first column provides the pattern number, the second column the pattern name, and the third column specifies whether the pattern requires a deontic classification. For example, some tasks in the *Sequence* and *Parallel Split* patterns can be classified as obligatory whereas in the *Synchronization* pattern several parallel paths converge into a single path without affecting the deontic classification.

Table 4.1: Overview Control-Flow Patterns based on [128]

No.	Pattern Name	Deontic Extension
Basic Control-Flow Patterns		
1	Sequence	Yes
2	Parallel Split	Yes
3	Synchronization	No
4	Exclusive Choice	Yes
5	Simple Merge	No
Advanced Branching and Synchronization Patterns		
6	Multi-Choice	Yes
7	Structured Synchronizing Merge	No
8	Multi-Merge	No
9	Structured Discriminator	No
28	Blocking Discriminator	No
29	Cancelling Discriminator	No
30	Structured Partial Join	No
31	Blocking Partial Join	No
32	Cancelling Partial Join	No
33	Generalized AND-Join	No
37	Local Synchronizing Merge	No
38	General Synchronizing Merge	No
41	Thread Merge	No
42	Thread Split	No
Multiple Instance Patterns		
12	Multiple Instances without Synchronization	No

No.	Pattern Name	Deontic Extension
13	Multiple Instances with *a priori* Design-Time Knowledge	No
14	Multiple Instances with *a priori* Run-Time Knowledge	No
15	Multiple Instances without *a priori* Run-Time Knowledge	No
34	Static Partial Join for Multiple Instances	No
35	Cancelling Partial Join for Multiple Instances	No
36	Dynamic Partial Join for Multiple Instances	No
State-based Patterns		
16	Deferred Choice	Yes
17	Interleaved Parallel Routing	No
18	Milestone	Yes
39	Critical Section	No
40	Interleaved Routing	No
Cancellation and Force Completion Patterns		
19	Cancel Task	No
20	Cancel Case	No
25	Cancel Region	No
26	Cancel Multiple Instance Activity	No
27	Complete Multiple Instance Activity	No
Iteration Patterns		
10	Arbitrary Cycles	Yes
21	Structured Loop	Yes
22	Recursion	No
Termination Patterns		
11	Implicit Termination	No
43	Explicit Termination	No
Trigger Patterns		
23	Transient Trigger	Yes
24	Persistent Trigger	Yes

Pattern 1: Sequence

The first pattern describes a sequence of tasks, where each task is enabled after the completion of the preceding task and no condition is associated with the control-flow edge [128]. The CPN of the *Sequence* pattern is shown in Fig. 4.9.

Figure 4.9: Pattern 1: Sequence (Source: [128])

The circles contain the places (input labels ($i1..in$), internal labels ($p1..pn$), and output labels ($o1..on$)), whereas the rectangles describe the transitions

$(A..Z)$ [110]. Places represent conditions, which can either be seen as precondition if placed before the transition or as postcondition if placed afterwards [127, p. 167]. The places and transitions are connected by edges that represent the control-flow (c). Since Petri nets are directed bipartite graphs, every edge has as source either a place or a transition and as target the respective other element [127, p. 165].

Considering the deontic classification, three cases are distinguished as shown in Fig. 4.10. The second and every further task of a sequence are obligatory and enabled after the completion of the preceding task. Thus, in all three cases these tasks are classified as obligatory under the precondition that the previous task was executed, e.g. $O(B|A)$. A forbidden statement is only necessary in cases where the previous task may be forbidden. The difference between the three cases shown in Fig. 4.10, however, is the classification of the first task.

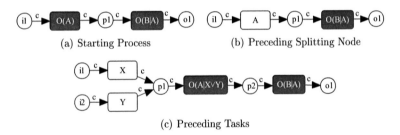

(a) Starting Process   (b) Preceding Splitting Node

(c) Preceding Tasks

Figure 4.10: Deontic Classification of *Sequence* Pattern

In the first case shown in Fig. 4.10(a), it is assumed that task A starts the process and there is no other preceding task or start event. In this case, task A is marked as obligatory $(O(A))$.

In the second case shown in Fig. 4.10(b), task A is addressed by a splitting node, for example, a parallel split or a choice. In this case, task A is deontically classified by the corresponding split or choice pattern and remains unclassified in the sequence pattern.

The third case is shown in Fig. 4.10(c) and comprises all scenarios where the first task of the sequence has one or more preceding tasks or events. In this case, task A is obligatory, but all preceding tasks or events must be summarized in the precondition, e.g. $O(A|X \vee Y)$ in case of a preceding multi-merge, $O(A|X \wedge Y)$ in case of parallel incoming paths, or $O(A|StartEvent)$ in case of a preceding start event.

However, according to the survey in section 4.3.4, preconditions decrease the understandability. Thus, a pragmatic approach is suggested, which allows to omit the preconditions (see Fig. 4.11) if the sequence is part of the main flow and the execution order is also expressed by sequence flows.

Figure 4.11: Pragmatic Approach of *Sequence* Pattern

Nevertheless, the preconditions must remain if the sequence follows an exclusive or multi-choice as shown by the BPMN example in Fig. 4.12(a) with the deontic classification provided in Fig. 4.12(b). The preconditions are necessary to define that if the first task is not executed, then also the further tasks may not be executed thereby representing the *Phi*-Path. Removing the preconditions (see Fig. 4.12(d)) would require to execute the further tasks and lead to the assumption that the former BPMN model only comprised task *A* within the choice and defined the other tasks after the merge as shown in Fig. 4.12(c).

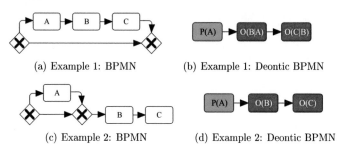

(a) Example 1: BPMN   (b) Example 1: Deontic BPMN

(c) Example 2: BPMN   (d) Example 2: Deontic BPMN

Figure 4.12: Examples of *Sequence* Pattern

Pattern 2: Parallel Split

The *Parallel Split* pattern describes the split of a branch in two or more parallel branches, which are executed concurrently as shown in Fig. 4.13 [128]. The parallel split does not define any conditions on the outgoing control-flow edges.

The deontic classification of the *Parallel Split* pattern is shown in Fig. 4.14. Tasks *B* and *C* are always executed and, thus, classified as obligatory under the precondition that the previous task has been completed ($O(B|A)$,

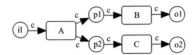

Figure 4.13: Pattern 2: Parallel Split (Source: [128])

$O(C|A)$). The preconditions can be omitted if the split is defined in the main flow, since in this case all parallel paths must be executed within every process instance ($B \wedge C = O(B) \wedge O(C)$).

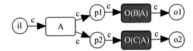

Figure 4.14: Deontic Classification of *Parallel Split* Pattern

Since parallel splits do not specify conditions, a possible *Phi*-Path has no additional semantics and can be removed:

$$B \wedge \Phi = B \qquad B \wedge C \wedge \Phi = B \wedge C$$

If there is only one other path besides the *Phi*-Path, then removing the *Phi*-Path also allows to remove the parallel split.

Pattern 4: Exclusive Choice

The *Exclusive Choice* pattern describes the divergence of one branch into two or more branches, but the thread of control is only passed to exactly one outgoing branch as shown in Fig. 4.15 [128]. The selection of the outgoing branch is based on an evaluation of the conditions defined for the outgoing paths [128]. Not specified is the behavior if several conditions evaluate to true, e.g. BPMN defines an ordering of the outgoing paths.

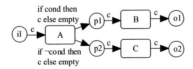

Figure 4.15: Pattern 4: Exclusive Choice (Source: [128])

The deontic classification depends on the type of choice (user vs. conditional) and on a possible *Phi*-Path (see Fig. 4.16). If the exclusive choice provides a user decision without *Phi*-Path, then all tasks are alternatives as shown in Fig. 4.16(a).

$$B \mathbin{\dot\vee} C = X(B) \mathbin{\dot\vee} X(C)$$

However, if one or more *Phi*-Paths exist, then these paths can be removed and all other tasks are classified as permissible as shown in Fig. 4.16(b). If there is only one other path apart from the *Phi*-Path, then also the exclusive choice can be removed.

$$B \mathbin{\dot\vee} \Phi = P(B) \qquad B \mathbin{\dot\vee} C \mathbin{\dot\vee} \Phi = P(B) \mathbin{\dot\vee} P(C)$$

However, if the exclusive choice provides a conditional decision, then the tasks are obligatory under the precondition that the condition is fulfilled as shown in Fig. 4.16(c), and possible *Phi*-Paths must remain.

$$(B|cond) \mathbin{\dot\vee} (C|\neg cond) = O(B|cond) \mathbin{\dot\vee} O(C|\neg cond)$$

All tasks specify as precondition the completion of the previous task. This precondition can be omitted if the choice is defined in the main flow.

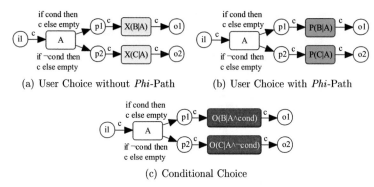

(a) User Choice without *Phi*-Path　　　(b) User Choice with *Phi*-Path

(c) Conditional Choice

Figure 4.16: Deontic Classification of *Exclusive Choice* Pattern

The preconditions are, however, necessary for nested choices as shown by the BPMN example in Fig. 4.17(a) with the deontic classification in Fig. 4.17(b). The preconditions are necessary to define that task B is only permissible if task A was executed before. Removing the preconditions (see Fig. 4.17(d)) would allow to execute task B in any case and lead to the assumption that the former BPMN model defined task A and task B within two different choices on the same level as shown in Fig. 4.17(c).

An extended deontic analysis of the exclusive choice pattern is provided in section 4.2.3.

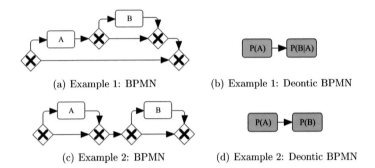

(a) Example 1: BPMN   (b) Example 1: Deontic BPMN

(c) Example 2: BPMN   (d) Example 2: Deontic BPMN

Figure 4.17: Examples of *Exclusive Choice* Pattern

Pattern 6: Multi-Choice

The *Multi-Choice* pattern describes the splitting of one branch into two or more branches, where the thread of control is immediately passed to one or more branches as shown in Fig. 4.15 [128]. The selection of the outgoing branches is based on an evaluation of the conditions defined for the outgoing paths [128].

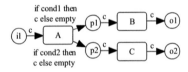

Figure 4.18: Pattern 6: Multi-Choice (Source: [128])

Similar to the exclusive choice pattern, the deontic classification of the multi-choice pattern depends on the type of choice (user vs. conditional) and on a possible *Phi*-Path (see Fig. 4.19). If the multi-choice provides a user decision without *Phi*-Path, then all tasks are permissible and obligatory if no alternative task will be executed as shown in Fig. 4.19(a).

$$B \lor C = (P(B) \land O(B|\neg C)) \lor (P(C) \land O(C|\neg B))$$

However, if one or more *Phi*-Paths exist, then these paths can be removed and all other tasks are classified as permissible as shown in Fig. 4.19(b). If there is only one other path apart from the *Phi*-Path, then also the multi-choice can be removed.

$$B \lor \Phi = P(B) \qquad B \lor C \lor \Phi = P(B) \lor P(C)$$

The deontic classification of tasks in a multi-choice with *Phi*-Path can be justified by considering all possible combinations of paths, e.g., the structure $(A \lor B \lor \Phi)$ can be transformed as follows:

$$\phi \; \dot\lor \; A \; \dot\lor \; B \; \dot\lor \; (A \land B) \; \dot\lor \; (A \land \phi) \; \dot\lor \; (B \land \phi) \; \dot\lor \; (A \land B \land \phi)$$
$$\phi \; \dot\lor \; A \; \dot\lor \; B \; \dot\lor \; (A \land B)$$
$$P(A \; \dot\lor \; B \; \dot\lor \; (A \land B))$$
$$P(A \lor B)$$

According to theorem OK6 of [104, p. 160], $P(A \lor B)$ is equal to $P(A) \lor P(B)$. Thus, all tasks following a multi-choice with *Phi*-Path are permissible.

However, if the multi-choice provides a conditional decision, then every task is obligatory under the precondition that the condition is fulfilled and possible *Phi*-Paths must remain (see Fig. 4.19(c)).

$$(B|cond1) \; \lor \; (C|cond2) = O(B|cond1) \; \lor \; O(C|cond2)$$

Furthermore, all tasks in Fig. 4.19 specify as precondition the completion of the previous task. This precondition can be omitted if the choice is defined in the main flow.

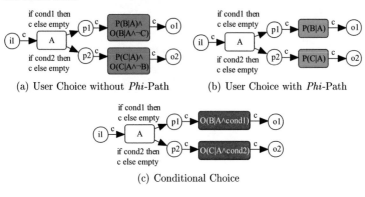

(a) User Choice without *Phi*-Path   (b) User Choice with *Phi*-Path

(c) Conditional Choice

Figure 4.19: Deontic Classification of *Multi-Choice* Pattern

An extended deontic analysis of the multi-choice pattern is provided in section 4.2.3.

Pattern 16: Deferred Choice

The *Deferred Choice* pattern offers the possibility to choose one of several outgoing branches based on an interaction with the operating system as shown in Fig. 4.20. In a first step, all branches are possible and the decision is made by initiating the first task, thereby withdrawing all other tasks [128].

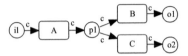

Figure 4.20: Pattern 16: Deferred Choice (Source: [128])

This pattern is similar to the exclusive choice pattern with conditions, but it is necessary to specify that only the branch of the first initiated task is taken. Thus, every task is obligatory if the previous task completed and the condition evaluates to true, but forbidden if already an alternative task is executed (see Fig. 4.21). If a further condition evaluates to true, then the corresponding task is simultaneously obligatory and forbidden leading to a contradiction, which assures that neither the task is executed nor a token is passed on (the latter would be the case if the task was only forbidden). All tasks specify as precondition the completion of the previous task. This precondition can be omitted if the choice is defined in the main flow.

$$(B|cond1) \dot\vee (C|cond2) = (O(B|cond1) \wedge F(B|C)) \vee (O(C|cond2) \wedge F(C|B))$$

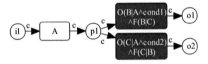

Figure 4.21: Deontic Classification of *Deferred Choice* Pattern

Pattern 18: Milestone

The *Milestone* pattern defines that a task is only enabled if the process instance has reached a specific state (milestone) and not progressed beyond this state (deadline) (see Fig. 4.22) [128].

For the deontic classification, the task must already be classified as obligatory, alternative, or permissible based on the other patterns. This classification is then extended with the precondition that the milestone must have been reached and a forbidden statement that prohibits the execution of the task if the deadline already expired.

$$(A|Milestone \wedge \neg Deadline) = O(A|Milestone) \wedge F(A|Deadline)$$

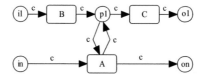

Figure 4.22: Pattern 18: Milestone (Source: [128])

This definition leads to a contradiction if both, the milestone and the deadline, have been reached, which assures that neither the task is executed nor a token is passed on. The deontic classification of three different tasks and the milestone pattern with an obligatory task is presented in Fig. 4.23. All tasks specify as precondition the completion of the previous task. This precondition can be omitted if the task is defined in the main flow.

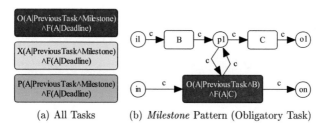

(a) All Tasks   (b) *Milestone* Pattern (Obligatory Task)

Figure 4.23: Deontic Classification of *Milestone* Pattern

The milestone pattern is only supported by the product COSA and partly by FLOWer [128]. However, an extension with deontic logic permits that also standards (or notations) like BPMN, UML ADs, and EPCs support this pattern.

Patterns 10 & 21: Arbitrary Cycles and Structured Loop

The two patterns, *Arbitrary Cycles* and *Structured Loop*, are both defined in this section, since the deontic classification is the same. The arbitrary cycles pattern is shown in Fig. 4.24 and represents cycles with more than one entry or exit point. In contrast, the structured loop pattern provides the possibility to execute a task or sub-process repeatedly within a loop that has a single entry and exit point. The structured loop pattern distinguishes between the pre-test or while loop (see Fig. 4.25(a)) and the post-test or repeat loop (see Fig. 4.25(b)) (cf. for this paragraph [128]).

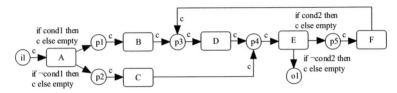

Figure 4.24: Pattern 10: Arbitrary Cycles (Source: [128])

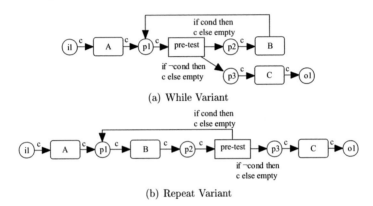

(a) While Variant

(b) Repeat Variant

Figure 4.25: Pattern 21: Structured Loop (Source: [128])

A cycle or loop has a limited deontic influence, since the elements in between are just repeated and the only question is how often a task is executed. In case of a repeat loop the elements in between are executed at least once $(1..n)$, whereas a while loop might not be executed at all $(0..n)$. Nevertheless, the elements in the loop are classified based on other patterns and the loop or cycle only affects the precondition of the tasks following the entry points as well as the classification of the task following the exit point in case the loop only defines one exit point.

Considering the deontic classification of the arbitrary cycles pattern (see Fig. 4.26), task D is the second task of a sequence and, thus, obligatory under the precondition that the previous task B was executed. This precondition is extended with task F based on the cycle. Furthermore, task D is comprised in a type of repeat loop and at least executed once, which corresponds to the obligatory classification. Task E follows the simple merge and is considered as a single task, whose deontic classification is explained in a subsequent section. Task E is classified as obligatory under the precondition that the previous tasks was executed and not affected by the cycle. Also not affected by the cycle is task *F*, which is classified based on the preceding exclusive choice (e.g., as alternative in case of a user choice). This task is comprised in a type of while loop and might not be executed at all, which corresponds to the deontic classification. Interesting, however, is the classification of a task following the exit point *o1*. Normally, the task would also be classified as alternative due to the preceding exclusive choice. However, since there is no other exit point within the cycle and this task must be executed sooner or later, the task can be classified as obligatory. In this case the classification of the exclusive choice pattern is overruled by the arbitrary cycle pattern.

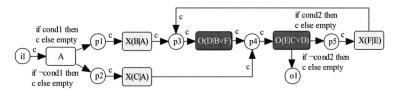

Figure 4.26: Deontic Classification of *Arbitrary Cycles* Pattern

The classification of tasks in a structured loop is shown in Fig. 4.27 with the while loop being presented in Fig. 4.27(a). Task *B* is classified as alternative due to the preceding exclusive choice (assumed to be a user choice) and the precondition refers to task *A* or *B*. The alternative classification corresponds to the fact that a while loop might not be executed at all. The task can also be classified as permissible if the exclusive choice with user decision has a preceding empty path (see explanation below). The loop further affects the classification of the task following the exit point, since this task will be executed sooner or later. Thus, task *C* is classified as obligatory under the precondition that either task *A* or *B* was completed before.

The classification of a structured repeat loop is presented in Fig. 4.27(b). In this case, task *B* is the second task of a sequence and classified as obligatory. This classification corresponds to the fact that a repeat loop must be executed at least once. The precondition further specifies that either task *A* or *B* must have been executed before. In addition, task *C* follows the loop and is classified as obligatory. The precondition only refers to task *B*, which is executed at least once and, thus, the only possible preceding task.

As mentioned earlier, a task in a structured while loop with an exclusive choice that provides a user decision and has a preceding empty (*Phi*) path may also be classified as permissible. For example, in Fig. 4.27(a) task *B* can be classified as permissible, since no task is defined between place *p1* and transition *pre-test*. Nevertheless, the gateways and sequence flows must

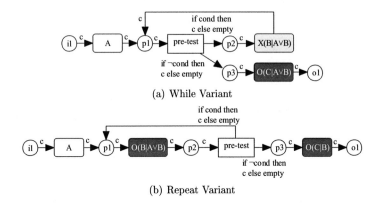

(a) While Variant

(b) Repeat Variant

Figure 4.27: Deontic Classification of *Structured Loop* Pattern

remain to express the loop. Thus, the definition of a task in a while loop without deontic classification ($[A]$) is different from that of a task with permissible classification ($[[A]]$), but the semantics is the same and the task can be executed as often as desired. The permissible classification corresponds to the classification of a task following an exclusive choice with user decision and *Phi*-Path in the main flow. However, if the path before the exclusive choice is not empty, then the task must not be classified as permissible. For example, the BPMN diagram shown in Fig. 4.28(a) ($A; [B; A]$) is semantically different from the Deontic BPMN diagram shown in Fig. 4.28(b) ($A; [[B]; A]$).

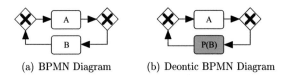

(a) BPMN Diagram   (b) Deontic BPMN Diagram

Figure 4.28: Example: Invalid Classification of *Structured Loop*

Patterns 23 & 24: Transient Trigger and Persistent Trigger

The two patterns *Transient Trigger* and *Persistent Trigger* are defined in one section, since the patterns are similar and the deontic classification is the same. The transient trigger pattern provides the possibility that a task is triggered by a signal from another part of the process or from the external environment. However, the triggers are transient and lost if the receiving task does not immediately act upon the trigger (see Fig. 4.29(a) for the unsafe variant of transient trigger). The persistent trigger pattern is very similar and also describes the triggering of a task by a signal. In contrast to transient triggers, persistent triggers are, however, retained by the process until the receiving task can act on the trigger (see Fig. 4.29(b)) (cf. for this paragraph [128]).

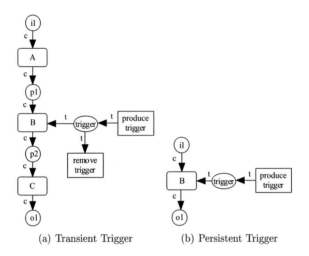

(a) Transient Trigger   (b) Persistent Trigger

Figure 4.29: Patterns 23 & 24: Transient & Persistent Trigger (Source: [128])

The deontic classification of different tasks that require a trigger is shown in Fig. 4.30(a). The tasks are already classified as obligatory, alternative, or permissible based on other patterns. This classification is extended with a forbidden statement that prohibits the execution of the task if no trigger is available. In this case, the task is simultaneously obligatory and forbidden, which assures that neither the task is executed nor a token is passed on.

$$(B|Trigger) = O(B) \wedge F(B|\neg Trigger)$$

The behavior in case of a contradiction can be defined individually and may range from throwing an exception as suggested in section 4.1.3 to reevaluating the expression regularly until all statements are fulfilled. Considering the trigger patterns, the second approach is recommended. The deontic classification does not differ between the transient and persistent trigger pattern, since it makes no difference whether the task receives a trigger signal from a buffer or directly from another source. The deontic classification of the

transient and persistent trigger patterns with an obligatory task is shown in
Fig. 4.30(b) and Fig. 4.30(c).

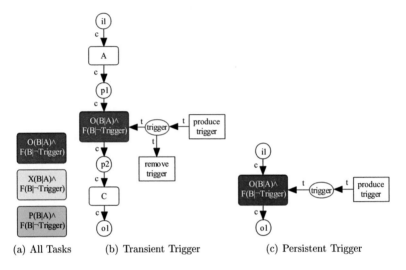

(a) All Tasks   (b) Transient Trigger   (c) Persistent Trigger

Figure 4.30: Deontic Classification of *Transient & Persistent Trigger* Patterns

BPMN 1.0 only supports the persistent trigger pattern through the use of
message events but not the transient trigger pattern [128]. However, in
BPMN 2.0 a signal event is provided, which is used for broadcasting and
may support the transient trigger pattern.

Single Task

The extension of the Control-Flow Patterns with deontic concepts allows to
highlight the modality of most tasks. However, not classified are some tasks
that may occur after an event or merge and are not part of a sequence. These
tasks are called *Single Tasks* and are studied in this section. For example, in
Fig. 4.31, tasks A, E, and F are single tasks and not classified by one of the
other Workflow Patterns.

Not a single task is, however, the first task after a splitting node, even if a
merge is defined in between, since this task is classified by the corresponding
split pattern. For example, in Fig. 4.31, task B is the first task after a
splitting node with a merge in between and, thus, not a single task. Instead,
task B requires multiple deontic classifications as explained in section 4.1.3.

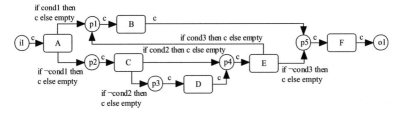

Figure 4.31: Single Task

The deontic classification of a single task is the same as for the first task of a sequence. The task is classified as obligatory under the precondition that all possible previous tasks and events have been completed as shown in Fig. 4.32. Furthermore, the precondition can be omitted if the task starts the process or if the task is part of the main flow (pragmatic approach).

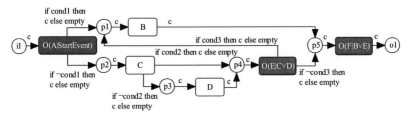

Figure 4.32: Deontic Classification of *Single Task*

4.2.3 Extended Choice

Up to now, the main goal of the deontic classification has been to highlight modalities, which in some cases allowed to reduce the number of gateways and sequence flows. However, in all other cases the process flow remained the same. Although this allows to validate Hypothesis 1, it also means that the decision whether a task is executed or not is on the one hand described by the choice construct and on the other hand by the deontically classified task. In [93], we have proven that these definitions are semantically equivalent but redundant.

This issue can be addressed by an extended deontic classification (see section 4.1.6), in which all choice constructs (inclusive and exclusive gateways) are replaced by parallel splits (parallel gateways), so that the resulting model ends up with a single gateway type. The decision semantics is no more redundant, since parallel gateways do not define conditions, and also the order of the outgoing sequence flows is irrelevant. However, the resulting deontic expressions are more complex, since it must also be specified when a task is forbidden. The resulting deontic expressions are hard to understand for humans, but simplify the execution by a process engine.

In the following, the replacement of the choice construct is defined for the exclusive choice and the multi-choice patterns.

Pattern 4: Exclusive Choice

The deontic classification again depends on the type of choice (user vs. conditional) and on a possible *Phi*-Path. If the exclusive choice is a user choice without *Phi*-Path, then the tasks are obligatory if no alternative task is executed and forbidden otherwise as shown in Fig. 4.33(a). So after the first task has been initiated, all other tasks are forbidden and the token is passed on to the parallel merge.

$$B \mathbin{\dot{\vee}} C = (O(B|\neg C) \wedge F(B|C)) \wedge (O(C|\neg B) \wedge F(C|B))$$

However, if one or more *Phi*-Paths exist, then all tasks are permissible and forbidden if an alternative task is executed as shown in Fig. 4.33(b).

$$B \mathbin{\dot{\vee}} \Phi = P(B) \quad B \mathbin{\dot{\vee}} C \mathbin{\dot{\vee}} \Phi = (P(B) \wedge F(B|C)) \wedge (P(C) \wedge F(C|B))$$

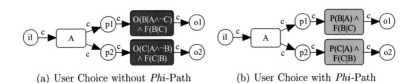

(a) User Choice without *Phi*-Path   (b) User Choice with *Phi*-Path

Figure 4.33: Extended Deontic Classification of *Exclusive Choice* Pattern with User Choice

Note that the petri nets in Fig. 4.33 now represent parallel splits. Furthermore, all tasks specify as precondition the completion of the previous task. This precondition can be omitted if the split is defined in the main flow.

The deontic classification of an exclusive choice with a conditional decision is more complex. First of all, we distinguish four decision types based on the scope (complete/incomplete) and the uniqueness (distinct/overlapping) of the conditions. In most cases, the Workflow Patterns assume a complete and distinct decision, for example, in Fig. 4.15 either the condition *cond* or ¬*cond* evaluates to true. However, the conditions of an exclusive choice can also be incomplete or overlapping. The difficulty to ensure that exactly one outgoing path is taken is also mentioned as possible issue in the description of the exclusive choice pattern (see [128]).

Considering the scope, a decision is complete if the conditions completely cover all possibilities. For example, the conditions (yes/no, true/false, red/green/default) are complete, but the conditions (red/green/yellow) are incomplete, since other colors like blue are missing. The Workflow Patterns recommend the use of default arcs as a possible solution. Default arcs always lead to complete decisions, since the default condition evaluates to true if every other condition evaluates to false. However, the behavior of the exclusive choice in case of an incomplete decision (no default arc) where none of the conditions evaluates to true is not specified. A possible solution could be to throw a runtime exception as defined, for example, in BPMN. In this case, the deontic classification must provide the possibility to throw an exception to be semantically equivalent.

The second important property of decisions is the uniqueness of the conditions. The conditions of a decision are distinct if only one of the conditions may evaluate to true, otherwise the conditions are overlapping. For example, the three roles student, assistant professor, and full professor are distinct if a concrete person can only have one role at a time, but overlapping if a concrete person can simultaneously be a student and an assistant professor. Since the exclusive choice pattern does not specify the behavior in case several conditions evaluate to true, an ordering is assumed as defined, for example, by BPMN. The BPMN specification defines that the first condition that evaluates to true is taken.

So a path after an exclusive choice is executed if and only if (material equivalence) the corresponding condition evaluates to true. In case of a distinct decision it is sufficient that the corresponding condition evaluates to true; however, in case of overlapping conditions also the previous conditions must evaluate to false. For example, an exclusive choice with three overlapping conditions is defined as follows:

$$(C1 \leftrightarrow A) \wedge ((\neg C1 \wedge C2) \leftrightarrow B) \wedge ((\neg C1 \wedge \neg C2 \wedge C3) \leftrightarrow C)$$

Note that the first expression $(C1 \leftrightarrow A)$ corresponds to the deontic expression $O(A|C1) \wedge O(\neg A|\neg C1)$, which can be simplified to $O(A|C1) \wedge F(A|\neg C1)$.

The extended deontic classification of the four decision types of exclusive choices can now be defined as follows:

Complete/Distinct (see Fig. 4.34(a)):

$$(O(A|C1) \wedge F(A|\neg C1)) \wedge$$
$$(O(B|C2) \wedge F(B|\neg C2)) \wedge$$
$$(O(C|C3) \wedge F(C|\neg C3))$$

Complete/Overlapping (see Fig. 4.34(b)):

$$(O(A|C1) \wedge F(A|\neg C1)) \wedge$$
$$(O(B|\neg C1 \wedge C2) \wedge F(B|C1 \vee \neg C2)) \wedge$$
$$(O(C|\neg C1 \wedge \neg C2 \wedge C3) \wedge F(C|C1 \vee C2 \vee \neg C3))$$

Incomplete/Distinct (see Fig. 4.34(c)):

$$(O(A|C1 \vee (\neg C2 \wedge \neg C3)) \wedge F(A|\neg C1)) \wedge$$
$$(O(B|C2 \vee (\neg C1 \wedge \neg C3)) \wedge F(B|\neg C2)) \wedge$$
$$(O(C|C3 \vee (\neg C1 \wedge \neg C2)) \wedge F(C|\neg C3))$$

Incomplete/Overlapping (see Fig. 4.34(d)):

$$(O(A|C1 \vee (\neg C2 \wedge \neg C3)) \wedge F(A|\neg C1)) \wedge$$
$$(O(B|\neg C1 \wedge (C2 \vee \neg C3)) \wedge F(B|C1 \vee \neg C2)) \wedge$$
$$(O(C|\neg C1 \wedge \neg C2) \wedge F(C|C1 \vee C2 \vee \neg C3))$$

Note that in case of an incomplete decision where none of the conditions evaluate to true, every task is at the same time obligatory and forbidden, which results in the desired runtime exception. However, I recommend to always define a default arc in case of incomplete decisions. Furthermore, the parallel splits shown in Fig. 4.34 are assumed to be defined in the main flow and, thus, do not specify task A within the precondition.

In addition, all *Phi*-Paths addressed by an exclusive choice with conditions can be removed. The following definitions are based on the extended deontic classification of the four decision types above, but the second outgoing path with condition $C2$ is assumed to be a *Phi*-Path:

Complete/Distinct:

$$(O(A|C1) \wedge F(A|\neg C1)) \wedge (O(C|C3) \wedge F(C|\neg C3))$$

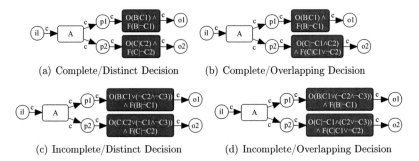

(a) Complete/Distinct Decision   (b) Complete/Overlapping Decision

(c) Incomplete/Distinct Decision   (d) Incomplete/Overlapping Decision

Figure 4.34: Extended Deontic Classification of *Exclusive Choice* Pattern with Conditional Choice

If the decision is complete and distinct and only condition $C2$ evaluates to true, then it is forbidden to execute task A or C. Since both tasks are not obligatory, there is no contradiction and the tokens are passed on without executing the tasks.

Complete/Overlapping:

$$(O(A|C1) \wedge F(A|\neg C1)) \wedge$$
$$(O(C|\neg C1 \wedge \neg C2 \wedge C3) \wedge F(C|C1 \vee C2 \vee \neg C3))$$

If the decision is complete and overlapping and only condition $C2$ evaluates to true, then again tasks A and C are forbidden and not obligatory. The two tasks are also forbidden and not obligatory if the conditions $C2$ and $C3$ evaluate to true. Note that the evaluation order remains the same, because condition $C2$ is expressed in the precondition of task C.

Incomplete/Distinct:

$$(O(A|C1 \vee (\neg C2 \wedge \neg C3)) \wedge F(A|\neg C1)) \wedge$$
$$(O(C|C3 \vee (\neg C1 \wedge \neg C2)) \wedge F(C|\neg C3))$$

If the decision is incomplete and distinct and only condition $C2$ evaluates to true, then also in this case tasks A and C are forbidden and not obligatory. However, if none of the three conditions evaluates to true, then both tasks are forbidden and obligatory resulting in a contradiction.

Incomplete/Overlapping:

$$(O(A|C1 \vee (\neg C2 \wedge \neg C3)) \wedge F(A|\neg C1)) \wedge$$
$$(O(C|\neg C1 \wedge \neg C2) \wedge F(C|C1 \vee C2 \vee \neg C3))$$

If the decision is incomplete and overlapping and only condition $C2$ evaluates to true, then again tasks A and C are forbidden and not obligatory. The two tasks are also forbidden and not obligatory if the conditions $C2$ and $C3$ evaluate to true. However, if none of the three conditions evaluates to true, then both tasks are forbidden and obligatory resulting in a contradiction.

Pattern 6: Multi-Choice

The extended deontic classification of the multi-choice pattern is similar and also depends on the type of choice (user vs. conditional) and on a possible *Phi*-Path. However, in case of a conditional choice only the scope (complete/incomplete) has to be considered. The uniqueness of the conditions is irrelevant, since after a multi-choice several outgoing paths may be taken.

If the multi-choice provides a user decision without *Phi*-Path, then all tasks are permissible and obligatory if no alternative task will be executed as shown in Fig. 4.35(a).

$$B \ \lor \ C = (P(B) \ \land \ O(B|\neg C)) \ \land \ (P(C) \ \land \ O(C|\neg B))$$

However, if one or more *Phi*-Paths exist, then the tasks are permissible as shown in Fig. 4.35(b).

$$B \ \lor \ \Phi = P(B) \qquad B \ \lor \ C \ \lor \ \Phi = P(B) \ \land \ P(C)$$

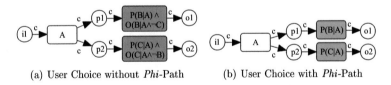

(a) User Choice without *Phi*-Path   (b) User Choice with *Phi*-Path

Figure 4.35: Extended Deontic Classification of *Multi-Choice* Pattern with User Choice

Note that the definitions correspond to those of section 4.2.2 and only the multi-choice has been replaced by a parallel split. Furthermore, all tasks specify as precondition the completion of the previous task. This precondition can be omitted if the choice is defined in the main flow.

In case of a multi-choice with conditional decision, the extended deontic classification of the complete and incomplete decision type corresponds to the complete/distinct and incomplete/distinct decision type of exclusive choice.

4.3 Deontic BPMN

In the previous sections, deontic classifications in general as well as an extension of the *Control-Flow Patterns* with deontic logic were presented. The main focus of this thesis, however, is on BPMN. Thus, in this section the concepts are applied to BPMN and the result is called *Deontic BPMN*.

This section starts with an overview of Deontic BPMN followed by a description of the path exploration approach to support the deontic analysis. The benefits of Deontic BPMN are then demonstrated by a case study and a preliminary survey.

4.3.1 Overview

The extension of BPMN with deontic logic corresponds to the deontic classification of the Control-Flow Patterns. The representation of the original 21 Control-Flow Patterns in UML 2.0 Activity Diagrams and BPMN 1.0 is described in [136]. Furthermore, in [139] also the Data and Resource Patterns are taken into account and compared with BPMN. According to this publication, BPMN provides good support for the control-flow perspective, medium support for the data perspective, but only low support for the resource perspective. In addition, a more recent analysis of the current 43 Control-Flow Patterns is provided in [110]. This publication states that BPMN fully supports 24 and partly supports 9 Control-Flow Patterns. However, all these publications consider BPMN 1.0, but further patterns like the *Transient Trigger* pattern are supported by BPMN 2.0. Considering the patterns that may have a deontic extension (see section 4.2.2), only the *Milestone* pattern is not directly supported by BPMN 2.0. Nevertheless, all patterns described in section 4.2.2 can be expressed in Deontic BPMN.

Note that all extensions suggested for Deontic BPMN are conform to the BPMN specification. According to this specification, an extended BPMN diagram may comprise new markers or indicators as well as new shapes representing a kind of artifact [99, p. 8]. In addition, graphical elements may be colored and the coloring may have a specified semantics or the line style of a graphical element may be changed if this change does not conflict with any other element. However, the extension shall not change the specified shape of a defined graphical element or marker (cf. for this paragraph [99]). Considering Deontic BPMN, the labels of BPMN elements are extended with a deontic operator. Regarding the adaption of labels, no restrictions are defined in the BPMN specification. In addition, activities (and in special cases sequence flows) are colored and every color has a specified semantics.

In the following, the BPMN elements are described and possible deontic classifications are presented. According to the BPMN 2.0 specification (see [99]), the elements are divided into five basic categories: *Flow Objects, Data, Connecting Objects, Swimlanes,* and *Artifacts* (see section 2.1). For the deontic classification of the process flow, only the categories *Flow-* and *Connecting Objects* are taken into account. Furthermore, the category *Swimlane* is considered in section 4.4.

Flow Objects

The category *Flow Objects* comprises *Activities, Gateways,* and *Events*.

Activity: Every concrete *Activity* can either be a *Task*, a *Sub-Process*, or a *Call Activity*. The activities can be classified as obligatory, permissible, forbidden, or alternative as described in section 4.1. In addition, multiple deontic classifications are necessary in case of unstructured diagrams.

The usage of sub-processes allows to define a hierarchy of deontic classifications and thereby increases the understandability of Deontic BPMN diagrams. The sub-process is classified according to the outer process, but whenever a token reaches the sub-process all comprised activities are executed similar to the main flow. So the pragmatic approach can be applied to reduce the number of preconditions. For example, in Fig. 4.36, the original Deontic BPMN diagram is shown on the left-hand side. The pragmatic approach was already applied to remove the precondition of task *A*. However, all other preconditions must remain. The diagram on the right-hand side defines a sub-process, which is marked as permissible. The comprised activities can then be classified as obligatory without any preconditions.

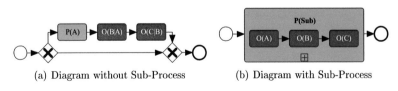

(a) Diagram without Sub-Process   (b) Diagram with Sub-Process

Figure 4.36: Deontic BPMN Diagram without and with Sub-Process

Gateway: BPMN distinguishes five different types of *Gateways*: *Parallel, Exclusive, Inclusive, Event-Based,* and *Complex Gateways*. For the deontic classification only the splitting gateways must be considered. The deontic classification of the paths following a *Parallel, Exclusive,* or *Inclusive Gateway* corresponds to the deontic extension of the *Parallel Split, Exclusive Choice,* or *Multi-Choice* pattern. The *Event-Based Gateway* represents a branching point in the process where the alternative paths are based on *Events* and only the path with the first triggered *Event* is taken [99]. Hence, this gateway corresponds to the *Deferred Choice* pattern. The *Complex Gateway* can be used to model complex synchronization behavior defined by an expression; however, in case of the splitting gateway, conditions define which of the outgoings paths receive a token [99]. Thus, the splitting *Complex Gateway* corresponds to the conditional *Multi-Choice* pattern.

Event: *Events* are distinguished based on their behavior (catch or throw), type (start-, intermediate-, or end event), and trigger (*None, Message, Timer, Error, Escalation, Cancel, Compensation, Conditional, Link, Signal, Terminate, Multiple,* or *Parallel Multiple*). In addition, all throw and most catch events are interrupting, but some catch events can also be non-interrupting.

The deontic classification of all activities following an event is the same; the activity is classified as obligatory under the precondition that the trigger of the preceding event has been sent or received. However, the classification is based on four different patterns (*Sequence, Parallel Split, Exclusive Choice* (conditional), and *Multi-Choice* (conditional)).

For example, if a throw event receives a token, then the trigger is thrown and a token is sent down the outgoing path of the throw event. Thus, all activities following a throw event are classified based on the *Sequence* pattern. The trigger of the throw event can be caught by zero or more corresponding catch events. All corresponding catch events receive the trigger in parallel, which, in case of several catch events, resembles the *Parallel Split* pattern. However, if a catch event has a *Link* trigger or no corresponding throw event, e.g. a start- or intermediate event with a *Timer* trigger, then again the classification is based on the *Sequence* pattern. Furthermore, if an activity has an interrupting boundary event, then either the outgoing path of the activity or of the boundary event is taken, which conforms to the *Exclusive Choice* pattern with conditions. Moreover, if an activity has several interrupting and non-interrupting boundary events, then further tokens might be sent down the outgoing paths of the non-interrupting boundary events, which corresponds to the conditional *Multi-Choice* pattern.

Although several different patterns can be applied in case of events, the result is always the same and all activities following an event are classified as obligatory under the precondition that the trigger of the preceding event was thrown or caught.

Connecting Objects

The category *Connecting Objects* comprises *Sequence Flows, Message Flows, Associations*, and *Data Associations*. A *Message Flow* is used to show the flow of messages, but no token traverses the flow. Thus, for the deontic classifications only *Sequence Flows* are considered.

Sequence Flow: A *Sequence Flow* is used to connect a source with a target *Flow Element* and thereby defines the order of the process flow. If no condition is defined for the sequence flow, then it is called an unconditional flow. An unconditional flow between two activities corresponds to the *Sequence* pattern and the second and every further activity is classified as obligatory under the precondition that the previous activity was executed. However, an activity may also have multiple incoming or outgoing sequence flows. If an activity has multiple outgoing sequence flows, then a token is sent down every outgoing path, which corresponds to the *Parallel Split* pattern. In case of multiple incoming sequence flows, the activity is executed upon every incoming token, which corresponds to the *Simple Merge* pattern.

If the sequence flow specifies a condition, then it is called a conditional sequence flow. Conditional sequence flows are defined after gateways or activities and at least two flows must originate from the same element. An element with multiple conditional outgoing sequence flows corresponds to the conditional *Multi-Choice* pattern. If the conditions are distinct and exactly one condition can be fulfilled, then the construct is conform to the conditional *Exclusive Choice* pattern.

Furthermore, BPMN supports the concept of default flows for exclusive, inclusive, and complex gateways as well as for activities. This flow will only be used if all other outgoing conditional flows are not true at runtime [99]. Considering the deontic classification, a default flow always implies a complete decision.

In seldom cases, the transformation from BPMN to Deontic BPMN requires the deontic classification of sequence flows. For example, in Fig. 4.37 all gateways provide user decisions and so the loop originates from a permissible path. In this case, the sequence flow representing the loop must be classified as permissible under the precondition that task *B* was executed before.

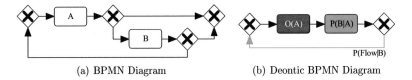

(a) BPMN Diagram   (b) Deontic BPMN Diagram

Figure 4.37: Sequence Flow with Deontic Classification

In summary, the extension of BPMN with deontic concepts largely corresponds to the deontic classification of the Control-Flow Patterns. The patterns are represented by various BPMN elements, but the classification is nevertheless the same.

4.3.2 Path Exploration

Up to now, the deontic classification has been done manually based on the patterns described in section 4.2. However, a BPMN diagram is a directed graph, which can have complex structures. This complicates the deontic classification, especially in case of cyclic or unstructured diagrams. As it is not possible to analyze the deontic constraints directly within the BPMN diagram, path exploration is used instead (see [89]).

In path exploration, all possible paths through the BPMN diagram are described within a tree structure that only includes the splits. Furthermore, references are necessary to cope with loops. The deontic analysis compares the paths afterwards and whenever an activity is found in every path, it is obligatory. If an activity is only found in some paths, it might be conditionally obligatory, permissible, or alternative, depending on whether the previous split is a user or conditional choice and whether it has an alternative *Phi*-Path. Since the path exploration approach duplicates the sequence flows and activities for different paths, it can neglect merging gateways and, nevertheless, reach all activities. Furthermore, this approach identifies activities with multiple deontic classifications as necessary, for example, for unstructured diagrams.

In a first step only structured acyclic BPMN diagrams are studied. An example is shown in Fig. 4.38(a) with the resulting path exploration being displayed in Fig. 4.38(b).

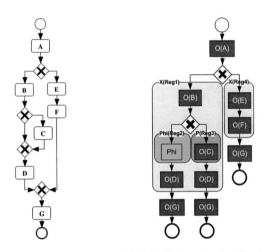

(a) Structured Acyclic Diagram   (b) Path Exploration for Fig. 4.38(a)

Figure 4.38: Path Exploration for Structured Acyclic Diagram

For the path exploration approach, a new element called *region* is defined. A region resembles a sub-process in BPMN and is deontically classified according to the outer process whereas the comprised activities are marked as in the main flow. Whenever a split is found in the BPMN diagram, a *region* is defined for each alternative path and marked according to the deontic classification. The region ends if an activity is part of each alternative path, e.g., task G is obligatory in all paths, therefore, the regions *Reg1* and *Reg4* end before task G. The deontic classification of a region can comprise preconditions, e.g. if the preceding split provides a conditional decision.

In the final Deontic BPMN diagram, the deontic classification of a region directly applies to its first activity and every further activity is marked based on the *Sequence* pattern, e.g., task C is classified as permissible. All regions including empty ones (*Phi*-Region) are then removed. In path exploration, the user can freely decide whether to provide an empty region or not, e.g., considering the example, it is allowed to remove the *Phi*-Region, the following tasks, and the preceding split, since task C is already marked as permissible. A major advantage of using regions is that they show a hierarchy of deontic classifications, e.g., task C is a permissible task in an alternative path.

The path exploration approach further distinguishes various splitting types:

Parallel Splits send a token on each outgoing path so all paths are executed and, therefore, obligatory regarding deontic logic. In path exploration, it is allowed to insert several paths for all possible ordering combinations, however, it is recommended to insert only one path with irrelevant order.

Exclusive Choices execute exactly one of the outgoing paths. Thus, every outgoing path is inserted as a possible path in the tree structure.

Multi-Choices are more complex, since all combinations of paths can be taken. In path exploration, every combination is inserted as a path, e.g., $A \vee B$ leads to three possible paths: A, B, and $A \wedge B$ (again with irrelevant order). If no default path is defined and zero outgoing paths can be taken, then the possibility of an exception has to be considered as described for incomplete decisions in section 4.2.3.

In path exploration, all paths are presented in a tree structure. Thus, several start events, as allowed by the BPMN specification [99], are not possible. This problem is solved by a virtual start event with a splitting gateway that references all original start events. The splitting gateway must be of the same type as the merging gateway that is used to join the branches of the original start events. In addition, BPMN allows several end events within a process flow. Whenever an end event finishes a path after a split, all other paths remain in their region until they reach their own end event.

The path exploration approach also supports the deontic analysis of unstructured acyclic diagrams with merging gateways joining paths from different splits. An example is shown in Fig. 4.39(a) with the path exploration being displayed in Fig. 4.39(b). Task J is once in a permissible and several times in an alternative path thereby representing multiple deontic classifications.

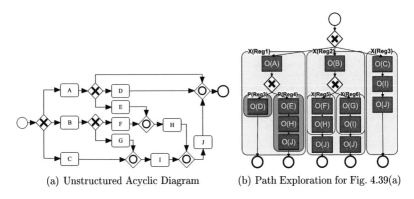

(a) Unstructured Acyclic Diagram   (b) Path Exploration for Fig. 4.39(a)

Figure 4.39: Path Exploration for Unstructured Acyclic Diagram

Considering cyclic graphs, a cycle or loop has a limited deontic influence, since the elements in between are just repeated and the only question is how often they are executed. In case of a repeat loop the elements in between are executed at least once whereas a while loop might not be executed at all (see description of *Arbitrary Cycles* and *Structured Loop* pattern in section 4.2.2). An example is shown in Fig. 4.40(a). Task *A* is defined in a repeat loop and executed at least once, so it is classified as obligatory as shown in Fig. 4.40(b). However, considering the split, the decision between task *B* and *C* is repeated until task *C* is chosen. So task *B* is defined in a while loop and might not be executed at all. Thus, it is an alternative to task *C*. However, task *C* is classified as obligatory, since it must be executed sooner or later.

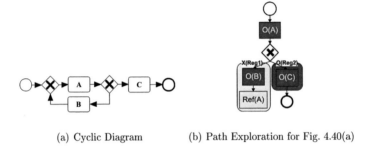

(a) Cyclic Diagram   (b) Path Exploration for Fig. 4.40(a)

Figure 4.40: Path Exploration for Cyclic Diagram

In summary, the path exploration approach supports the deontic analysis and the classification of BPMN diagrams. In chapter 5, an automatic transformation from BPMN to Deontic BPMN based on the algebraic graph transformation approach is presented. However, this transformation is currently limited to structured diagrams and a basic set of BPMN elements. Thus, in case of manual classification as well as for unstructured or cyclic BPMN diagrams, the path exploration approach is recommended.

4.3.3   Case Study

In order to study the suitability of Deontic BPMN for practical scenarios, this section provides a case study with workflows taken from a business environment. The case study comprises two workflows implemented in an industrial project for the prevention domain of the *Austrian Social Insurance Company for Occupational Risks* (AUVA). The goal of the prevention domain is to suggest possibilities to improve the employees' safety and health conditions at their workplaces. For this purpose, the prevention workers receive requests to visit the companies. Thus, the two major workflows implemented within the industrial project describe the process of an order execution and of a business travel. Since both workflows are typical for many companies, they are taken as basis for this case study.

Within the scope of the project, the workflows were only documented textually and by a matrix describing the initial and target states. These sources are taken to define the BPMN models. Especially the order execution process is quite complex, since the customers asked for a flexible workflow in which the prevention workers can freely decide. I presented an extract of the order execution process and its transformation to Deontic BPMN in [89]. Furthermore, the business travel process was studied in [92] and a BPMN model was suggested. The BPMN diagram presented in this section is based on this original model, but has been slightly adapted to correct some minor mistakes and make it better understandable.

The BPMN diagram of the order execution process is shown in Fig. 4.41. The process comprises the following tasks: *Create Request* (CR), *Modify Request* (MR), *Delete Request* (DR), *Reject Request* (RJR), *Approve Order* (AO), *Create/Modify Appointment* (CMA), *Remove Appointment* (RA), *Approve Appointment* (AA), *Reject Appointment* (RJA), *Order in Progress* (OP), *Execute Order* (EO), *Create Report* (RC), *Modify Report* (RM), *Formally Correct Report* (RFC), *Formally Incorrect Report* (RFI), and *Close Order* (CO). These tasks are specified within three lanes that describe the roles *Assistant*, *Consultant*, and *Approver*.

Essentially, the order execution process defines that a request can be created by one of the three roles. If an assistant or consultant creates the request, then this request can be modified by the consultant and is afterwards either deleted or sent to the approver for approval. However, if the approver creates a request, then this request is automatically approved. The approved order is then sent to the consultant who may define an appointment or specify that the order is in progress. Subsequently, every order must be executed by the consultant. The consultant can then create and modify a report, which might be sent to the approver for approval. Finally, the consultant closes the order.

Although it is possible to discuss some aspects of the process flow, e.g., the optional creation of appointments or reports, this model describes an actual workflow taken from an industrial project based on real customer requirements. For example, appointments are optional, since prevention workers may visit companies spontaneously if they are nearby.

Considering the order execution process, all splitting gateways provide user choices and do not depend on any states or data. The entire diagram consists of 26 gateways and 64 sequence flows and is quite complex. Thus, it is difficult to identify the permissible and obligatory tasks.

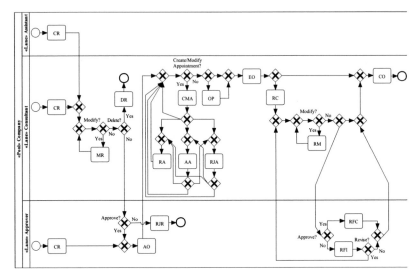

Figure 4.41: Order Execution Process: BPMN Diagram

The path exploration for the order execution process is shown in Fig. 4.42. In total, 20 regions were defined and most of them have a deontic classification. The only exceptions are the regions *Reg4* and *Reg10*, which support the reuse of sub-trees in different paths. Furthermore, several regions are nested, which allows to define, for example, that *Order in Progress* (OP) is a permissible task (since it is the only task in a permissible region) in a multiple alternative path.

The task *Create Order* (CR) is defined as first task in three alternative paths. Thus, someone might suggest to define the task only once and classify it as obligatory. The difference between the three paths, however, is the executing role, which effects possible further tasks. Hence, it is necessary to define all three paths as alternative.

Furthermore, some tasks are specified in different paths, which indicates that the tasks require multiple deontic classifications. However, in most cases the classification is the same in all paths, e.g., considering the task *Close Order* (CO) all occurrences are obligatory in an alternative path.

Finally, cycles and loops are expressed with references to splitting gateways (e.g., Ref(S2)) or to tasks (e.g., Ref(RA)). If all paths within a sub-tree end with a reference that addresses an element in or before the sub-tree, then the alternative path describes the process flow after the cycle or loop and is, thus, obligatory. For example, considering region *Reg11*, all paths end with a reference, so the alternative path starting with region *Reg15* must be executed sooner or later.

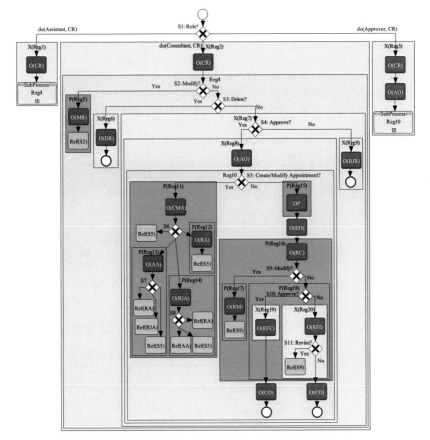

Figure 4.42: Order Execution Process: Path Exploration

The corresponding Deontic BPMN diagram is shown in Fig. 4.43. The process flow between *Approve Order* (AO) and *Close Order* (CO) is considered as main flow. This is obvious from the perspective of the approver, but considering the other roles, two end events allow to finish the process flow in advance. However, considering the entire process, the merging gateway before *Approve Order* (AO) is the first gateway that merges the paths from all start events and the path following this gateway is the only one in which an order is really executed. Thus, every complete order execution requires that a request is created (by any of the three roles) and that the order is approved, executed and closed. All other tasks are permissible or describe an abort of the order execution process.

So the Deontic BPMN diagram highlights that it is obligatory to create a request and to approve, execute, and close the order. In addition, it defines that the two tasks *Delete Request* (DR) and *Reject Request* (RJR) are alternatives to the main flow. All other tasks are permissible. It is further necessary to deontically classify two sequence flows as conditionally permissible, since a report may only be modified or sent for approval if it was created before. This classification, however, highlights that the two tasks *Formally Correct Report* (RFC) and *Formally Incorrect Report* (RFI) are alternatives in a permissible structure.

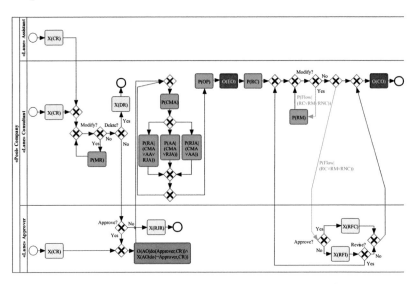

Figure 4.43: Order Execution Process: Deontic BPMN Diagram

The Deontic BPMN diagram provides two advantages with respect to understandability. First, the resulting Deontic BPMN diagram only consists of 18 gateways and 49 sequence flows. So it was possible to remove 8 gateways and 15 sequence flows and thereby reduce the structural complexity of the process flow. Second, obligatory and permissible tasks can be distinguished at first sight based on the colored highlighting. It is still necessary to decide whether a permissible task is executed or not, but instead of describing this decision through separate gateways and alternative paths, the decision is described within the corresponding task. The advantages are accompanied by additional deontic constructs requiring a basic understanding by the user. However, the complex constructs (e.g., preconditions) are only relevant for a more detailed understanding of the process.

The second workflow describes a business travel process and the BPMN diagram is shown in Fig. 4.45. The process comprises the tasks: *Create BT*, *Modify BT*, *Send for Approval*, *Review BT*, *Reject Review*, *Approve BT*, *Reject BT*, and *Execute & Close BT*. The abbreviation *BT* stands for *Business Travel*. These tasks are specified within three lanes that describe the roles *Owner*, *Reviewer*, and *Approver*.

This process essentially defines that a business travel is created by its owner and can then be modified. Afterwards, the business travel is sent for approval to either a reviewer or an approver. If the business travel is sent to a reviewer, then the reviewer reviews it and either resends it for approval or rejects the review in which case the owner is supposed to modify the business travel. If, however, the recipient of the business travel is an approver, then the approver has to review the business travel and can either resend or approve/reject it. If the approver rejects the business travel, then the owner is again supposed to modify it, but if the approver approves the business travel, then the owner has the permission to execute and close the business travel.

Again it is possible to discuss some aspects of the process flow, for example, the definition of a reviewer or the possibility to reject an approved business travel. Considering the role reviewer, the question arises why the business travel is not sent to the approver in the first place. The reason is that the reviewer exculpates the approver by identifying most of the invalid business travel requests in advance. Furthermore, an approver who approved a business travel is allowed to change his/her mind until (s)he sends the business travel back to the owner.

Considering the business travel process, again all splitting gateways provide user choices and the entire BPMN model consists of 10 gateways and 28 sequence flows. So although this BPMN model is less complex than that of the order execution process, it is still difficult to identify the obligatory and permissible tasks at first sight.

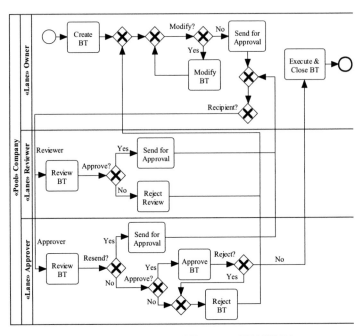

Figure 4.44: Business Travel Process: BPMN Diagram

The path exploration for the business travel process is shown in Fig. 4.45. In this case, only 7 regions were defined and all of them have a deontic classification. Furthermore, it is easy to identify the main flow, since only one end event is defined. All other paths end with a reference and, therefore, describe cycles and loops. Region *Reg1* comprises the only loop with a *Phi*-Path before the splitting gateway and is, thus, the only permissible region. Furthermore, no multiple deontic classifications are necessary, since every duplicated task has the same deontic classification in all paths, e.g., the task *Reject BT* is addressed by two splitting gateways but always classified as an alternative.

Note that in this case, the path exploration is very simple and seems better understandable than the BPMN model with several arbitrary cycles. Furthermore, in a next step all regions that comprise only one task can be removed and the deontic classification directly applies to the task. Thus, the only remaining region is *Reg2*, which specifies that the tasks *Send for Approval* and *Reject Review* defined within the reviewer lane are alternatives tasks in an alternative path.

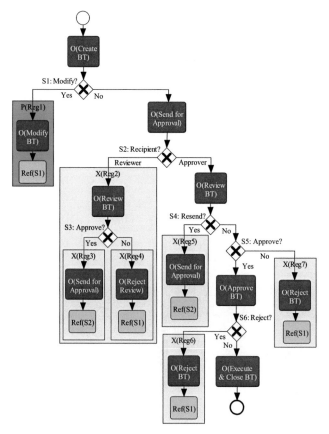

Figure 4.45: Business Travel Process: Path Exploration

The corresponding Deontic BPMN diagram is shown in Fig. 4.46. The tasks *Create BT*, *Send for Approval* (by the owner), *Review BT* (by an approver), *Approve BT*, and *Execute & Close BT* are obligatory. All tasks executed by a reviewer as well as the tasks *Send for Approval* and *Reject BT* specified within the approver lane are alternatives. The only permissible task is *Modify BT*, which is defined within a loop and may be executed as often as desired.

In this case, the deontic classification does not affect the structure of the process flow and the number of gateways and sequence flows remains the same. However, the deontic classification nevertheless increases the understandability, since obligatory and permissible tasks can be distinguished at first sight.

Furthermore, the business travel process provides an example that does not require complex deontic constructs like preconditions, classified paths, or multiple deontic classifications.

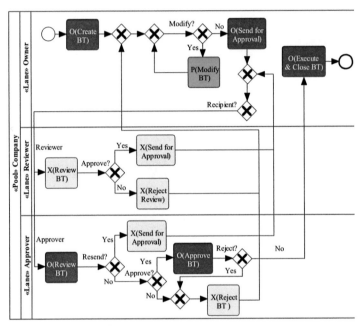

Figure 4.46: Business Travel Process: Deontic BPMN Diagram

In summary, this section demonstrated the transformation from BPMN to Deontic BPMN within a case study consisting of an order execution and a business travel process. In the first case, some complex deontic operators were necessary, but the modalities were highlighted and the structural complexity was reduced. In the second case, the structural complexity remained the same, but only simple deontic operators were necessary to highlight the modalities. So the examples showed two extremes and other process flows might only have a few complex deontic operators but still decrease the structural complexity. Nevertheless, it seems that the understandability is increased in both cases. To confirm this statement, the understandability of Deontic BPMN is further studied within a preliminary survey in the next section.

4.3.4 Preliminary Survey

This section provides a preliminary survey to study the understandability of Deontic BPMN. A short overview of the preliminary survey was presented in [89].

Although the structural complexity of every Deontic BPMN diagram is equal or less compared to the BPMN diagram, this does not automatically conclude better understandability. For example, Gemino and Wand explore differences between two modeling techniques based on a combination of ontological analysis and cognitive theory (see [43]). After proving that the modeling grammars are informationally equivalent, they conducted an experiment with 77 participants answering problem solving questions. Interestingly, the evaluation showed that the more complex modeling technique provides better clarity. Since reduced complexity does not automatically imply better clarity, it is also necessary to study the understandability of Deontic BPMN within a controlled experiment as provided by the preliminary survey.

The preliminary survey executed for Deontic BPMN was answered by 22 post-graduate computer scientists. It is called a preliminary survey, since the number of respondents is too small for a significant survey. Nevertheless, it provides some interesting results and identifies possible problems.

The survey starts with an introduction to BPMN and Deontic BPMN including several examples and some pretest questions concerning the experience with (process) modeling languages in general and BPMN in particular.

Question	Yes	No
Experience with general modeling languages (UML, ...)?	22	0
Experience with process modeling languages (BPMN, ...)?	15	7

Afterwards four examples are presented, each expressed with a BPMN and a Deontic BPMN model. Examples 1-3 are shown in Fig. 4.47, 4.48 and 4.49. Example 4 provides an extract of the order execution process presented in section 4.3.3 and is shown in Fig. 4.50.

To avoid a recognition of models expressing the same example, corresponding tasks received different names and the order of examples (e.g. first BPMN or Deontic BPMN diagram), elements (e.g. first parallel or exclusive gateway) and questions varies. For example, the diagrams in the survey are ordered as follows: Example 1 (BPMN), Example 2 (Deontic BPMN), Example 3 (Deontic BPMN), Example 4 (BPMN), Example 1 (Deontic BPMN), Example 2 (BPMN), Example 3 (BPMN), and Example 4 (Deontic BPMN).

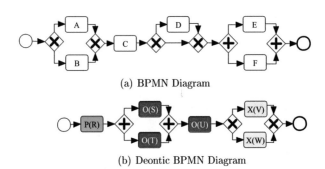

(a) BPMN Diagram

(b) Deontic BPMN Diagram

Figure 4.47: Survey: Example 1

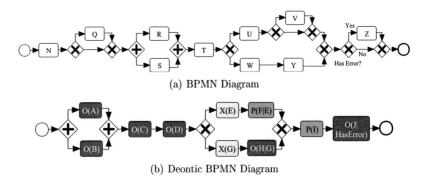

(a) BPMN Diagram

(b) Deontic BPMN Diagram

Figure 4.48: Survey: Example 2

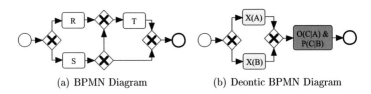

(a) BPMN Diagram   (b) Deontic BPMN Diagram

Figure 4.49: Survey: Example 3

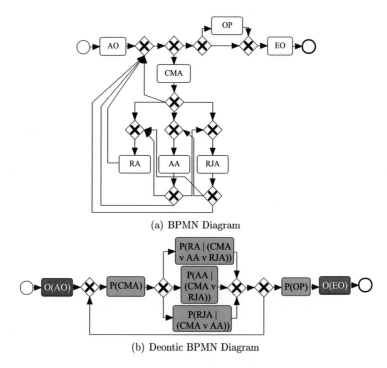

(a) BPMN Diagram

(b) Deontic BPMN Diagram

Figure 4.50: Survey: Example 4

The respondents then answered 17 questions for each model type:

- Example 1:

    - Q1: Which tasks are mandatory without any condition?
    - Q2: Which tasks are optional?
    - Q3: Which tasks are alternative?
    - Q4: What happens if task A (or W) cannot be executed?
    - Q5: What happens if task D (or R) cannot be executed?
    - Q6: What happens if task E (or S) cannot be executed?

- Example 2:

    - Q7: Which tasks are mandatory without any condition?
    - Q8: Which tasks are optional?

- Q9: What happens if task U (or E) cannot be executed?
- Q10: What happens if task V (or F) cannot be executed?

- Example 3:

    - Q11: Must task T (or C) be executed after task R (or A)?
    - Q12: Must task T (or C) be executed after task S (or B)?
    - Q13: Which tasks might have been executed before task T (or C)?

- Example 4:

    - Q14: Which tasks are mandatory without any condition?
    - Q15: Which tasks are optional?
    - Q16: Which steps are possible after Reject (or Approve) Appointment?
    - Q17: Which steps are possible before Approve (or Reject) Appointment?

The understandability of process models was also studied in [80]. Four aspects were identified to be relevant for the structural understanding: *concurrency*, *exclusiveness*, *order*, and *repetition*. Relevant for a comparison of BPMN and Deontic BPMN are *exclusiveness*, which describes whether a task is always, sometimes or never executed within a process instance, and *order*. All questions within the preliminary survey address these two aspects.

Furthermore, an experiment showed that *exclusiveness* is more difficult to understand than *order* (see [80]). Deontic BPMN addresses exactly this issue by classifying those tasks as obligatory that are always executed and others as permissible or alternative if they are only sometimes executed. The classification is highlighted by a simple deontic operator and by a distinct background color. In addition, the aspect *order* is addressed by preconditions, defining that a task can only be executed after another one. However, the concept of preconditions requires experience to support the identification of the *order*.

After finishing the survey, the wrong answers are divided into false-positives (FP) (answer is selected although wrong) and false-negatives (FN) (answer is not selected although true). If a question only allows a single answer (Q4-6, Q9-13), then an answer is only counted once as FP (otherwise every mistake would be doubled). An overview of all mistakes is shown in Fig. 4.51.

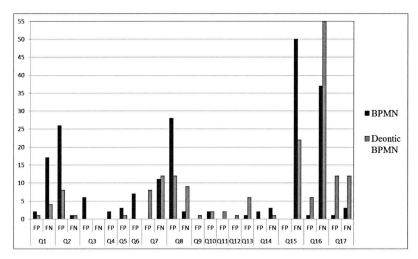

Figure 4.51: Summary of Mistakes in BPMN and Deontic BPMN Diagrams

In summary, 205 mistakes emerged in the BPMN models compared to 176 mistakes in the Deontic BPMN models. So the number of mistakes could be reduced by 14.1%, which implies that Deontic BPMN increases the understandability. In addition, there are two major reasons why the percentage is not higher:

1. Known BPMN vs. Unknown Deontic BPMN: According to the pretest questions most respondents have experience with BPMN but nobody was familiar with Deontic BPMN. Thus, several respondents mixed the colors or the deontic concepts. A longer training or workshop with Deontic BPMN would have led to better and more comparable results.

2. Preconditions: The survey showed problems with preconditions, especially in combination with multiple deontic classifications (see example 3). In total, 53 mistakes were made in Deontic BPMN models due to a misunderstanding of preconditions. So without preconditions, it would have been possible to reduce the number of mistakes by up to 40%. Hence, it is either necessary to revise the notation of preconditions within further work or, since the notation of conditional commitments is quite common, to provide better explanations for the users.

All in all, the results of the preliminary survey are satisfying and indicate that Deontic BPMN increases the understandability of a process model. Furthermore, all respondents were asked whether they preferred the BPMN or the Deontic BPMN diagram. The answers are shown in Fig. 4.52. The BPMN diagram was only favored in example 3, since this example required multiple deontic classifications and preconditions in Deontic BPMN, but did not decrease the structural complexity. In all other examples, the Deontic BPMN model was preferred, especially for more complex process flows as provided by the extract of the order execution process in example 4. Considering the fourth example, the respondents made slightly more mistakes by answering the questions of Deontic BPMN, which can be explained by the great number of preconditions. Nevertheless, almost all respondents prefer the Deontic BPMN diagram, which indicates that a reduction of structural complexity and a highlighting of modalities are beneficial even if complex deontic operators are necessary.

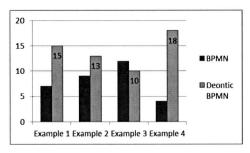

Figure 4.52: Preferences of Respondents

4.4   Deontic BPMN with Actor Modeling

In the previous sections, BPMLs in general and BPMN in particular were extended with deontic concepts to highlight modalities and reduce the structural complexity of the process flow. In addition, another issue that can be addressed with deontic logic is the limited support for actor modeling in BPMN. Thus, this section provides the motivation for supporting actors in BPMN, proposes a new approach for actor modeling based on deontic logic, and applies the approach to the case study and the resource perspective of the *Workflow Patterns*. All in all, the approach for actor modeling based on deontic logic is slightly more complex but far more expressive than the existing *Pool* and *Lane* concepts of the BPMN specification.

4.4.1 Motivation

According to the BPMN specification (see [99]), BPMN only supports those concepts of modeling that are applicable to business processes, whereas, for example, the definition of organizational models and resources is out of the scope of BPMN. Nevertheless, the category *Swimlane* provides *Pools* and *Lanes* that can used to model participants. These two concepts are frequently used by BPMN modelers as shown by an analysis of 1210 BPMN models in which more than 60% of the models comprised pools and lanes (only sequence flows, tasks, and start/end events are used more often) (see [65]). However, the modeling of participants (or actors) is limited by the fact that an activity can only be located in at most one lane. This results in the following issues:

1. Inaccuracy: If lanes are defined, then all types of elements may be located in these lanes including those that are automatically executed.

2. Redundancy: If an activity can be executed by two or more roles, then this activity must be duplicated for every additional lane.

3. Expressiveness: It is not possible to express that an activity (e.g., a sub-process) can be executed by two or more roles in collaboration.

Similar problems were also identified by other researchers. For example, Recker presented a global survey with 590 BPMN users in [105]. Beneath a detailed description of BPMN users (who uses BPMN where, how and why), five major issues were identified, one of it being organizational modeling with the ambiguity of the pool and lane concept. The ambiguity that comes with the flexible semantics is contradictory to the ease with which the two concepts can be used for process modeling. Thus, further effort is required to specify the meaning of the two concepts, and the multiple purposes of pools and lanes should be differentiated (cf. for this paragraph [105]).

Recker et al. also presented an evaluation of BPMN based on the Bunge-Wand-Weber (BWW) ontology and on interviews in [106]. The ontological evaluation revealed, beneath other issues, lack of completeness and clarity regarding the pool and lane concept, since both concepts represent several BWW constructs. The two concepts have also been voted in the highest problem category during the following interview (cf. for this paragraph [106]).

Furthermore, Wohed et al. studied the suitability of BPMN for business process modeling and used the Workflow Patterns as an evaluation framework (see [139]). According to this publication, BPMN provides good support for the control-flow perspective, medium support for the data perspective, but only low support for the resource perspective. Considering the resource perspective, BPMN supports only 8 out of 43 Resource Patterns, since *Swimlanes* are specified in a restrictive manner. Thus, it is important that the resource perspective is more widely acknowledged as an integral part of business process modeling. In addition, although the BPMN specification states that organizational modeling and resources are out of the scope of BPMN, the pool and lane concepts reveal the need (cf. for this paragraph [139]).

To address the problems with actor modeling, several extensions to BPMN have been suggested. For example, Awad et al. propose a task-based human resource allocation and extended the BPMN metamodel with the Object Constraint Language (OCL) to express resource allocation constraints [11]. Task-based authorization constraints for BPMN supporting different patterns like separation of duty, role-based allocation or case handling have further been presented by Wolter and Schaad in [140]. In addition, a BPMN extension considering security requirements like access control, non-repudiation, privacy, or integrity is proposed by Rodríguez et al. in [108]. Furthermore, Korherr and List extended BPMN with goals and performance measures [62] and Milanović et al. provide a rule-based extension of the BPMN metamodel based on the REWERSE Rule Markup Language (R2ML) [85]. However, although several extensions suggest a task-based approach for actor modeling, they still use the pool and lane concept to express the role hierarchy resulting in a mixture of different resource definitions. In addition, it is not possible to specify generic restrictions (e.g., every business travel must be approved by the corresponding manager) or dependencies between tasks concerning the executing roles. Thus, in the following section a further extension of Deontic BPMN that supports actor modeling is suggested.

4.4.2   Approach for Actor Modeling

This section starts with an overview of the suggested approach for actor modeling in Deontic BPMN. Afterwards, the main concepts as, for example, task-based deontic classification, the definition of an organizational model, the specification of additional rules, inference of further rules, and the extension with speech acts are explained in detail. Considering these concepts, different gradations concerning the extent to which actor modeling is supported are distinguished. Higher gradings are, for example, more complex but also more expressive.

Overview

An overview of the approach for actor modeling in Deontic BPMN is shown in Fig. 4.53 and consists of three different views. The first view is called the *Process View* and comprises the process flow. All activities in the process flow are deontically classified according to the description of Deontic BPMN in section 4.3. In addition, the deontic classification of manual or human activities (or abstract activities with a human executor) is extended with the modal operator for agency (*Do*) and a definition of the executing role (several roles can be concatenated with conjunction or disjunction). Instead of the modal operator for agency, speech acts may also be defined. Speech act theory treats communication as action and distinguishes between five different types of speech acts: representatives (e.g., inform), directives (e.g., request), commissives (e.g., commit), declarations (e.g., declare), and expressives (e.g., thank) [142, p. 132ff]. The last type (expressives) is not relevant for process modeling, but all other types may be used to support collaboration of actors. In summary, the process flow provides a task-based definition of possible actors based on deontic logic and speech act theory. Thus, the pool and lane concepts are no more required and should be omitted.

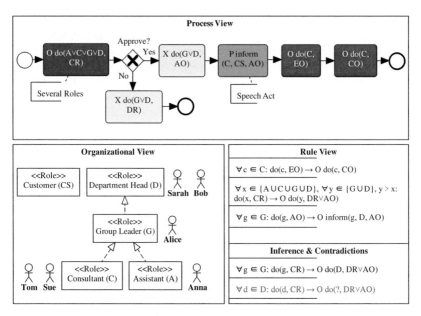

Figure 4.53: Actor Modeling in Deontic BPMN

The second view is called the *Organizational View* and provides a specification of possible roles and groups, the definition of the role hierarchy and an assignment of individuals to the roles and groups. Thus, this view comprises the dependencies and relationships between roles, groups, and individuals.

The third view is called the *Rule View* and comprises additional rules that are defined based on deontic logic and speech act theory. These rules specify restrictions that can hardly be defined in the process flow. For example, the first rule shown in Fig. 4.53 specifies that the individual c of role C (written as $c \in C$ or $C(c)$) who is executing the order (EO) must also close the order (CO). The second rule specifies that the individual y who is deleting the request (DR) or approving the order (AO) must have a higher role than the individual x who created the request (CR). In addition, the third rule defines that if a group leader g approves an order (AO), (s)he must inform a department head about the approved order (AO). The defined rules are then evaluated and with the help of inference new rules are derived and contradictions are identified, e.g., if a group leader creates a request (CR), then a department head must delete the request (DR) or approve the order (AO), but if a department head creates a request (CR), then no higher role can execute the following activities.

Considering the suggested concepts for supporting actor modeling in Deontic BPMN, not all of them are required for every process model. For example, in order to transform an existing BPMN diagram with pools and lanes into a Deontic BPMN diagram, only the *Process View* with deontic classifications and the definition of at most one role or actor as well as the *Organizational View* with roles, a role hierarchy, and individuals are necessary. However, the usage of further concepts increases the expressiveness. Thus, the following gradations to which extent the suggested concepts can be used for actor modeling are distinguished:

1. Task-Based Assignment: All activities in the process flow are deontically classified according to the definition of Deontic BPMN described in section 4.3. In addition, if an activity is executed by a human actor, then deontic logic with agency is used to define the executing role. The organizational model further comprises roles, the role hierarchy, and individuals. This gradation has the same expressiveness as standard BPMN, but allows to remove all pools and lanes from the process model. Thus, the first problem mentioned in section 4.4.1, which states that all types of elements can be located in a lane and are, therefore, assigned to a participant, is solved.

2. Extended Actor Modeling: The next step is to extend actor modeling by supporting several roles. Several roles or actors that execute an activity either together (concatenated with conjunction) or alternative (concatenated with disjunction) can be defined based on deontic logic with agency. This small extension allows to solve the other two problems described in section 4.4.1. For example, activities that can be executed by two or more roles must not be duplicated any more thereby reducing the structural complexity of the process flow. Furthermore, it is possible to specify that activities, e.g. a sub-process, can be executed by two or more roles in collaboration.

3. Deontic Rules: Further deontic rules are defined in the *Rule View*. Although such rules increase the complexity of the diagram, they also allow to define restrictions that could not have been specified within the process flow. For example, the restriction that the first task can be executed by an arbitrary individual of a given role but the subsequent task must be executed by another individual (*Separation of Duties* pattern) is often required but cannot be expressed with the pool and lane concepts of standard BPMN.

4. Inference: The deontic rules are evaluated based on inference in order to derive new rules and to identify contradictions. This extension does not increase the expressiveness of the diagram but it reduces the complexity from the perspective of the modeler, since derived rules explicitly express already existing knowledge and contradictions support the modeler by highlighting mistakes in the original rule definitions.

5. Speech Acts: In a last step, the approach is extended with speech act theory in order to support communication, coordination and cooperation between actors. Speech acts can be defined within the process flow or as additional rules and are then also considered in the inference. Speech acts are easy to understand and only slightly increase the complexity of the diagram, but allow to express collaboration of actors, e.g., actor r requests actor s to execute an activity A followed by a commitment of actor s to actor r to execute activity A.

Since it has been claimed that the expressiveness in every gradation is increased or remains the same, the entire approach for actor modeling in Deontic BPMN should increase the expressiveness as stated by Hypothesis 2. This hypothesis will be validated by a comparison of BPMN and Deontic BPMN with actor modeling based on the *Resource Patterns* (see section 4.4.4).

However, it should be noted that also Deontic BPMN with actor modeling supports only a restricted number of Resource Patterns, since the focus of BPMN (and also Deontic BPMN) is on business process modeling and not on workflows and resources. In contrast, several workflow systems like Staffware, WebSphere MQ Workflow, or COSA provide an extended organizational model that also includes concepts like work lists or queues and supports further Resource Patterns [109]. In addition, if a more resource-centric approach for business process modeling is required, then subject-oriented business process management (S-BPM) (see [36]) is recommended.

Task-Based Approach

The approach for actor modeling in Deontic BPMN provides a task-based definition of possible roles and actors based on deontic logic with agency (e.g., $O\ do(role, Activity)$). The advantage of the task-based definition is that every activity has its own specification of allowed roles and actors and several roles can be combined within a list. Thus, this approach is more flexible and more expressive than the pool and lane concept.

Other approaches that extend BPMN with task-based definitions of roles and actors were presented in section 4.4.1. However, these extensions use the task-based approach in combination with the pool and lane concepts resulting in a mixture of different resource definitions.

Considering other BPMLs, most of them provide a task-based definition of resources. Actors in *UML Activity Diagrams* (UML ADs) can, for example, either be expressed by swimlanes similar to BPMN diagrams or they are defined above the activity name in parenthesis thereby representing a task-based approach. Several partition names can be specified within a comma-delimited list expressing that the node is contained in more than one partition (cf. for this paragraph [101, p. 352f]). Another BPML that uses a task-based approach are *Event-Driven Process Chains* (EPCs), which define an own element for organization units that is referenced by a function [114]. In addition, also *Yet Another Workflow Language* (YAWL) provides a task-based approach to specify participants [2].

The consistency of task-based authorization constraints was studied by Tan et al. in [124]. The authors define a formal model with a set of consistency rules for constraints that guarantee a sound constrained workflow authorization schema (cf. for this paragraph [124]). Similar to our approach is the role-based access control and the task-based definition of constraints.

Organizational Model

The organizational model is kept simple and consists of groups, roles, hierarchical relationships between roles, and individuals that can be assigned to roles and groups. The hierarchical relationships are necessary to achieve the same expressiveness as standard BPMN, since also lanes can be nested thereby expressing hierarchical dependencies.

Enterprise architecture frameworks like ARIS or the Zachman Framework comprise several views also including process and organizational models. ARIS, for example, consists of five views that are symbolically presented in the form of a house, the so-called ARIS house, with the *Organization View* as the roof, the *Data, Control*, and *Function View* as the three pillars, and the *Output View* as basis of the house [112, 113]. According to Scheer, the designations "function", "process" and "activity" are used synonymously [112, p. 36], thus the *Function View* is similar to our *Process View*. Furthermore, the *Organization View* of ARIS comprises a hierarchical organizational model with organization units and concrete instances [113, p. 52ff] and resembles the *Organization View* of Deontic BPMN with actor modeling.

In addition, the *Zachman Framework* consists of six rows for the viewpoints (*Scope, Enterprise* (or *Business*) *Model, System Model, Technology Model, Detailed Representations*, and *Functioning Enterprise*) and six columns for the aspects (*Data, Function, Network, People, Time*, and *Motivation*). The aspect *Function* contains the business process model and is similar to our *Process View*. Furthermore, the aspect *People* contains the workflow or organizational model with organization units and hierarchical dependencies defined between them (cf. for this paragraph [86, 143]).

Finally, also the business process modeling language YAWL supports three different perspectives: control-flow, data, and resources. The resource perspective provides an organizational model that comprises the participants of an organization, their roles and capabilities, as well as managerial hierarchies (cf. for this paragraph [2]).

Additional Rules

Additional rules that cannot be expressed within the process flow are defined in the *Rule View* based on deontic logic and speech act theory. Furthermore, predicate logic may be used to define quantifiers and higher or lower roles may be expressed with the operators $\prec$ and $\succ$. Then the rules can, for example, specify that two activities assigned to the same role must be executed by the same individual (*Retain Familiar* pattern) or that the executor of one activity must have a higher role than that of another activity.

Considering related work, the use of deontic rule sets to connect the organizational model to the activities in the process flow is recommended by Hohwiller et al. in [56]. In addition, Grossi et al. propose a semantic framework based on dynamic logic with deontic expressions in which responsibilities between groups and agents are divided into three dimensions (power (delegation), coordination (information), and control (monitoring)) and formally characterized [50]. Furthermore, also the *Semantics of Business Vocabulary and Rules* (SBVR), which is like BPMN a standard of OMG, recommends deontic logic for specifying business rules [98].

However, an open issue of the approach for actor modeling in Deontic BPMN are actors that violate obligations. If actors do not execute the activities they are obliged to perform, the process must be adapted and the activity, e.g., assigned to another actor. The specification of error-tolerant software agents based on deontic logic has, for example, been studied by Eiter et al. in [35]. In addition, Governatori and Milosevic present a formal system based on deontic concepts for reasoning about violations of obligations in contracts [49].

Inference and Contradictions

Up to now, assignments of actors and restrictions in the execution have been specified based on formal rules either within the process flow or as additional rules in the *Rule View*. However, these rules have not been validated. Thus, in a next step, inference techniques are used to analyze the rules and to derive new rules thereby making implicit knowledge explicit. Furthermore, with the help of inference, contradictions in the rule definitions can be identified and are highlighted for the modeler. All derived rules and potential contradictions are shown at the bottom of the *Rule View*.

Inference has also been used for the *BPMN 2.0 Ontology* described in chapter 3 to derive additional information and to check the syntactical correctness of BPMN models. In fact, inference of deontic rules is very similar to inference (or reasoning) in description logics (DLs). In both bases, the formal definitions are based on predicate logic including conjunction, disjunction, negation, and universal and existential quantifiers. In addition, individuals resemble individuals in the ABox, roles are similar to concepts in the TBox, which can be defined in a hierarchical structure and denote sets of individuals, and the modal operator *Do*, which links roles or actors to activities, resembles a role (or relationship) in DL. Furthermore, a major challenge of both approaches is the balance between the expressiveness of the language and the complexity of reasoning. Due to the similarities and the fact that most DLs are more expressive than the language used for the deontic rules, it is referred to the description of inference in DLs (see [88]) for further details and possible extensions (e.g., number restrictions) (cf. for this paragraph [88]).

Speech Act Theory

Speech act theory was introduced by Austin in 1962 and extended by Searle in 1969. It treats communication as action with the assumption that speech actions are performed by agents like any other action. Speech act theory further distinguishes three different aspects of speech acts: locutionary act (act of making an utterance), illocutionary act (action performed in saying something), and prelocution (effect of the act). In the following, only illocutionary acts are considered, which are further classified as representatives (e.g., inform), directives (e.g., request), commissives (e.g., commit), declarations (e.g., declare), and expressives (e.g., thank) (cf. for this paragraph [142, p. 132ff]). The last type (expressives) is not relevant for process modeling, but all other types may be used to support collaboration of actors.

In order to support collaboration (communication, coordination, and cooperation) of actors in Deontic BPMN, the following speech acts may be defined within the process flow or in additional rules in the *Rule View* (speaker s, hearer h, proposition φ, action α (based on [142, p. 132ff])):

- inform(s, h, φ)

- request(s, h, α)

- commit(s, h, α)

- declare(s, h, φ)

So, for example, in the process flow shown in Fig. 4.53, the consultant informs the customer about the proposition that the order was approved. Hence, the speech act *inform* supports *communication* between actors. Furthermore, all speech acts together support *coordination* and *cooperation*. Every speech act can then be extended with deontic concepts to define that the speech act is obligatory, permissible, or forbidden.

In addition, the inference techniques described before must be extended to support rules with speech acts. Also speech acts can be expressed with roles in DL, however, speech acts require ternary relations. Some DLs support n-ary relations and, thus, also provide inference concepts for such roles. However, if the description logic does not support n-ary relations, then the concept of reified relationships must be used and a new concept with n properties (functional roles) is created for the relationship (see [15]).

Considering related work, Dignum and Weigand combined illocutionary and dynamic deontic logic to model communication processes [26, 27]. The authors distinguish four basic speech acts (request, commit, assert, and declare), which are executed by agents based on charity, power, or authorization. The work of Dignum and Weigand inspired the extension of Deontic BPMN with actor modeling. Furthermore, Colombetti introduced an agent communication language based on speech acts that supports conversations of agents [22].

4.4.3   Case Study

In order to study the suitability of Deontic BPMN with actor modeling for practical scenarios, this section provides a case study based on the order execution and business travel process presented in section 4.3.3. The Deontic BPMN diagrams of both processes are considered and transformed to Deontic BPMN with actor modeling.

The Deontic BPMN diagram of the order execution process is shown in Fig. 4.43 and comprises 3 start events, 18 tasks, 18 gateways, and 49 sequence flows. The transformation to Deontic BPMN with actor modeling replaces the pools and lanes with an organizational model and a task-based authorization as shown in Fig. 4.54. This, on the one hand, allows a flexible positioning of the elements that is no more restricted by lanes and, on the other hand, the three *Create Request* (CR) tasks can be unified in one task that is executed by either one of the three roles. The resulting task is classified as obligatory (which is more appropriate than three alternative tasks) and two start events, two tasks, two gateways, and six sequence flows can be removed thereby reducing the structural complexity of the process flow.

Furthermore, it was not possible to specify in the BPMN or Deontic BPMN diagram that the creation of an appointment as well as the execution and closure of the order must be done by the same consultant (*Retain Familiar* pattern). In Deontic BPMN with actor modeling, this restriction can be defined by additional rules in the *Rule View*.

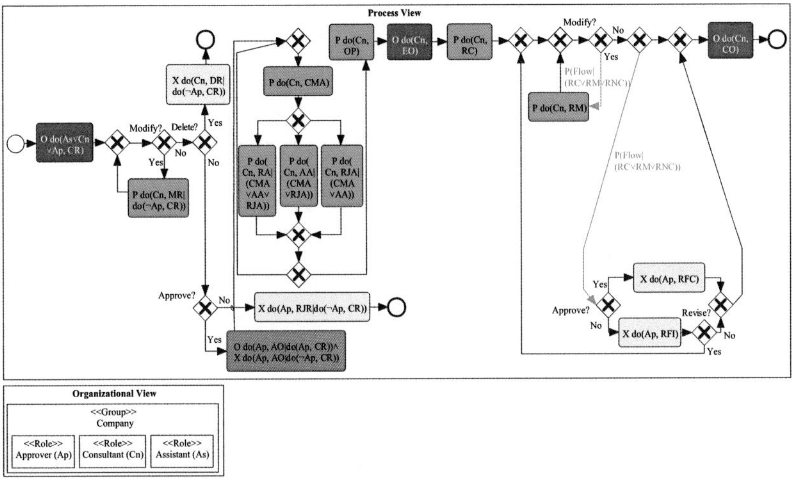

Figure 4.54: Order Execution Process: Deontic BPMN with Actor Modeling

The Deontic BPMN diagram of the business travel process is shown in Fig. 4.46 and consists of 11 tasks, 10 gateways, and 28 sequence flows. The resulting Deontic BPMN diagram with actor modeling comprises 8 tasks, 10 gateways, and 24 sequence flows and is shown in Fig. 4.55. In a first step, the two tasks *Review BT* are unified in one task, which allows a reduction of one task and two sequence flows. The exclusive gateway with the question "Recipient?" is placed after the unified task. In addition, the three *Send for Approval* tasks are unified in one task resulting in a reduction of two tasks and two sequence flows. If, however, only the two *Send for Approval* tasks that are either executed by the *Reviewer* or the *Approver* are unified in one task, then an additional merging gateway and a further sequence flow would have been necessary. Thus, the modeler can freely decide whether to unify tasks or not.

Furthermore, if a hierarchical dependency is defined between the roles *Approver* and *Reviewer* in the *Organizational View*, then it would be possible to specify only *Reviewer* instead of (*Reviewer* ∨ *Approver*) as executing role of a task. However, this abbreviation is only recommended if *Reviewer* is the standard role, which is sometimes substituted by an *Approver*. Considering the task *Review BT*, both roles should be specified to highlight that an *Approver* is not only a substitute, but is required to execute the task at least once in every process instance.

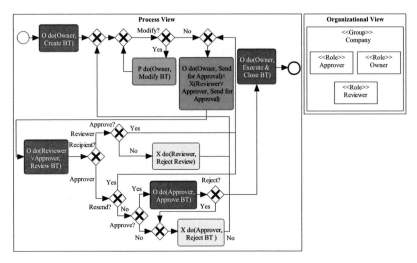

Figure 4.55: Business Travel Process: Deontic BPMN with Actor Modeling

In summary, this section demonstrated the extension of Deontic BPMN with actor modeling within a case study consisting of an order execution and a business travel process. In both cases, the number of tasks could have been reduced by unifying duplicated tasks which, in most cases, also reduced the number of gateways and sequence flows. However, in one case the unification of tasks would require an additional merging gateway. Thus, the modeler can freely decide whether to unify tasks or not. So without unification of tasks, the structure of the process flow remains the same resulting in the same structural complexity. In addition, the unification of some tasks provides the possibility to reduce the structural complexity of the process flow. Thus, there is at least one transformation from Deontic BPMN to Deontic BPMN with actor modeling with an equal or reduced structural complexity.

However, the main objective of Deontic BPMN with actor modeling is to increase the expressiveness. In the case study, the resulting Deontic BPMN diagrams with actor modeling had the same expressiveness due to the transformation. It has only been mentioned for the order execution process that additional rules are necessary to define that some tasks must be executed by the same individual. Since it was not possible to study the increased expressiveness within the case study, the expressiveness of Deontic BPMN with actor modeling is evaluated based on the *Workflow Resource Patterns* in the next section.

4.4.4 Workflow Resource Patterns

In this section the 43 *Workflow Resource Patterns* are studied, which are used
to capture the various ways in which resources are represented and utilized
in workflows and business processes [109]. An overview of the 43 Resource
Patterns is given in Tab. 4.2. The first column provides the pattern number, the second column the pattern name and the third and fourth column
specify whether the pattern is supported in BPMN and Deontic BPMN with
actor modeling (abbreviated with *Actors*). For example, the pattern *Case
Handling* is only supported by Deontic BPMN with actor modeling. Furthermore, the pattern *Role-Based Distribution* is supported by BPMN, but
the support in Deontic BPMN with actor modeling is more comprehensive.

Table 4.2: Overview Workflow Resource Patterns based on [128]

No.	Pattern Name	BPMN	Actors
Creation Patterns			
1	Direct Distribution	Yes	Yes
2	Role-Based Distribution	Yes	Yes(+)
3	Deferred Distribution	No	No
4	Authorization	No	No
5	Separation of Duties	No	Yes
6	Case Handling	No	Yes
7	Retain Familiar	No	Yes
8	Capability-Based Distribution	No	No(+)
9	History-Based Distribution	No	No
10	Organizational Distribution	No	Yes
11	Automatic Execution	Yes	Yes
Push Patterns			
12	Distribution by Offer - Single Resource	No	No(+)
13	Distribution by Offer - Multiple Resources	No	No(+)
14	Distribution by Allocation - Single Resource	Yes	Yes
15	Random Allocation	No	No
16	Round Robin Allocation	No	No
17	Shortest Queue	No	No
18	Early Distribution	No	Yes
19	Distribution on Enablement	Yes	Yes
20	Late Distribution	No	No
Pull Patterns			
21	Resource-Initiated Allocation	No	Yes
22	Resource-Initiated Execution - Allocated Work Item	No	Yes
23	Resource-Initiated Execution - Offered Work Item	No	No
24	System-Determined Work Queue Content	No	No
25	Resource-Determined Work Queue Content	No	No
26	Selection Autonomy	No	No

No.	Pattern Name	BPMN	Actors
Detour Patterns			
27	Delegation	No	No
28	Escalation	No	No
29	Deallocation	No	No
30	Stateful Reallocation	No	No
31	Stateless Reallocation	No	No
32	Suspension-Resumption	No	No
33	Skip	No	No
34	Redo	No	No
35	Pre-Do	No	No
Auto-Start Patterns			
36	Commencement on Creation	Yes	Yes
37	Commencement on Allocation	No	No
38	Piled Execution	No	No
39	Chained Execution	Yes	Yes
Visibility Patterns			
40	Configurable Unallocated Work Item Visibility	No	No
41	Configurable Allocated Work Item Visibility	No	No
Multiple Resource Patterns			
42	Simultaneous Execution	Yes	Yes
43	Additional Resources	No	No

So BPMN only supports 8 out of 43 Resource Patterns. A major reason for the limited support is the restrictive manner in which the pool and lane concepts are specified. In addition, most patterns are not supported because BPMN does not provide a work list or queue and does not support dynamic reallocation or collaboration (see pull and detour patterns). Several of these patterns are also not supported by Deontic BPMN with actor modeling due to the missing work list and the static definition at design-time. However, Deontic BPMN with actor modeling provides full support for 15 patterns and partial or enhanced support for 4 further patterns. In the following, the patterns supported by Deontic BPMN with actor modeling are described in detail.

Pattern 1: Direct Distribution

The *Direct Distribution* pattern describes the ability to specify at design-time the individual (or resource) to which instances of the task will be distributed at runtime. This pattern is supported in BPMN with the pool and lane concept, since pools and lanes may also denote individuals (cf. for this paragraph [128]).

In Deontic BPMN with actor modeling, this pattern is supported by the definition of individuals in the *Organizational View* and the assignment of these individuals to activities.

Pattern 2: Role-Based Distribution

The *Role-Based Distribution* pattern defines the ability to specify at design-time one or more roles to which instances of the task will be distributed at runtime. This pattern is supported in BPMN with the pool and lane concept, since pools and lanes may also denote general roles (cf. for this paragraph [128]).

However, the BPMN support for this pattern is limited, since tasks can only be located in at most one lane. Thus, the assignment to several roles is only supported if the roles have a hierarchical relationship and the lanes are nested. In all other cases, several roles require a duplication of the task. Furthermore, it is not possible to specify that an activity (e.g., a sub-process) is executed by several roles in collaboration.

In Deontic BPMN with actor modeling, one or more roles can be assigned to a task without the necessity to duplicate the task. Several roles can be concatenated with conjunction or disjunction. Thus, it can also be specified that an activity is executed by several roles in collaboration. So Deontic BPMN with actor modeling provides a more comprehensive support for the *Role-Based Distribution* pattern.

Pattern 5: Separation of Duties

The fifth pattern describes the ability to specify that two tasks must be executed by different individuals in a given process instance. This pattern is not supported by BPMN (cf. for this paragraph [128]).

However, the *Separation of Duties* pattern is supported by Deontic BPMN with actor modeling by the definition of additional rules. For example, it can be specified in the process flow that two tasks are executed by the same role (X), but an additional rule defines that the individuals must be different (e.g., $\forall x \in X : do(x, A1) \rightarrow F\ do(x, A2)$).

Pattern 6: Case Handling

The sixth pattern describes the ability to allocate all work items within a process instance to the same individual. This pattern is not supported by BPMN (cf. for this paragraph [128]).

However, the *Case Handling* pattern is supported by Deontic BPMN with actor modeling by the definition of additional rules. For example, it can be specified in the process flow that every task is executed by the same role (X) and additional rules define for every task that also the individuals must be the same (e.g., $\forall x \in X : do(x, A1) \rightarrow O\ do(x, A2)$, $\forall x \in X : do(x, A1) \rightarrow O\ do(x, A3)$, ...).

Pattern 7: Retain Familiar

The *Retain Familiar* pattern describes the ability to allocate a work item within a process instance to the same individual that undertook a preceding work item. In contrast to the *Case Handling* pattern, this pattern applies to single work items and not to all work items within a process instance. This pattern is not supported by BPMN (cf. for this paragraph [128]).

However, the *Retain Familiar* pattern is supported by Deontic BPMN with actor modeling by the definition of additional rules. For example, it can be specified in the process flow that two tasks are executed by the same role (X) and an additional rule defines that also the individuals must be the same (e.g., $\forall x \in X : do(x, A1) \rightarrow O\ do(x, A2)$).

Pattern 8: Capability-Based Distribution

The eighth pattern describes the ability to distribute work items to individuals based on specific capabilities they possess. The capabilities are defined for individuals as part of the organizational model. This pattern is not supported by BPMN (cf. for this paragraph [128]).

The *Capability-Based Distribution* is currently also not supported by Deontic BPMN with actor modeling. However, the organizational model can be easily extended to also comprise the capabilities of actors. Furthermore, additional rules can be defined to restrict the assignment of a task to those actors that provide the required capabilities. Thus, a minor extension of Deontic BPMN with actor modeling would allow to support this pattern.

Pattern 10: Organizational Distribution

The *Organizational Distribution* pattern describes the ability to distribute work items to resources based on their position within the organization and their relationship with other resources. This pattern is not supported by BPMN (cf. for this paragraph [128]).

The *Organizational Distribution* pattern is, however, supported by Deontic BPMN with actor modeling. Roles and groups are defined in the *Organizational View* and then assigned to activities in the process flow. In addition, Deontic BPMN with actor modeling supports the distribution of work items based on the relationship with other resources by additional rules in the *Rule View*. For example, an additional rule may defined that an order created by any employee must be approved by a higher role (e.g., $\forall x \in \{A \cup B \cup C\}, \forall y \in \{A \cup B \cup C\}, y \succ x : do(x, CO) \rightarrow O\ do(y, AO))$.

Pattern 11: Automatic Execution

The *Automatic Execution* pattern describes the ability of a task instance to execute without needing to utilize the services of a resource. The automatic execution of tasks that do not involve human interaction is not effected by actor modeling and, thus, supported by BPMN and Deontic BPMN with actor modeling (cf. for this paragraph [128]).

Pattern 12: Distribution by Offer - Single Resource

The *Distribution by Offer - Single Resource* pattern describes the ability to distribute a work item to an individual on a non-binding basis. The actor is informed of the work item being offered but is not committed to execute it. This pattern is not supported by BPMN (cf. for this paragraph [128]).

However, this pattern is partly supported in Deontic BPMN with actor modeling by additional tasks with speech acts. For example, a task in the process flow can specify that an actor $x \in R$ requests an actor $y \in R$ to perform task A (e.g., $O\ request(x, y, A)$). Two further tasks addressed by an exclusive gateway then define that actor y can either commit or decline to execute the task (e.g., $X\ commit(y, x, A)$ or $X\ commit(y, x, \neg A)$). If actor y commits to execute the task, then actor y is obliged to perform task A (e.g., $O\ do(y, A)$). If actor y declines, then another actor $z \in R$ can be asked to execute the task (e.g., $O\ request(x, z, A)$). Note that actor y can decide at runtime whether to commit or decline the execution of the task. However, the actors and the order in which they are asked must be defined at design-time within the tasks in the process flow. Thus, this pattern is only partly supported by Deontic BPMN with actor modeling.

Pattern 13: Distribution by Offer - Multiple Resources

The *Distribution by Offer - Multiple Resources* pattern describes the ability to distribute a work item to a group of selected resources on a non-binding basis. This pattern is not supported by BPMN (cf. for this paragraph [128]).

However, the *Distribution by Offer - Multiple Resources* pattern is partly supported in Deontic BPMN with actor modeling by additional tasks with speech acts. For example, a task in the process flow can specify that all actors of a given group are requested to perform task A (e.g., $O\ request(system, G1, A)$). Every actor of the group can then either commit or decline to execute the task (e.g., $X\ commit(x, system, A)$ or $X\ commit(x, system, \neg A)$ and $X\ commit(y, system, A)$ or $X\ commit(y, system, \neg A)$). As soon as the first actor commits to execute the task, all other actors are interrupted and, in addition, forbidden to execute the task (e.g., $commit(x, system, A) \rightarrow F\ do(y, A)$ and $commit(y, system, A) \rightarrow F\ do(x, A)$). If all actors decline to execute the task, then the task can be assigned to another group (e.g., $O\ request(system, G2, A)$). However, similar to the previous pattern, the communication must be defined at design-time. Thus, also this pattern is only partly supported by Deontic BPMN with actor modeling.

Pattern 14: Distribution by Allocation - Single Resource

The *Distribution by Allocation - Single Resource* pattern describes the ability to distribute a work item to a specific resource for execution on a binding basis. This pattern is supported in BPMN by the pool and lane concept (cf. for this paragraph [128]).

The *Distribution by Allocation - Single Resource* pattern is also supported by the task-based approach of Deontic BPMN with actor modeling. If an obligatory task is assigned to an actor or role (e.g., $O\ do(x, A)$), then the actor or role is obliged to execute the task.

Pattern 18: Early Distribution

The *Early Distribution* pattern describes the ability to advertise and potentially distribute a work item to resources ahead of the moment at which it is actually enabled, but the notification does not imply that the work item is ready for execution. This pattern is not supported by BPMN (cf. for this paragraph [128]).

However, the pattern is supported in Deontic BPMN with actor modeling by the speech act *inform*. For example, an additional rule can define that the consultant c must inform the approver a after the creation of a business travel about its upcoming approval (e.g., $do(c, Create\ BT) \rightarrow O\ inform(c, a, Approve\ BT)$), although the consultant can still modify the business travel before sending it to the approver.

Pattern 19: Distribution on Enablement

The *Distribution on Enablement* pattern describes the ability to distribute a work item to resources at the moment that the task to which it corresponds is enabled for execution. This pattern is supported in BPMN by the pool and lane concept (cf. for this paragraph [128]).

The *Distribution on Enablement* pattern is also supported by the task-based approach of Deontic BPMN with actor modeling. If an obligatory task is enabled for execution, then this task is immediately distributed to the assigned actor or role.

Pattern 21: Resource-Initiated Allocation

This pattern describes the ability of an actor to commit to undertake a work item without needing to commence working on it immediately. This pattern is not supported by BPMN (cf. for this paragraph [128]).

However, the pattern is supported in Deontic BPMN with actor modeling by the speech act *commit*. An actor that is requested to execute a task (e.g., $O\ request(x, y, A)$) can commit (e.g., $X\ commit(y, x, A)$). After the commitment, a further task in the process flow defines that the actor is obligated to perform task A (e.g., $O\ do(y, A)$). However, the actor can start task A later and, e.g., execute tasks on parallel paths before.

Pattern 22: Resource-Initiated Execution - Allocated Work Item

This pattern describes the ability of an actor to commence work on a work item that is allocated to it and that it has committed to execute. Furthermore, the actor should have the possibility to inform others about the commencement. This pattern is not supported by BPMN (cf. for this paragraph [128]).

However, this pattern is supported in Deontic BPMN with actor modeling by speech acts. After an actor has committed to execute a task (e.g., $X\ commit(y, x, A)$), (s)he can start the task at an arbitrary point in time. Furthermore, the actor can inform others about the commencement (e.g., $do(y, start(A)) \rightarrow P\ inform(y, x, start(A))$).

Pattern 36: Commencement on Creation

The *Commencement on Creation* pattern describes the ability of a resource to commence execution on a work item as soon as it is created. This pattern is supported by BPMN, since an activity is enabled as soon as it receives the required token(s) (cf. for this paragraph [128]).

This pattern is also supported by the task-based approach of Deontic BPMN with actor modeling. If an obligatory task is assigned to an actor or role (e.g., $O\ do(x, A)$), then the actor or role can commence execution as soon as the task is enabled.

Pattern 39: Chained Execution

The *Chained Execution* pattern describes the ability to automatically start the next work item in a process instance once the previous one has completed. This pattern is supported by BPMN, since once an activity is completed, subsequent activities receive a token and are triggered immediately (cf. for this paragraph [128]).

This pattern is also supported by the task-based approach of Deontic BPMN with actor modeling. If an activity has completed, subsequent activities are triggered immediately.

Pattern 42: Simultaneous Execution

The *Simultaneous Execution* pattern describes the ability of an actor to execute more than one work item simultaneously. This pattern is supported by BPMN, since there are no constraints on how many instances of a task specified within a pool or lane can be active (cf. for this paragraph [128]).

This pattern is also supported by the task-based approach of Deontic BPMN with actor modeling. Several instances of a task can be active simultaneously (e.g., multi-instance activity) and are executed by the same actor.

In summary, Deontic BPMN with actor modeling supports almost twice as much patterns as BPMN including essential ones like *Separation of Duties* and *Retain Familiar*. However, in order to support the remaining patterns, a more resource-centric approach with work lists and dynamic collaboration is necessary. Nevertheless, it has been shown that Deontic BPMN with actor modeling is, concerning the resource perspective, more expressive than BPMN thereby validating Hypothesis 2.

4.5 Summary

In this chapter, an extension of BPMLs with deontic concepts to highlight modalities was presented. The first section started with an introduction to the deontic classification of activities including monadic and dyadic deontic logic, multiple deontic classifications, as well as deontic logic with agency. In addition, user and conditional choices were distinguished and different gradations of deontic classifications presented. Afterwards, the *Control-Flow Patterns* by van der Aalst et al. (see [129]) were extended with deontic concepts. This extension allows to identify obligatory, permissible, and alternative activities on first sight and can be applied to several BPMLs including BPMN, UML ADs, and EPCs. In the third section, the deontic extension was applied to BPMN called *Deontic BPMN*. The deontic analysis is supported by a path exploration approach and the benefits of Deontic BPMN were demonstrated by a case study and a preliminary survey. Subsequently, Deontic BPMN was extended with actor modeling. The approach for actor modeling is based on deontic logic for agency and speech acts and supports a task-based assignment of actors and roles. After a detailed description of the approach, the suitability was studied within a case study and the expressiveness was evaluated based on the *Workflow Resource Patterns*.

Chapter 5

Graph Transformation: BPMN ⇒ Deontic BPMN

This chapter describes a graph transformation from BPMN to Deontic BPMN called *DeonticBpmnGTS*. After specifying the basic definitions of algebraic graph transformation, DeonticBpmnGTS is presented including the type graph and several transformation rules. Moreover, it is proven that DeonticBpmnGTS is strictly AC-confluent and terminating, which implies that the transformation is globally deterministic. This chapter concludes with a discussion of the results.

5.1 Basic Definitions

In the following, the most important definitions concerning algebraic graph transformation are presented as, for example, *graph*, *graph morphism*, *type graph*, and *confluence*. Further definitions can be found in [31].

The first definition defines a *graph* consisting of nodes and directed edges.

Definition 1. *Graph [31, p. 21]:*

> "A [directed] graph $G = (V, E, s, t)$ consists of a set V of nodes (also called vertices), a set E of edges, and two functions $s, t :$ $E \to V$, the source and target functions."

The definition of *graph morphism* specifies how two graphs are related by defining a mapping between the nodes and edges of the graphs [31, p. 22].

Definition 2. *Graph Morphism [31, p. 22]:*

"*Given graphs G_1, G_2 with $G_i = (V_i, E_i, s_i, t_i)$ for i = 1, 2, a graph morphism $f : G_1 \to G_2$, $f = (f_V, f_E)$ consists of two functions $f_V : V_1 \to V_2$ and $f_E : E_1 \to E_2$ that preserve the source and target functions, i.e. $f_V \circ s_1 = s_2 \circ f_E$ and $f_V \circ t_1 = t_2 \circ f_E$.*"

"*A graph morphism f is injective (or surjective) if both functions f_V, f_E are injective (or surjective, respectively); f is called isomorphic if it is bijective, which means both injective and surjective.*"

Further important definitions are those of a *type graph*, *typed graph*, and *typed graph morphism*. A *type graph* specifies node and edge types and the relationships between them. A specific graph with nodes and edges based on types is then called a *typed graph*. Furthermore, a *typed graph morphism* defines a graph morphism between two typed graphs.

Definition 3. *Type Graph, Typed Graph, and Typed Graph Morphism [31, p. 22f]:*

"*A type graph is a distinguished graph $TG = (V_{TG}, E_{TG}, s_{TG}, t_{TG})$. V_{TG} and E_{TG} are called the vertex and the edge type alphabets, respectively.*

A tuple $(G, type)$ of a graph G together with a graph morphism $type : G \to TG$ is then called a typed graph.

Given typed graphs $G_1^T = (G_1, type_1)$ and $G_2^T = (G_2, type_2)$, a typed graph morphism $f : G_1^T \to G_2^T$ is a graph morphism $f : G_1 \to G_2$ such that $type_2 \circ f = type_1$."

An extension of typed graphs are attributed typed graphs over an attributed type graph (ATG). This extension requires the definition of an E-graph, which has two kinds of nodes (graph (V_G) and data nodes (V_D)) and three kinds of edges (usual graph edges (E_G) and special edges for node (E_{NA}) and edge attribution (E_{EA})). The main difference between graphs and E-graphs is that edges in a graph may only connect to nodes whereas in E-graphs the source of edge attribute edges (E_{EA}) are graph edges (E_G). An attributed graph is then defined to be an E-graph combined with an algebra over a data signature $DSIG$ with attribute value sorts $S_D' \subseteq S_D$ (cf. for this paragraph [31, p. 171ff]).

An attributed type graph may also define node type inheritance with a distinguished set of abstract nodes and inheritance relations between the nodes [31, p. 260f]. Since DeonticBpmnGTS defines abstract nodes and inheritance relations with the type graph, the definition of an attributed type graph with inheritance (ATGI) is necessary.

Definition 4. *Attributed Type Graph with Inheritance [31, p. 260f]:*

> "*An* attributed type graph with inheritance $ATGI = (TG, Z, I, A)$ *consists of an attributed type graph* $ATG = (TG, Z)$ *[...], where* TG *is an E-graph* $TG = (TG_{V_G}, TG_{V_D}, TG_{E_G}, TG_{E_{NA}}, TG_{E_{EA}}, (source_i, target_i)_{i \in \{G, NA, EA\}})$ *with* $TG_{V_G} = S'_D$ *and final DSIG-algebra* Z; *an inheritance graph* $I = (I_V, I_E, s, t)$ *with* $I_V = TG_{V_G}$; *and a set* $A \subseteq I_V$, *called the abstract nodes. For each node* $n \in I_V$, *the inheritance clan is defined by* $clan_I(n) = \{n' \in I_V \mid \exists \text{ path } n' \xrightarrow{*} n \text{ in } I\} \subseteq I_V$ *with* $n \in clan_I(n)$."

So an ATG consists of a type graph TG that is an E-graph and a final *DSIG*-algebra Z. The *DSIG*-algebra Z is called final if it is "the unique (up to isomorphism) final algebra in the category $Alg(\Sigma)$" [31, p. 357]. An ATGI further comprises an inheritance graph I and a set of abstract nodes A. The inheritance clan of a node represents all its subnodes [31, p. 260].

An ATGI can be flattened to an ATG in order to benefit from the definitions of typed attributed graph transformation. The equivalence of typed attributed graph grammars with and without inheritance is shown in [31, p. 278f]. Considering graph morphisms, a bijective correspondence between ATGI-clan morphisms and normal type morphisms can be shown. An ATGI-clan morphism $type : AG \to ATGI$ corresponds uniquely to a normal type morphism $\overline{type} : AG \to \overline{ATG}$, where $\overline{ATG}$ is the abstract flattening (or abstract closure) of *ATGI*. In the abstract closure of a type graph all inheritance relations are flattened and the remaining abstract nodes are removed in the concrete closure [123]. An ATGI-clan morphism is called concrete if there are no abstract nodes in the graph (cf. for this paragraph [31, p. 261ff]).

Another important concept of algebraic graph transformation are labeled graphs, which consist of a label alphabet L with node and edge labels ($L = (L_V, L_E)$) [31, p. 23f]. A labeled graph corresponds to the type graph as follows [31, p. 24]:

- $V_{TG} = L_V$,

- $E_{TG} = L_V \times L_E \times L_V$,

- $s_{TG} : E_{TG} \to V_{TG} : (a, x, b) \mapsto a$,

- $t_{TG} : E_{TG} \to V_{TG} : (a, x, b) \mapsto b$.

Since every node type must have a distinct label, the node label corresponds to the node type. However, one edge label can be used for different combinations of nodes whereas an edge type is restricted to the defined source and target node. For example, in DeonticBpmnGTS all edges represent sequence flows (SF) and may be used between different node types. Therefore, different edge types are necessary, e.g., *SF1* may connect two tasks, *SF2* a start event and a task and so on. To avoid various names for the same concept, DeonticBpmnGTS defines one edge label with the name *SF*. This label is then reused for all combinations of nodes, e.g., {Task × SF × Task} represents one edge type and {StartEvent × SF × Task} another one.

If the source or target node of a labeled edge is an abstract node or defines inheritance relations, then the abstract combination can be flattened to further concrete combinations. The difference between a labeled graph and an E-graph is that labels are preserved during rule application whereas an E-graph uses node and edge attribute edges, so that attributes may be changed during a transformation step [31, p. 171ff].

For the application of rules it is also necessary to define *pushouts*, which have been mentioned shortly in section 2.3. The definition of pushouts requires the concept of categories, which are defined to be a mathematical structure with objects, morphisms, a composition operation on the morphisms and an identity morphism for each object. For a categorical framework, the morphism classes of monomorphisms, epimorphisms and isomorphisms are defined, which correspond in case of graph and typed graph categories with injective, surjective and bijective functions (cf. for this paragraph [31, p. 25ff]).

Definition 5. *Pushout [31, p. 29]:*

"*Given morphisms $f : A \to B$ and $g : A \to C$ in a category $\mathbf{C}$, a pushout (D, f', g') over f and g is defined by*

- *a pushout object D and*

- *morphisms $f' : C \to D$ and $g' : B \to D$ with $f' \circ g = g' \circ f$*

such that the following universal property is fulfilled: For all objects X and morphisms $h : B \to X$ and $k : C \to X$ with $k \circ g = h \circ f$, there is a unique morphism $x : D \to X$ such that $x \circ g' = h$ and $x \circ f' = k$:"

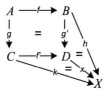

The pushout object D results from gluing two objects along a common subobject [31, p. 29]. The dual construction of a pushout is a *pullback*, which can be seen as a generalized intersection of objects over a common object [31, p. 33].

Definition 6. *Pullback [31, p. 33]:*

"Given morphisms $f : C \to D$ and $g : B \to D$ in a category C, a pullback (A, f', g') over f and g is defined by

- a pullback object A and
- morphisms $f' : A \to B$ and $g' : A \to C$ with $g \circ f' = f \circ g'$

such that the following universal property is fulfilled: For all objects X with morphisms $h : X \to B$ and $k : X \to C$ with $f \circ k = g \circ h$, there is a unique morphism $x : X \to A$ such that $f' \circ x = h$ and $g' \circ x = k$:"

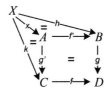

A further important definition for graph transformation is that of a *graph rule* (also called *graph production*). The application of a rule to a graph is called a direct graph transformation [31, p. 37].

Definition 7. *Graph Production [31, p. 37]:*

> *"A (typed) graph production $p = (L \xleftarrow{l} K \xrightarrow{r} R)$ consists of (typed) graphs, L, K, and R, called the left-hand side, gluing graph, and the right-hand side respectively, and two injective (typed) graph morphisms l and r.*
>
> *Given a (typed) graph production p, the inverse production is defined by $p^{-1} = (R \xleftarrow{r} K \xrightarrow{l} L)$."*

So a direct (typed) graph transformation $(G \overset{r,m}{\Rightarrow} H)$ requires a graph rule r and a graph morphism m, called the match, of the rule's left-hand side L in G ($m : L \to G$). If a rule comprises abstract nodes, then a flattening approach can be used to achieve concrete rules. A sequence $G_0 \Rightarrow G_1 \Rightarrow ... \Rightarrow G_n$ of direct (typed) graph transformations is called a (typed) graph transformation $(G_0 \overset{*}{\Rightarrow} G_n)$ and a graph transformation system (GTS) consists of a set of graph rules. A GTS can be nondeterministic if for a given rule several matches are possible and one has to be chosen, or if several rules are applicable and one is chosen arbitrarily (cf. for this paragraph [31, p. 9f, 38, 273]).

The overall goal is to prove global determinism of DeonticBpmnGTS, even if there is local nondeterminism. Global determinism means that the target graphs H_1 and H_2 of every terminating graph transformation $G \overset{*}{\Rightarrow} H_1$ and $G \overset{*}{\Rightarrow} H_2$ are isomorphic [31, p. 59]; so regardless of the chosen match or the order of the rule application, the resulting graph is always the same.

According to Ehrig et al., every confluent GTS is globally deterministic [31, p. 59]. A GTS is confluent if for all graph transformations $G \overset{*}{\Rightarrow} H_1$ and $G \overset{*}{\Rightarrow} H_2$, there exists a graph X with graph transformations $H_1 \overset{*}{\Rightarrow} X$ and $H_2 \overset{*}{\Rightarrow} X$. Hence, confluence implies the uniqueness of X [19, p. 198f]. In order to prove confluence, it is either necessary to show that each rule pair is parallel independent for all possible matches or, in case of parallel dependent rules, that the GTS is terminating and locally confluent. A GTS is locally confluent if all its critical pairs (parallel dependent and minimal) are strictly confluent (see definition in section 5.4) (cf. for this paragraph [31, p. 59ff, 144]).

The question whether two rules can be applied in arbitrary order requires the definition of parallel and sequential independence. Two rules are parallel independent if all nodes and edges in the intersection of the two matches are gluing items, i.e. are not deleted by the rule, for both transformations.

This means that all elements of graph G that are part of both matches must not be deleted by one of the two rules. Two consecutively applied rules are sequentially independent if all nodes and edges in the intersection of the comatch $R_1 \to H_1$ and the second rule's match are gluing items with respect to both transformations (cf. for this paragraph [31, p. 44f, 47ff]). So all elements that are part of the comatch $R_1 \to H_1$ of the first rule and match $L_2 \to G$ of the second rule must not be deleted by one of the two rules. If, e.g., the second rule deletes a gluing item, then this rule cannot be applied before the other rule resulting in a sequential dependency. The dependency between parallel and sequential independence is defined by the *Local Church-Rosser Theorem*.

Theorem 1. *Local Church-Rosser Theorem for GTSs [31, p. 50f]:*

> *"Given two parallel independent direct (typed) graph transformations $G \overset{p_1,m_1}{\Rightarrow} H_1$ and $G \overset{p_2,m_2}{\Rightarrow} H_2$, there is a (typed) graph G' together with direct (typed) graph transformations $H_1 \overset{p_2,m_2'}{\Rightarrow} G'$ and $H_2 \overset{p_1,m_1'}{\Rightarrow} G'$ such that $G \overset{p_1,m_1}{\Rightarrow} H_1 \overset{p_2,m_2'}{\Rightarrow} G'$ and $G \overset{p_2,m_2}{\Rightarrow} H_2 \overset{p_1,m_1'}{\Rightarrow} G'$ are sequentially independent.*
>
> *Given two sequentially independent direct (typed) graph transformations $G \overset{p_1,m_1}{\Rightarrow} H_1 \overset{p_2,m_2'}{\Rightarrow} G'$, there are a (typed) graph H_2 and direct (typed) graph transformations $G \overset{p_2,m_2}{\Rightarrow} H_2 \overset{p_1,m_1'}{\Rightarrow} G'$ such that $G \overset{p_1,m_1}{\Rightarrow} H_1$ and $G \overset{p_2,m_2}{\Rightarrow} H_2$ are parallel independent:"*

So the Local Church-Rosser Theorem states that two parallel independent graph transformations can be applied in arbitrary order. Furthermore, the *Parallelism Theorem* in [31, p. 53] shows that two parallel independent graph transformations can also be applied in parallel (cf. for this paragraph [31, p. 50ff]).

If each pair of rules is parallel independent for all possible matches, then this implies that the GTS is confluent. However, for all parallel dependent rules, a critical pair can be identified, and local confluence must be proven. A GTS is locally confluent if each pair of direct graph transformations $G \Rightarrow H_1$ and $G \Rightarrow H_2$ is strictly confluent (see Fig. 5.1) (cf. for this paragraph [31, p. 59f, 144]).

Figure 5.1: Confluence and Local Confluence (Source: [31, p. 59])

Critical pairs, strict (local) confluence and termination will be explained in more detail in the corresponding sections 5.4 and 5.5.

5.2   DeonticBpmnGTS: An Overview

The following sections describe a graph transformation from BPMN to Deontic BPMN. The transformation is called *DeonticBpmnGTS* and consists of an attributed type graph with inheritance and 18 transformation rules with positive and negative application conditions distributed across 4 layers. Concrete BPMN models are taken as input and then transformed to Deontic BPMN models thereby highlighting the deontic concepts.

Since every rule in the transformation leads to equally many or fewer gateways and/or sequence flows, Hypothesis 1 will be confirmed for all definitions that are part of DeonticBpmnGTS. Furthermore, it will be proven that DeonticBpmnGTS is globally deterministic thereby affirming Hypothesis 3.

DeonticBpmnGTS comprises the basic transformations described in chapter 4, but is limited to:

- Structured Diagrams: See section 4.1.3 for an explanation and comparison of structured and unstructured diagrams.

- Basic Set of BPMN Elements: DeonticBpmnGTS supports sequence flows, parallel, exclusive and inclusive gateways without conditions, tasks, and start/end events. All supported node and edge types are presented in section 5.3.1.

- One Task per Path: DeonticBpmnGTS is limited to one task per path following a splitting gateway and is also prohibiting most types of nested gateways.

Forbidden are also mixed gateways as well as several incoming or outgoing sequence flows of an activity. In most cases, these constructs can synonymically be expressed with an additional gateway except some rare cases in which, for example, several incoming sequence flows generate new process instances. In addition, different markers used for tasks or events are not relevant for the current deontic classification and thus not distinguished.

According to the BPMN specification (see [99]), all exclusive and inclusive gateways must have conditions on the outgoing sequence flows except for the default flow. Therefore, unconditional gateways in the context of Deontic BPMN denote all those gateways with conditions, where the user can freely decide. These conditions are also called *User Choice* and subsequent tasks might be permissible. In DeonticBpmnGTS, the gateways are shown without any condition, since the decision is normally described by a simple question, e.g. "Execute Task?". On the contrary, conditional gateways denote all those gateways with conditions, where the outgoing path is selected based on a state, data or rule. In this case, the user is not free to decide and a subsequent task is obligatory or forbidden. This differentiation is described in more detail in section 4.1.5.

The transformation from BPMN to Deontic BPMN is supported by the tool *Attributed Graph Grammar* (AGG). AGG allows to define typed attributed graph transformations and offers analysis techniques as for consistency checking, critical pair analysis (CPA), and termination evaluation (see section 2.3).

5.3 Type Graph and Rules

The following subsections present the type graph with all node and edge types as well as the 18 transformation rules of DeonticBpmnGTS. The transformation from BPMN to Deontic BPMN is further demonstrated by an example.

5.3.1 Type Graph

In a first step, the node types and the edge label of the graph transformation system are specified as shown in Fig. 5.2. DeonticBpmnGTS comprises four node types for gateways *(Gateway, ParallelGateway, InclusiveGateway,* and *ExclusiveGateway)*, two for BPMN tasks *(BpmnTask* and *Task)*, eight for deontic tasks *(DeonticTask, O(Task), X(Task), P(Task), O(Task|Precondition), X(Task|Precondition), P(Task|Precondition),* and *P(Task)&O(Task|Precon-*

dition)), and three for events *(Event, StartEvent,* and *EndEvent)*. The deontic tasks are colored as suggested in chapter 4. One further node type is
called *MeasuredValues* and used to store meta-information like the number
of gateways and sequence flows in order to study the reduction of structural
complexity. This node is not relevant for the deontic transformation and,
thus, excluded from the CPA. In addition, DeonticBpmnGTS provides one
edge label called *SF* for sequence flows representing several edge types.

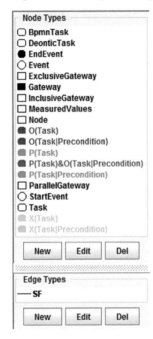

Figure 5.2: Node Types and Edge Label of *DeonticBpmnGTS*

In a second step, the type graph is specified, which defines the generalization and dependency relationships between the node types. For Deontic-
BpmnGTS an attributed type graph with inheritance is defined and shown
in Fig. 5.3. The basic element of the type graph is *Node* with the derived
types *Gateway, DeonticTask, BpmnTask,* and *Event*.

The type graph of DeonticBpmnGTS includes the following information:

- Abstract/Concrete Node Types: The five node types (*Node, Gateway,
  DeonticTask, BpmnTask,* and *Event*) are abstract as highlighted by the
  curly brackets and italic font. All other node types are concrete.

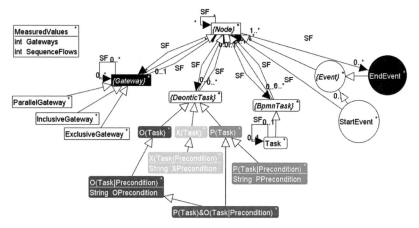

Figure 5.3: Type Graph of *DeonticBpmnGTS*

- Multiplicity of Node Types: The multiplicity of a node type is specified in the upper right corner of the rectangle and defines how many nodes of a given type may be used within a typed graph. All node types of the current type graph show an asterisk and can thus be used as often as required.

- Attributes: Some node types define attributes as for example preconditions or the number of gateways and sequence flows. These attributes may change during a transformation step.

- Inheritance Relationships: The ATGI definition permits inheritance relationships between different node types also with multiple inheritance as used for the node type *P(Task)&O(Task|Precondition)*. The attributes specified within a superclass are inherited by all subclasses; e.g., *P(Task)&O(Task|Precondition)* inherits the attribute *OPrecondition* from the node type *O(Task|Precondition)*.

- Dependency Relationships with Multiplicity: The source, target, and cardinality of a sequence flow is specified by dependency relationships. Although all edges are labeled as SF, every dependency relationship represents a distinct edge type. The cardinality defines how many relationships are allowed in a typed graph. For example, a *BpmnTask* or *DeonticTask* may not have more than one outgoing sequence flow whereas a *Gateway* may reference several further *Nodes*.

Considering the inheritance relationships between deontic tasks, a colleague suggested to reverse the hierarchy and to classify deontic tasks with preconditions as superclasses as shown in Fig. 5.4 [63]. Deontic tasks with the same operator but with less or no preconditions (assumed to be true) are then defined as subclasses. This suggestion, however, conflicts with the Liskov substitution principle, which requires that a sub-type preserves the behavior of the super-type methods [69]. In case of the deontic tasks, a super-type *O(Task|Precondition)* might have methods like SetPrecondition() and SkipTaskExecution(), which are not supported with the same behavior by the sub-type *O(Task)*, since the sub-type is always obligatory.

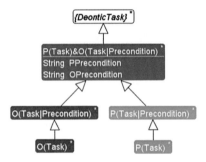

Figure 5.4: Type Graph with Reversed Hierarchy

The concrete gateways (parallel, inclusive, and exclusive) can either be represented as colored rectangles with the name or as images corresponding with the BPMN specification (see Fig. 5.5). The gateways in the following rules and transformation will be shown as colored rectangles, since this representation displays the mapping number.

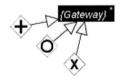

Figure 5.5: Image View of Gateways in Type Graph

Within the tool AGG, the extent to which the type graph is used can be specified and ranges from taking no multiplicity into account to considering both, the minimum and the maximum value of all multiplicities. DeonticBpmnGTS uses the highest level so that all information specified within the type graph is taken into account for the graph transformation.

Possible extensions of the type graph have been investigated and could cover:

- Sub-Processes: The type graph could be extended to support sub-processes by changing the node type *BpmnTask* to *BpmnActivity* with two derived classes *Task* and *SubProcess*. The internal details of a sub-process can be described within a further graph. This extension would support nested gateways and several tasks per path if the elements are combined within a sub-process.

- Conditional Gateways: Further node types for extended conditional gateways can be defined and derived from the inclusive and exclusive gateway. Two boolean attributes will specify whether the conditions are complete and distinct. This extension further requires a new edge label *ConditionalSF* for conditional sequence flows, which specifies two attributes: (i) the text of the condition and (ii) the order number of this sequence flow. A short outline of this extension is provided in section 5.3.3.

- Attributes: Further attributes could store additional information, for example, the name of a task or its markers.

5.3.2 Rules with Application Conditions

This section introduces the 18 transformation rules of DeonticBpmnGTS together with their application conditions. The rules cover sequences, gateways (parallel, exclusive and inclusive) and iterations and are distributed across four different layers.

Layering offers a kind of ordering, since all rules of one layer are applied as long as possible before the next layer is considered. Thus, layering provides a sequentialization of some rules and also avoids conflicts between rules of different layers. A set of graph rules R is defined to be layered if for each graph rule $r \in R$ there is a rule layer $rl(r)$ with $0 \leq rl(r) \leq k_0$, where $k_0 + 1$ is the number of layers [31, p. 250]. In DeonticBpmnGTS, all rules are assigned to one of the four layers ($0 \leq rl(r) \leq 3$; $k_0 + 1 = 4$). Note that layer 0 is called the first layer, layer 1 the second layer and so on.

The application of rules is restricted by application conditions (AC), which can either be positive or negative. A negative application condition (NAC) of the form $NAC(x)$ with graph morphism $x : L \to X$ is satisfied by a graph morphism $m : L \to G$ if there does not exist an injective graph morphism

$p : X \to G$ with $p \circ x = m$. This means that if there is an occurrence of the left-hand side L in G, then the NAC is satisfied if X is not also part of that match in G. A positive application condition (PAC) is the analogy to a NAC and satisfied if such an injective graph morphism exists. ACs are further allowed to contain L only partially ($s : L_{Sub} \to L$ and $x : L_{Sub} \to X$). In the following rule descriptions, the NACs and PACs do not include the *Measured Values* element (cf. for this paragraph [31, p. 64, 67ff, 309]).

Furthermore, dangling conditions might be violated if the application of a rule results in a dangling edge. Since DeonticBpmnGTS uses the double-pushout approach (DPO), an exception will be thrown during the graph transformation. The number of possible violations is minimized by specifying the cardinality of the sequence flows within the type graph and by further NACs.

Layer 0

The first layer comprises four transformation rules in order to address duplicate *Phi*-Paths and to transform loops and sequences of tasks.

SeveralPhiReductionRule: The rule *SeveralPhiReductionRule* addresses duplicate *Phi*-Paths between two gateways by removing one of them (see Fig. 5.6). Since both sequence flows are unconditional, they are semantically equivalent and nothing (Φ) has to be done if a token traverses a path. Therefore, it makes no difference whether the first or the second *Phi*-Path or both are executed.

(a) LHS   (b) RHS

Figure 5.6: SeveralPhiReductionRule

The intersection K of the left- and right-hand side ($K = LHS \cap RHS$) is for the given rule equal to the right-hand side ($K = RHS$). In general, it can be said that all elements with a preceding number on the *RHS* are defined on both sides and, thus, part of K, whereas all other elements are either created or deleted by the rule. Note that elements which are deleted by the rule may have a preceding number on the *LHS* if the element has a morphism image in an application condition.

The element *Gateway* describes an abstract type and can be instantiated by *ParallelGateway, InclusiveGateway* and *ExclusiveGateway*. Thus, the two abstract *Gateways* may lead to nine combinations of concrete gateways. The element *MeasuredValues* shows that every rule application leads to a reduction of one sequence flow.

IterationRepeatUntilRule: Iterations have a limited impact on the deontic classification of a task, since the elements in between are just repeated. Thus, an iteration does not allow to decide between tasks, but only how often a task is executed. The two major loop types supported within BPMN are the *While* and *Do-While* (or *Repeat-Until*) loop. Both types consist of a splitting gateway with a boolean condition. The condition covers all possibilities (true and false) and is, therefore, complete and distinct. Conditional gateways are not part of DeonticBpmnGTS, however, considering the *Repeat-Until* loop, the tasks in between are at least executed once and, thus, obligatory. Therefore, the rule *IterationRepeatUntilRule* classifies a task within a *Repeat-Until* loop as obligatory as shown in Fig. 5.7.

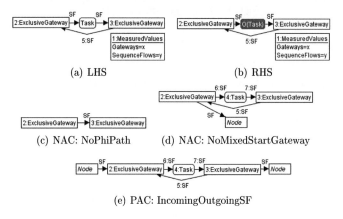

Figure 5.7: IterationRepeatUntilRule

In addition, two NACs specify that the first gateway is only a merging gateway and does not address a further node or a *Phi*-Path. Furthermore, the PAC defines that the first gateway has an incoming sequence flow and the second gateway references an outgoing sequence flow. The *MeasuredValues* element points out that the transformation does not affect the number of gateways and sequence flows.

A *Repeat-Until* loop may also include more complex constructs, for example, an exclusive gateway with two alternative tasks. In this case, the tasks are marked as alternative based on the corresponding rule *ExclusiveWithoutPhiRule*. The decision between the two alternative tasks might be made several times, however, the tasks remain alternatives.

SequenceRuleBase: The rule *SequenceRuleBase* classifies the second task within a sequence of tasks as obligatory under the precondition that the previous task was executed (see Fig. 5.8). This transformation does not affect the number of gateways and sequence flows.

(a) LHS   (b) RHS

Figure 5.8: SequenceRuleBase

The purpose of the precondition "PreviousTask" is to show that a task is only obligatory if the former task was executed. If, for example, an exclusive gateway references a *Phi*-Path and an alternative path with a sequence of tasks, then the first task of the sequence is classified as permissible and all further tasks are obligatory under the precondition that the previous task was executed. The preconditions are necessary to define that if the first task is not executed, then also the further tasks may not be executed.

However, according to the survey in section 4.3.4, preconditions increase the complexity and decrease the understandability. Therefore, preconditions referencing a previous task in the main flow might be removed if the order is also expressed through a sequence flow. The preconditions are deleted by two pragmatic rules, namely the *SequenceBpmnRulePragmatic* and *SequenceDeonticRulePragmatic*.

SequenceRuleExtended: The rule *SequenceRuleExtended* is used to classify the third and every further task within a sequence as obligatory under the precondition that the previous task was executed (see Fig. 5.9). This rule does not affect the number of gateways and sequence flows.

(a) LHS   (b) RHS

Figure 5.9: SequenceRuleExtended

Layer 1

The second layer comprises only one rule, which also applies to sequences of tasks. This rule is defined within its own layer, as it must not be applied before the rules *SequenceRuleBase* and *SequenceRuleExtended*. Theoretically, the second and third layer can be integrated into one layer; however, the scope of the first and second layer comprises rules for sequences whereas the focus of the third layer is on gateways.

SequenceRuleFinish: The third rule defined for sequences of tasks is called *SequenceRuleFinish* and shown in Fig. 5.10. This rule classifies the first task of a sequence in the main flow as obligatory without any precondition. All further tasks in the sequence were already transformed in the first layer. The NAC specifies that the task must not be addressed by a splitting node and is, thus, neither alternative nor permissible. The transformation does not reduce the number of gateways and sequence flows as highlighted by the *MeasuredValues* element.

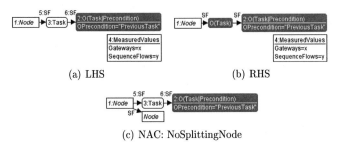

(a) LHS   (b) RHS

(c) NAC: NoSplittingNode

Figure 5.10: SequenceRuleFinish

In fact, three different cases were distinguished in section 4.2.2 and only the second case is forbidden by the NAC leaving two other cases. However, since DeonticBpmnGTS is restricted to sequences in the main flow, the first task is always obligatory and a differentiation of the remaining cases not necessary. The preconditions of all further tasks are later removed by the two pragmatic rules.

Considering an example with five sequentially arranged tasks in the main flow, *SequenceRuleBase* is applied first to transform a task (2-5). Afterwards, either *SequenceRuleBase*, *SequenceRuleExtended*, or both rules are applied to classify the other three tasks. In a last step, the first task is transformed by *SequenceRuleFinish*.

Layer 2

The third layer provides 11 rules for transforming parallel, exclusive and inclusive gateways with user choice. The rules for exclusive and inclusive gateways are very similar and only slightly different from those of parallel gateways. Since DeonticBpmnGTS is limited to splitting gateways with at most one task per path also prohibiting most types of nested gateways, preconditions referencing the previous task are not necessary.

ParallelWithPhiDualRule: The rule *ParallelWithPhiDualRule* replaces every occurrence of a parallel gateway addressing one task and one *Phi*-Path with an obligatory task as shown in Fig. 5.11. The NAC forbids that the splitting gateway references further nodes and thereby avoids dangling edges. If further nodes exist, then the rule *ParallelRule* may be used. The element *MeasuredValues* shows that the transformation leads to a reduction of two gateways and three sequence flows.

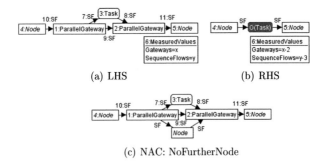

(a) LHS   (b) RHS

(c) NAC: NoFurtherNode

Figure 5.11: ParallelWithPhiDualRule

Note that DeonticBpmnGTS is currently limited to structured diagrams and one task per path following a splitting gateways. Thus, the abstract *Node* addressed by the NAC may only be replaced by a single *Bpmn-* or *DeonticTask*. However, one of the mentioned extensions is the introduction of a *Sub-Process*, which can comprise a complex sub-graph. An abstract *Node* can then be replaced by a *Sub-Process* without an adaptation of rules or ACs.

ParallelRule: The rule *ParallelRule* can be applied several times to classify an arbitrary number of tasks being referenced by a parallel gateway as obligatory as shown in Fig. 5.12.

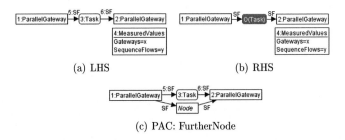

(a) LHS   (b) RHS

(c) PAC: FurtherNode

Figure 5.12: ParallelRule

The PAC specifies that at least one further node is referenced. This application condition assures that the first gateway addresses not only one further *Phi*-Path (*ParallelWithPhiDualRule* should be used) and that it is not a merging gateway with a subsequently task followed by a splitting gateway. According to the *MeasuredValues* element, this rule does not reduce the number of gateways and sequence flows.

ParallelRuleFinish: After all tasks following a parallel split are classified as obligatory, the rule *ParallelRuleFinish* removes a possible *Phi*-Path. This rule is applied if at least two tasks are obligatory and no further BPMN task exists as defined by the NAC. This rule leads to a reduction of one sequence flow.

A *Phi*-Path after a parallel split has no additional meaning and is executed in parallel with all other paths. Thus, this construct is dispensable and it would be best practice to not use it at all. However, since this construct is not forbidden by the BPMN specification, a transformation rule is necessary.

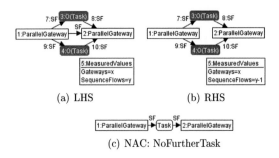

(a) LHS   (b) RHS

(c) NAC: NoFurtherTask

Figure 5.13: ParallelRuleFinish

ExclusiveWithPhiDualRule: The rule *ExclusiveWithPhiDualRule* takes
an exclusive gateway with a task and a *Phi*-Path and transforms it to a
permissible task (see Fig. 5.14). The NAC forbids further alternative nodes
and thereby avoids dangling edges. The rule *ExclusiveWithPhiRule* may be
used in case of further tasks. The transformation leads to a reduction of two
gateways and three sequence flows.

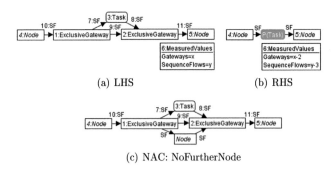

(a) LHS   (b) RHS

(c) NAC: NoFurtherNode

Figure 5.14: ExclusiveWithPhiDualRule

ExclusiveWithPhiRule: The next rule is called *ExclusiveWithPhiRule*
and transforms a task of an exclusive gateway with a *Phi*-Path into a permissible task (see Fig. 5.15). The rule can be applied several times to classify
an arbitrary number of tasks. The PAC specifies that a further node exists,
since otherwise the rule *ExclusiveWithPhiDualRule* should be applied. This
transformation rule does not reduce the number of gateways and sequence
flows.

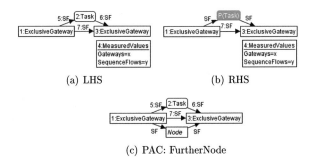

(a) LHS   (b) RHS

(c) PAC: FurtherNode

Figure 5.15: ExclusiveWithPhiRule

The *Phi*-Path must remain until the last BPMN task is transformed. In a former version of DeonticBpmnGTS, two rules were defined to classify all permissible tasks. The first rule classified two tasks as permissible and removed the *Phi*-Path. A second rule then searched for exclusive gateways with already two permissible tasks and classified every further task as permissible. The problem with this specification was that exclusives gateways might also reference tasks with different deontic classifications if nested gateways are used as shown in Fig. 5.16. In this case, the two nested gateways are replaced by permissible tasks, however, the other tasks must be classified as alternatives. Although nested gateways are currently out of the scope of DeonticBpmnGTS, the transformation of nested gateways with only one path beneath the *Phi*-Path is already supported. Thus, the deontic classification of every permissible task must be based on a *Phi*-Path.

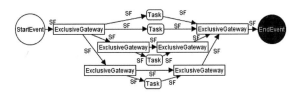

Figure 5.16: Example with Nested Exclusive Gateways

ExclusiveWithPhiRuleFinish: The rule *ExclusiveWithPhiRuleFinish* is applied after the rule *ExclusiveWithPhiRule* and removes the *Phi*-Path as shown in Fig. 5.17. The left-hand side of the rule requires two permissible tasks as well as a *Phi*-Path and the NAC forbids further not transformed tasks. The transformation leads to a reduction of one sequence flow.

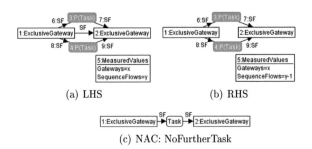

(a) LHS   (b) RHS

(c) NAC: NoFurtherTask

Figure 5.17: ExclusiveWithPhiRuleFinish

ExclusiveWithoutPhiRule: The rule *ExclusiveWithoutPhiRule* classifies the task of an exclusive gateway without a *Phi*-Path as an alternative task (see Fig. 5.18). This rule can be applied several times to transform an arbitrary number of tasks.

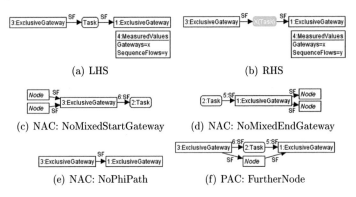

(a) LHS   (b) RHS

(c) NAC: NoMixedStartGateway   (d) NAC: NoMixedEndGateway

(e) NAC: NoPhiPath   (f) PAC: FurtherNode

Figure 5.18: ExclusiveWithoutPhiRule

Three NACs define that neither the first nor the second gateway has multiple incoming and outgoing sequence flows (mixed gateway) and that no *Phi*-Path exists. The PAC specifies that at least one further node is addressed, which ensures that the first gateway is a splitting gateway. The transformation does not reduce the number of gateways and sequence flows.

InclusiveWithPhiDualRule: The first rule used for inclusive gateways is called *InclusiveWithPhiDualRule* and transforms an inclusive gateway with one task and a *Phi*-Path into a permissible task as shown in Fig. 5.19.

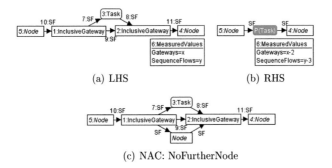

(a) LHS   (b) RHS

(c) NAC: NoFurtherNode

Figure 5.19: InclusiveWithPhiDualRule

The NAC forbids further nodes and thereby avoids dangling edges. The transformation leads to a reduction of two gateways and three sequence flows.

InclusiveWithPhiRule: The rule *InclusiveWithPhiRule* converts a task of an inclusive gateway with a *Phi*-Path into a permissible task (see Fig. 5.20). The rule can be applied several times to classify an arbitrary number of tasks.

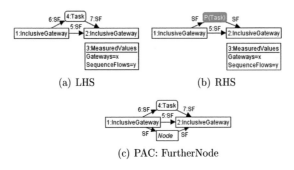

(a) LHS   (b) RHS

(c) PAC: FurtherNode

Figure 5.20: InclusiveWithPhiRule

The PAC specifies that a further node exists, since otherwise the rule *InclusiveWithPhiDualRule* should be used to remove the gateways. This rule does not reduce the number of gateways and sequence flows.

InclusiveWithPhiRuleFinish: The rule *InclusiveWithPhiRuleFinish* is applied after the rule *InclusiveWithPhiRule* and removes a *Phi*-Path as shown in Fig. 5.21.

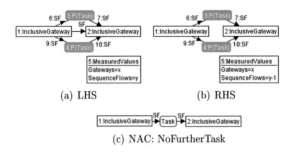

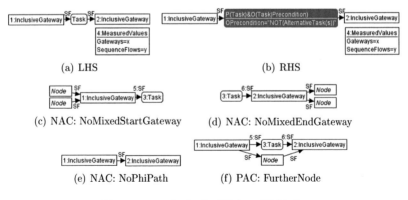

Figure 5.21: InclusiveWithPhiRuleFinish

The rule requires at least two permissible tasks and a *Phi*-Path addressed by an inclusive gateway. The NAC forbids further not transformed BPMN tasks. The transformation leads to a reduction of one sequence flow.

InclusiveWithoutPhiRule: The rule *InclusiveWithoutPhiRule* classifies a task of an inclusive gateway without a *Phi*-Path as a permissible task that is obligatory under the precondition that no other task will be executed (see Fig. 5.22). This rule can be applied several times to transform an arbitrary number of tasks.

Figure 5.22: InclusiveWithoutPhiRule

Three NACs define that neither the first nor the second gateway has multiple incoming and outgoing sequence flows (mixed gateway) and that no *Phi*-Path exists. The PAC specifies that at least one further node is addressed, which ensures that the first gateway is a splitting gateway. The transformation does not reduce the number of gateways and sequence flows.

The obligatory part of the classification includes a precondition, which is defined as an attribute. This precondition references all alternative tasks. In fact, this precondition should address all tasks individually, e.g.: P(A) ∧ O(A|¬B ∧ ¬C). However, since the tasks in DeonticBpmnGTS are currently not named, the precondition "NOT(AlternativeTask(s))" is used instead.

Layer 3

The fourth layer comprises two pragmatic rules, which remove preconditions of obligatory tasks in the main flow if the order is also expressed through sequence flows. These rules were inserted in DeonticBpmnGTS, since the survey in section 4.3.4 identified problems with the understanding of preconditions. The pragmatic rules must not be applied to paths following a splitting gateway. If, for example, the first task of a sequence following an exclusive gateway with a *Phi*-Path is classified as permissible and all further tasks are obligatory under the precondition that the previous task was executed (e.g., *P(A)*, *O(B|A)*, and *O(C|B)*), then not executing the first task allows to not execute the further tasks thereby representing the *Phi*-Path. DeonticBpmnGTS is currently limited to one task per path following a gateway thereby prohibiting sequences outside the main flow.

SequenceBpmnRulePragmatic: The first pragmatic rule is called *SequenceBpmnRulePragmatic* and transforms an obligatory task with precondition "PreviousTask" into an obligatory task without precondition as shown in Fig. 5.23. This transformation is only executed if the obligatory task is addressed by exactly one incoming sequence flow from a BPMN task and is, thus, always executed after this task. The transformation from an obligatory task with precondition to an obligatory task without precondition is a generalization, since a subclass is transformed into its superclass. The application of the rule does not reduce the number of gateways and sequence flows.

The restriction to exactly one incoming sequence flow cannot be ensured by the type graph due to the inheritance relationships. However, the multiplicities of the dependency relationships forbid that only one NAC is defined with a further *Node* element referencing the obligatory task with precondition. Instead three NACs are necessary to forbid further incoming sequence flows from *BpmnTasks*, *DeonticTasks*, or *Gateways*.

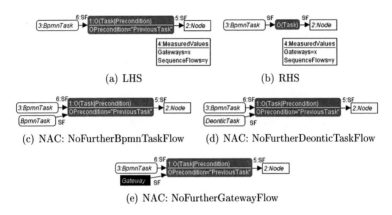

Figure 5.23: SequenceBpmnRulePragmatic

SequenceDeonticRulePragmatic: The second pragmatic rule is called
SequenceDeonticRulePragmatic and also transforms an obligatory task with
precondition "PreviousTask" into an obligatory task without precondition
(see Fig. 5.24).   The difference compared to the rule *SequenceBpmnRule-
Pragmatic* is that this rule requires a preceding deontic task. The application
of the rule does not reduce the number of gateways and sequence flows.

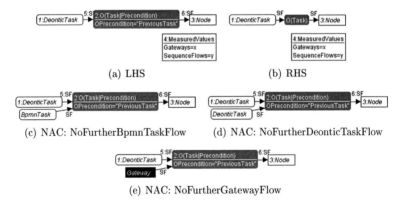

Figure 5.24: SequenceDeonticRulePragmatic

Alternatively to the two pragmatic rules, one rule could have been defined
for both cases, if *BpmnTask* and *DeonticTask* are derived from a common
superclass where neither *Gateway* nor *Event* is derived from.

Consistency Constraints: In sum, five NACs were specified in Deontic-BpmnGTS to forbid gateways with incoming and outgoing sequence flows (mixed gateways). In addition, further NACs for other rules like *Exclusive-WithPhiDualRule* could avoid a possible violation of the dangling condition and would have been necessary in case of the single-pushout approach (SPO). Instead of defining a large number of similar NACs, graph constraints can be specified. Graph constraints allow to formulate properties for graphs independent of a particular rule as, for example, the existence or non-existence of a certain subgraph.

A graph constraint is a boolean formula over atomic graph constraints. An atomic graph constraint is defined to be a morphism $c : P \to C$, where P is called the premise and C the conclusion. An atomic graph constraint is satisfied by a graph G if for all morphisms $p : P \to G$ there is a morphism $q : C \to G$ such that $q \circ c = p$. In addition, atomic graph constraints may specify several conclusions, but it is sufficient if at least one conclusion is satisfied (cf. for this paragraph [31, p. 64f, 312ff]). In summary, if a graph G contains the premise P of an atomic graph constraint, then it must also contain one of the conclusions C_i.

A graph constraint is then defined like a boolean formula using the atomic graph constraints as variables [3, p. 50]. An atomic constraint that defines mixed gateways and a further graph constraint that forbids those mixed gateways are shown in Fig. 5.25.

(a) Atomic Constraint: MixedGateway   (b) Graph Constraint: !MixedGateway

Figure 5.25: Consistency Constraints

However, consistency constraints are currently not used in DeonticBpmnGTS due to the following reasons:

- The atomic constraint specifies a mixed gateway and the graph constraint forbids it. Thus, for every graph only one of the consistency checks provided by AGG, either the atomic check or the constraint check, is satisfied, e.g., a valid graph does not fulfill the atomic constraint. In this case, only the graph constraint should be checked, however, the reported violation of the atomic constraint might be confusing for the user.

- The second and more problematic reason is that consistency constraints do not reduce the number of critical pairs in DeonticBpmnGTS. Although it can be defined that consistency checks should be included in the critical pair analysis, a note within the tool AGG (see [4]) remarks that it is not always possible to check all graph consistency constraints. In case of DeonticBpmnGTS, invalid critical pairs were reported, which could be avoided by using NACs.

5.3.3   Extension: Conditional Gateways

This section introduces a possible extension of DeonticBpmnGTS to address the extended conditional gateways described in section 4.2.3. First of all, a new edge label called *ConditionalSF* with two attributes for *Condition* and *Order* is defined. In addition, two conditional gateways with boolean attributes for *Distinct* (only in case of exclusive gateway) and *Complete* are specified and derived from the corresponding gateways without conditions. Moreover, three node types are defined for forbidden deontic tasks: *F(Task)*, *F(Task|Precondition)* and *O(Task|Precondition)&F(Task|Precondition)*. The type graph of the extended graph transformation is shown in Fig. 5.26.

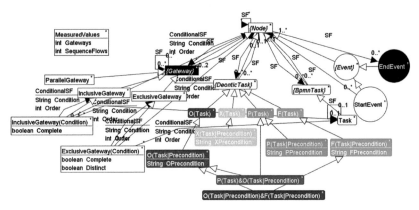

Figure 5.26: Type Graph with Conditions

The following rules are then defined to transform exclusive gateways with complete and distinct decisions. Further transformation rules for inclusive gateways with complete decisions were also defined, but are not presented in the current work, since the rules are very similar to those of exclusive gateways.

Layer 4

The fifth layer provides three rules to transform the tasks of exclusive gateways with complete and distinct conditions, either with or without *Phi-Paths*. The corresponding rules for inclusive gateways with complete conditions are also specified within this layer. The replacement of the exclusive (or inclusive) gateway by a parallel gateway is defined within the sixth layer.

ExclusiveWithPhiCompleteDistinctDualRule: The first rule is called *ExclusiveWithPhiCompleteDistinctDualRule* and converts an exclusive gateway with complete and distinct conditions addressing a task and a *Phi*-Path into a deontic task (see Fig. 5.27). The deontic task is classified as obligatory if condition *c1* is satisfied and forbidden otherwise.

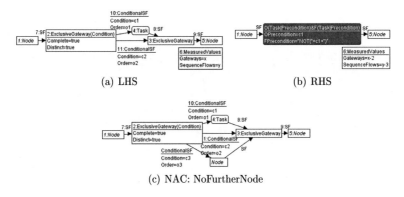

Figure 5.27: ExclusiveWithPhiCompleteDistinctDualRule

The NAC forbids further addressed nodes. This transformation leads to a reduction of two gateways and three sequence flows as highlighted by the *MeasuredValues* element.

ExclusiveCompleteDistinctRule: The second rule is called *Exclusive-CompleteDistinctRule* and transforms a task referenced by an exclusive gateway with complete and distinct conditions into a deontic task (see Fig. 5.28). The deontic task is classified as obligatory if condition *c* is true and forbidden otherwise. This rule can be applied several times in order to transform an arbitrary number of tasks.

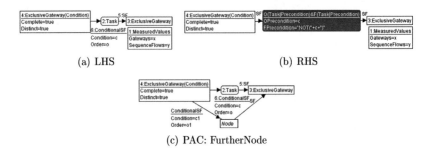

(a) LHS   (b) RHS

(c) PAC: FurtherNode

Figure 5.28: ExclusiveCompleteDistinctRule

The PAC specifies that at least one further node is referenced by the exclusive gateway. This ensures that the first gateway is a splitting gateway and that not only one alternative *Phi*-Path exists. In case of only one further *Phi*-Path the rule *ExclusiveWithPhiCompleteDistinctDualRule* should be applied. This transformation does not reduce the number of gateways and sequence flows as highlighted by the *MeasuredValues* element.

Note that the conditional sequence flow on the left-hand side (LHS) is replaced by an unconditional sequence flow on the right-hand side (RHS). The condition is now defined within the deontic task and the order can be omitted, because the exclusive gateway will be replaced by a parallel gateway within the next layer and all outgoing paths will be executed in parallel.

ExclusiveWithPhiCompleteDistinctRuleFinish: The last rule of this layer is called *ExclusiveWithPhiCompleteDistinctRuleFinish* and removes a *Phi*-Path (see Fig. 5.29). This rule is applied after the rule *ExclusiveCompleteDistinctRule* as ensured by the NAC, which defines that no further BPMN task might exist. The transformation leads to a reduction of one sequence flow.

The deletion of the *Phi*-Path is possible, since the condition is complete and distinct and it is, therefore, sufficient to define when the other tasks are obligatory or forbidden. The parallel gateway will send a token on each outgoing path and if no other condition is satisfied, none of the tasks will be executed.

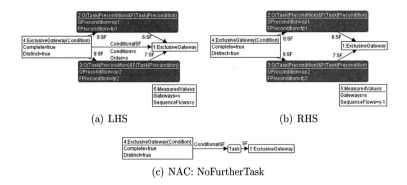

(a) LHS   (b) RHS

(c) NAC: NoFurtherTask

Figure 5.29: ExclusiveWithPhiCompleteDistinctRuleFinish

Layer 5

The sixth layer describes the replacement of the exclusive (or inclusive) gateway with a parallel gateway within three rules. This replacement is necessary for all conditional gateways.

The entire replacement does not change the number of gateways and sequence flows. The first rule *ExclusiveReplaceGatewayRuleBase* increases the number of both elements, however, the rule is only applied once per conditional gateway and the corresponding rule *ExclusiveReplaceGatewayRuleFinish* will in any case be executed afterwards and decreases the number of gateways and sequence flows by the same amount.

ExclusiveReplaceGatewayRuleBase: In a first step, the rule *ExclusiveReplaceGatewayRuleBase* creates two parallel gateways and reassigns two deontic tasks to these parallel gateways (see Fig. 5.30). Three NACs ensure that the first gateway is only a splitting gateway, that the second gateway is only a merging gateway and that no parallel gateway is already addressed by the node arranged in front of the exclusive gateway. The transformation increases the number of gateways and sequence flows by two in each case, which will later be reversed by the rule *ExclusiveReplaceGatewayRuleFinish*.

ExclusiveReplaceGatewayRuleExtended: Afterwards, the rule *ExclusiveReplaceGatewayRuleExtended* reassigns further deontic tasks from the exclusive to the parallel gateway (see Fig. 5.31). This rule can be applied several times to reassign an arbitrary number of deontic tasks.

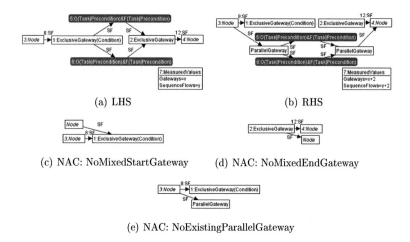

(a) LHS   (b) RHS

(c) NAC: NoMixedStartGateway   (d) NAC: NoMixedEndGateway

(e) NAC: NoExistingParallelGateway

Figure 5.30: ExclusiveReplaceGatewayRuleBase

Two NACs ensure that the first is a splitting gateway and the second a merging gateway. This rule does not reduce the number of gateways and sequence flows.

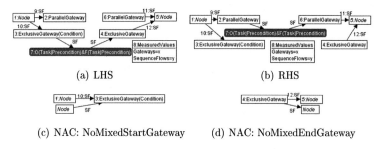

(a) LHS   (b) RHS

(c) NAC: NoMixedStartGateway   (d) NAC: NoMixedEndGateway

Figure 5.31: ExclusiveReplaceGatewayRuleExtended

ExclusiveReplaceGatewayRuleFinish: Finally, the rule *ExclusiveReplaceGatewayRuleFinish* deletes the exclusive gateways as shown in Fig. 5.32. The NAC ensures that no further node is referenced by the exclusive gateways and thereby avoids a violation of the dangling condition. This rule is the complement to the rule *ExclusiveReplaceGatewayRuleBase* and decreases the number of gateways and sequence flows by two in each case as highlighted by the *MeasuredValues* element.

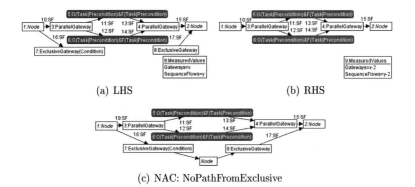

(a) LHS   (b) RHS

(c) NAC: NoPathFromExclusive

Figure 5.32: ExclusiveReplaceGatewayRuleFinish

Other gateways with overlapping or incomplete conditions have not been studied in detail but can be transformed analogical. The only challenge might be that the deontic tasks require a reference to single alternative tasks within the preconditions.

A major advantage of transforming conditional gateways is that exclusive/inclusive gateways can be replaced by parallel gateways and the order of the SFs can be omitted thereby simplifying the complexity of the diagram. The transformation of conditional gateways has only been outlined shortly and neither confluence nor termination will be proven.

5.3.4   An Example

After defining the transformation rules of DeonticBpmnGTS, a typed graph can be created for a concrete BPMN model and is then transformed to Deontic BPMN. This is demonstrated by an example whose BPMN model is shown in Fig. 5.33 in the image view. According to the *MeasuredValues* element, the BPMN model consists of eight gateways and twenty-nine sequence flows.

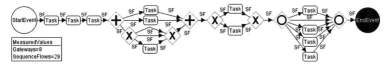

Figure 5.33: Example: BPMN Model

The graph transformation in AGG can be executed non-deterministically (NT), by rule layers (LT), rule priorities (PT) or rule sequences (ST). Every transformation in DeonticBpmnGTS is executed based on the rule layers.

After starting the transformation, every rule of the first layer may be executed. In the given example, *SeveralPhiReductionRule*, *SequenceRuleBase* and optionally *SequenceRuleExtended* are applied. *SequenceRuleExtended* is optional, since either *SequenceRuleBase* is executed once followed by *SequenceRuleExtended* or *SequenceRuleBase* is applied twice. The order of the rule application within a layer is arbitrary but restricted by the matching of the left-hand side of a rule and its application conditions.

After all rules of the first layer have been executed for as long as possible, the second layer is considered. *SequenceRuleFinish* is the only rule defined within this layer and applied once to transform the first task of the sequence.

Afterwards the third layer is taken into account to transform all further BPMN tasks. For the given example, the following rules are applied: *ParallelRule* (2x), *ExclusiveWithPhiDualRule* (1x), *ExclusiveWithoutPhiRule* (2x), *InclusiveWithPhiRule* (4x) and *InclusiveWithPhiRuleFinish* (1x).

Finally, the rule *SequenceDeonticRulePragmatic* of the fourth layer is applied twice to remove the preconditions within the sequence of tasks.

The resulting Deontic BPMN model is shown in Fig. 5.34. This model consists of six gateways and twenty-four sequence flows. Thus, the transformation leads to a reduction of two gateways and five sequence flows. In addition, the obligatory, alternative and permissible tasks can be distinguished on first sight based on their prefix and color.

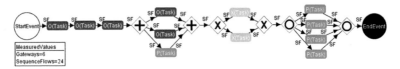

Figure 5.34: Example: Deontic BPMN Model

5.4 Strict AC-Confluence

This section starts with the foundations and main definitions of strict AC-confluence. Afterwards the critical pair analysis of DeonticBpmnGTS is presented followed by the proof that DeonticBpmnGTS is locally confluent.

5.4.1 Foundations of Strict AC-Confluence

The requirements for proving local confluence changed within the last few years. In 2006, a GTS was defined to be locally confluent if all its critical pairs are *strictly confluent* [31, p. 61].

This definition requires in a first step the identification of all critical pairs. A critical pair is defined as a pair of direct graph transformations that are parallel dependent and minimal. Two direct graph transformations are parallel dependent if they are not parallel independent as defined in section 5.1. In addition, a pair of graph transformations is minimal if each item in K has a preimage in the left-hand side L of one of the two graph transformations (cf. for this paragraph [31, p. 47f, 60]).

If no critical pairs are identified, then the GTS is already locally confluent. Otherwise strict confluence must be proven for each critical pair. A critical pair $P_1 \Leftarrow K \Rightarrow P_2$ is confluent if a graph K' together with graph transformations $P_1 \overset{*}{\Rightarrow} K'$ and $P_2 \overset{*}{\Rightarrow} K'$ exists. Furthermore, the confluence is called strict if the largest common subgraph N of K, P_1 and P_2 is preserved by $P_1 \overset{*}{\Rightarrow} K'$ and $P_2 \overset{*}{\Rightarrow} K'$ (cf. for this paragraph [31, p. 60f]).

In 2008, the definition of local confluence was extended to capture also NACs of rules and required to show *strict NAC-confluence*. A critical pair is NAC-confluent if it is confluent via some transformations $t_1 : K \Rightarrow P_1 \overset{*}{\Rightarrow} K'$ and $t_2 : K \Rightarrow P_2 \overset{*}{\Rightarrow} K'$ and it is NAC-confluent for t_1 and t_2. This means that for every morphism $k_0 : K \to G$, which is NAC-consistent with respect to $K \Rightarrow P_1$ and $K \Rightarrow P_2$, it follows that k_0 is also NAC-consistent with respect to t_1 and t_2 (cf. for this paragraph [67]).

This means that if every NAC is satisfied by the two given graph transformations, then it must not be possible to violate a NAC in the further graph transformations $P_1 \overset{*}{\Rightarrow} K'$ and $P_2 \overset{*}{\Rightarrow} K'$. Otherwise, a graph transformation to K' might exist, but cannot be applied due to a NAC. Critical pairs for rules with NACs are already implemented in AGG [31, p. 314].

In 2010, the definition was further extended to capture all ACs and now requires to prove *strict AC-confluence* in order to show local confluence [66]. The definition of strict AC-confluence is as follows.

Definition 8. *Strict AC-Confluence [66, p. 20]:*

"*A critical pair* $P_1 \overset{p_1,o_1}{\Leftarrow} K \overset{p_2,o_2}{\Rightarrow} P_2$ *for* $< p_1, p_2 >$ *with induced* ac_K *and* ac_K^* *on* K *is called* strictly AC-confluent, *if*

1. *The pair is plain strictly confluent, i.e. strictly confluent [...] with AC-disregarding transformations t_1 and t_2.*

2. *The extended AC-disregarding transformations $\bar{t}_i = K \overset{p_i,o_i}{\Rightarrow} P_i \overset{*,t_i}{\Rightarrow} K'$ ($i = 1, 2$) with derived ACs $ac(\bar{t}_i)$ on K are AC-compatible, i.e. $ac_K \wedge ac_K^* \Rightarrow ac(\bar{t}_1) \wedge ac(\bar{t}_2)$."*

Strict AC-confluence is, thus, an extension of strict NAC-confluence and requires that all ACs, both NACs and PACs, are satisfied during further graph transformations.

5.4.2   Critical Pair Analysis

This section presents an overview of the critical pair analysis (CPA). The critical pairs are determined by the tool AGG, which identifies all conflicting rule applications by computing the minimal critical graphs to which rules can be applied in a conflicting way [31, p. 314]. The CPA distinguishes two types of critical pairs [3, p. 54]:

- *Conflicts* in case of parallel dependent rule applications and

- *Dependencies* in case of sequential dependent rule applications.

Before starting the analysis, the element *MeasuredValues* is removed from the type graph and all transformation rules. This element is used to store meta-information, but does not affect the transformation to Deontic BPMN. However, the element *MeasuredValues* would increase the number of critical pairs, since the attributes for counting the number of gateways and sequence flows may change.

Afterwards the CPA is executed by AGG and the CPA-Graph is shown in Fig. 5.35. This graph provides an overview of all conflicts (red edges) and dependencies (blue edges) identified between the rules of a given graph transformation system [3, p. 57]. Directed edges represent asymmetric and undirected edges symmetric conflicts/dependencies [3, p. 57]. In the CPA-Graph of DeonticBpmnGTS the only undirected edge describes conflicts between the rules *SequenceRuleBase* and *SequenceRuleExtended*.

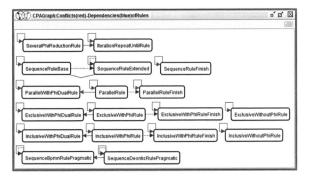

Figure 5.35: CPA-Graph of DeonticBpmnGTS calculated by AGG

Considering the CPA for parallel dependent rule applications, 45 conflicts are computed and shown in Tab. 5.1. The layers are taken into account and critical pairs are only calculated for rules of the same layer. If the rules are defined on different layers, then the cell in the table is left empty. Otherwise the number of critical pairs is displayed.

As can be seen in Tab. 5.1, the number and alignment of the conflicts identified for the three different gateways in the third layer are similar. Especially the conflicts for exclusive and inclusive gateways are almost the same and only slightly different from that of parallel gateways, which do not distinguish transformation rules with and without *Phi*-Paths.

Three kinds of conflicts are distinguished by AGG (cf. [3, p. 52f]):

1. Delete-Use Conflict: One rule application deletes an element, which is part of the match of the other rule.

2. Produce-Forbid Conflict: One rule produces an element such that a graph structure occurs that is prohibited by a NAC of the other rule.

3. Change-Use Attribute Conflict: One rule changes attributes that are in the match of the other rule.

In DeonticBpmnGTS all valid conflicts are classified as delete-use conflicts.

However, the critical pair analysis provided by the tool AGG computed several very similar critical pairs as, for example, the two critical pairs of

Table 5.1: CPA for Parallel Dependent Rule Applications

	1	2	3	4	5	6	7	8	9	10	11	12	13	14	15	16	17	18
1	2	1	0	0														
2	0	1	0	0														
3	0	0	2	1														
4	0	0	1	1														
5					1													
6						1	0	0	0	0	0	0	0	0	0	0		
7						1	1	0	0	0	0	0	0	0	0	0		
8						0	0	7	0	0	0	0	0	0	0	0		
9						0	0	0	1	0	0	0	0	0	0	0		
10						0	0	0	1	1	0	0	0	0	0	0		
11						0	0	0	0	0	7	0	0	0	0	0		
12						0	0	0	0	0	0	1	0	0	0	0		
13						0	0	0	0	0	0	0	1	0	0	0		
14						0	0	0	0	0	0	0	1	1	0	0		
15						0	0	0	0	0	0	0	0	0	7	0		
16						0	0	0	0	0	0	0	0	0	0	1		
17																	1	0
18																	1	1

Rule Numbers:

[1] SeveralPhiReductionRule
[2] IterationRepeatUntilRule
[3] SequenceRuleBase
[4] SequenceRuleExtended
[5] SequenceRuleFinish
[6] ParallelWithPhiDualRule
[7] ParallelRule
[8] ParallelRuleFinish
[9] ExclusiveWithPhiDualRule

[10] ExclusiveWithPhiRule
[11] ExclusiveWithPhiRuleFinish
[12] ExclusiveWithoutPhiRule
[13] InclusiveWithPhiDualRule
[14] InclusiveWithPhiRule
[15] InclusiveWithPhiRuleFinish
[16] InclusiveWithoutPhiRule
[17] SequenceBpmnRulePragmatic
[18] SequenceDeonticRulePragmatic

SeveralPhiReductionRule and further pairs identified for the rules *Parallel-*, *ExclusiveWithPhi-*, and *InclusiveWithPhiRuleFinish*. Furthermore, the three critical pairs identified for the rule combinations 7/6, 10/9, and 14/13 are invalid, since the corresponding first rule defines a PAC *FurtherNode*, which is not considered by the AGG tool. The CPA of AGG currently only considers the NACs [31, p. 314]. The invalid critical pairs can be disregarded for the strict AC-confluence proof.

The critical pairs for parallel dependent rule applications (conflicts) together with the corresponding proof of strict AC-confluence are described in more detail in section 5.4.3.

The sequential dependent rule applications of DeonticBpmnGTS are shown in Tab. 5.2. The thirteen dependencies denote that one rule must be executed before the other, e.g. *SequenceRuleBase* must at least once be executed before *SequenceRuleExtended*. These critical pairs are, however, not relevant for the local confluence proof of DeonticBpmnGTS.

Table 5.2: CPA for Sequential Dependent Rule Applications

	1	2	3	4	5	6	7	8	9	10	11	12	13	14	15	16	17	18
1	0	0	0	0														
2	0	0	0	0														
3	0	0	0	1														
4	0	0	0	1														
5					0													
6						0	0	0	0	0	0	0	0	0	0	0		
7						0	0	3	0	0	0	0	0	0	0	0		
8						0	0	0	0	0	0	0	0	0	0	0		
9						0	0	0	0	0	0	0	0	0	0	0		
10						0	0	0	0	0	3	0	0	0	0	0		
11						0	0	0	0	0	0	0	0	0	0	0		
12						0	0	0	0	0	0	0	0	0	0	0		
13						0	0	0	0	0	0	0	0	0	0	0		
14						0	0	0	0	0	0	0	0	0	3	0		
15						0	0	0	0	0	0	0	0	0	0	0		
16						0	0	0	0	0	0	0	0	0	0	0		
17																	1	0
18																	0	1

Rule Numbers:

1 SeveralPhiReductionRule
2 IterationRepeatUntilRule
3 SequenceRuleBase
4 SequenceRuleExtended
5 SequenceRuleFinish
6 ParallelWithPhiDualRule
7 ParallelRule
8 ParallelRuleFinish
9 ExclusiveWithPhiDualRule

10 ExclusiveWithPhiRule
11 ExclusiveWithPhiRuleFinish
12 ExclusiveWithoutPhiRule
13 InclusiveWithPhiDualRule
14 InclusiveWithPhiRule
15 InclusiveWithPhiRuleFinish
16 InclusiveWithoutPhiRule
17 SequenceBpmnRulePragmatic
18 SequenceDeonticRulePragmatic

5.4.3 Proof: Local Confluence

In this section the critical pairs (CPs) are presented in detail and strict AC-confluence is proven for each critical pair. Thus, DeonticBpmnGTS is locally confluent.

Remark: For the confluence proofs, the naming of the graphs corresponds to Fig. 5.1 where graph G denotes the original graph, graphs H_1 and H_2 show the resulting graphs after an application of the two parallel dependent rules, and graph X presents the final graph that is achieved through extended transformations to prove confluence.

SeveralPhiReductionRule/SeveralPhiReductionRule:

Two very similar critical pairs are identified for the rule *SeveralPhiReductionRule* and shown in Fig. 5.36. The CPs comprise two gateways with three *Phi*-Paths in between. The cause of the CPs is that the first rule considers the two *Phi*-Paths *3:SF* and *4:SF* and removes *4:SF*, whereas the second rule considers *4:SF* and *5:SF* and either removes *4:SF* (CP2) or *5:SF* (CP1). The two rules are parallel dependent, since the deletion of *4:SF* by the first rule prevents the application of the second rule.

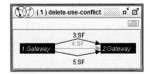 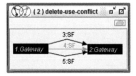

Figure 5.36: SeveralPhiReductionRule/SeveralPhiReductionRule

However, the dependency is only based on the mapping names of the sequence flows and the parallel application of both rules results in isomorphic graphs as shown in Fig. 5.37.

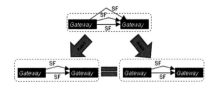

Figure 5.37: Strict AC-Confluence of CPs shown in Fig. 5.36

Since the resulting graphs (H_1, H_2) are isomorphic, no further transformation is necessary to prove confluence and no application conditions may be violated. Furthermore, every parallel application of rules resulting in isomorphic graphs is also strict, since the largest subgraph N (marked by a dashed line in Fig. 5.37) is equal to the resulting graphs $(N = H_1 = H_2 = X)$.

Thus, the CPs are strictly AC-confluent. Within a further step, it would be possible to apply the rule once again with new mappings leading to two gateways with only one *Phi*-Path.

SeveralPhiReductionRule/IterationRepeatUntilRule:

The two rules *SeveralPhiReductionRule* and *IterationRepeatUntilRule* are parallel dependent as shown by the critical pair in Fig. 5.38. The CP comprises a *Repeat-Until* loop with two backward-going sequence flows. The two rules are parallel dependent, since the first rule considers the flows *3:SF* and *4:SF* and removes *4:SF*, whereas the second rule also considers *4:SF* and transforms the task.

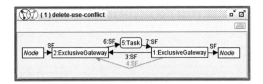

Figure 5.38: SeveralPhiReductionRule/IterationRepeatUntilRule

The main problem are again the mapping names defined by AGG, since the second rule could also use *3:SF*. Then the respective other rule can be applied afterwards to prove confluence as shown in Fig. 5.39.

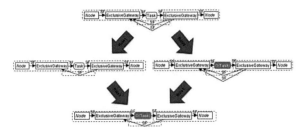

Figure 5.39: Strict AC-Confluence of CP shown in Fig. 5.38

Considering AC-confluence, the rule *SeveralPhiReductionRule* does not define any application conditions. However, the rule *IterationRepeatUntilRule* specifies three ACs, namely the NACs *NoPhiPath* and *NoMixedStartGateway* as well as the PAC *IncomingOutgoingSF*. These ACs must be fulfilled by graph *G* in order to execute *IterationRepeatUntilRule* within the first transformation step leading to graph H_2. Since the first application of *SeveralPhiReductionRule* leading to graph H_1 does not create a *Phi*-Path or a splitting start gateway nor does it affect the incoming and outgoing sequence flows, it can be concluded that H_1 fulfills all three ACs and the extended transformation is AC-compatible. Furthermore, the largest subgraph N of G, H_1, and H_2 comprises two nodes, two gateways, and one sequence flow and is also part of X as highlighted by the dashed line in Fig. 5.39. Therefore, this critical pair is strictly AC-confluent.

IterationRepeatUntilRule/IterationRepeatUntilRule:

A further critical pair is identified for the rule *IterationRepeatUntilRule* as shown in Fig. 5.40. The CP shows a *Repeat-Until* loop with two backwards going sequence flows. The two rules are parallel dependent, since the first rule considers *4:SF* and transforms the task, whereas the second rule considers *7:SF* and also transforms the task.

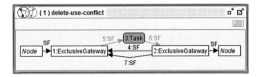

Figure 5.40: IterationRepeatUntilRule/IterationRepeatUntilRule

After the application of the two rules, the graphs H_1 and H_2 are isomorphic and, thus, strictly AC-confluent as shown in Fig. 5.41. Within a further step, *SeveralPhiReductionRule* may be applied to reduce the number of *Phi*-Paths.

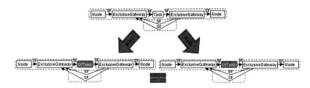

Figure 5.41: Strict AC-Confluence of CP shown in Fig. 5.40

SequenceRuleBase/SequenceRuleBase:

If applied in parallel, the rule *SequenceRuleBase* entails two critical pairs as shown in Fig. 5.42.

Figure 5.42: SequenceRuleBase/SequenceRuleBase

The first CP occurs, because the first rule transforms *2:Task* whereas the second rule transforms *3:Task*. After an application of the second rule leading to graph H_2, the rule *SequenceRuleBase* can be applied once more resulting in graph X as shown in Fig. 5.43. However, an extended transformation of graph H_1 leading to graph X is more complex, since *SequenceRuleBase* cannot be applied anymore. Instead, the rule *SequenceRuleExtended* is used for the transformation $H_1 \Rightarrow X$. Thus, the transformation is confluent. The transformation is also AC-confluent due to the fact that both rules do not specify any ACs. Moreover, the largest subgraph N of G, H_1, and H_2 consists of the first task and the node and is also preserved by graph X.

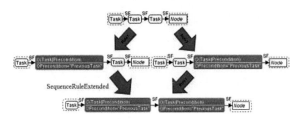

Figure 5.43: Strict AC-Confluence of first CP shown in Fig. 5.42

The second CP is caused by the two rules both transforming *2:Task*. Since the two resulting graphs H_1 and H_2 are isomorphic as shown in Fig. 5.44, strict AC-confluence can be concluded.

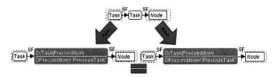

Figure 5.44: Strict AC-Confluence of second CP shown in Fig. 5.42

SequenceRuleBase/SequenceRuleExtended:

Parallel dependent are also the rules *SequenceRuleBase* and *SequenceRuleExtended* as shown by the critical pair in Fig. 5.45. In this case, *SequenceRuleBase* transforms *2:Task* resulting in graph H_1 whereas *SequenceRuleExtended* deontically classifies *1:Task* leading to graph H_2.

Figure 5.45: SequenceRuleBase/SequenceRuleExtended

In order to prove confluence for these rules, *SequenceRuleExtended* must be applied for both further transformations, $H_1 \Rightarrow X$ and $H_2 \Rightarrow X$, as shown in Fig. 5.46. *SequenceRuleExtended* does not specify any application conditions, so the critical pair is AC-confluent. Furthermore, the largest subgraph N of G, H_1, and H_2 consists of the first obligatory task with precondition and the node and is also part of graph X. Thus, the CP is strictly AC-confluent.

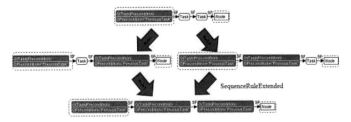

Figure 5.46: Strict AC-Confluence of CP shown in Fig. 5.45

SequenceRuleExtended/SequenceRuleBase:

The rules *SequenceRuleExtended* and *SequenceRuleBase* are parallel dependent as shown by the critical pair in Fig. 5.47. This CP is very similar to the former one between the rules *SequenceRuleBase* and *SequenceRuleExtended*. In this case, *SequenceRuleExtended* transforms *2:Task* whereas *SequenceRuleBase* transforms *3:Task*.

Again, *SequenceRuleExtended* must be applied for both further transformations and the confluence is shown in Fig. 5.48. The CP is AC-confluent,

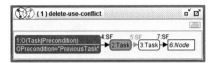

Figure 5.47: SequenceRuleExtended/SequenceRuleBase

since *SequenceRuleExtended* does not specify any application conditions. In addition, the largest subgraph N consisting of the first obligatory task with precondition and the node is preserved by X, so the CP is strictly AC-confluent.

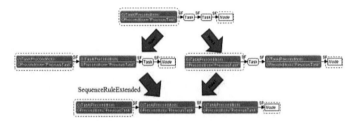

Figure 5.48: Strict AC-Confluence of CP shown in Fig. 5.47

SequenceRuleExtended/SequenceRuleExtended:

The next critical pair is identified for the rule *SequenceRuleExtended* and shown in Fig. 5.49.

Figure 5.49: SequenceRuleExtended/SequenceRuleExtended

Given that the two resulting graphs H_1 and H_2 are isomorphic as shown in Fig. 5.50, strict AC-confluence can be concluded.

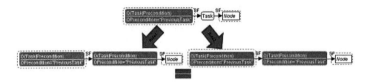

Figure 5.50: Strict AC-Confluence of CP shown in Fig. 5.49

SequenceRuleFinish/SequenceRuleFinish:

The rule *SequenceRuleFinish* is also parallel dependent as shown by the critical pair in Fig. 5.51.

Figure 5.51: SequenceRuleFinish/SequenceRuleFinish

The two resulting graphs H_1 and H_2 are isomorphic as shown in Fig. 5.52 and strict AC-confluence can be concluded.

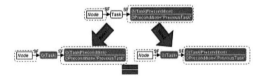

Figure 5.52: Strict AC-Confluence of CP shown in Fig. 5.51

(Parallel/Exclusive/Inclusive)WithPhiDualRule/ (Parallel/Exclusive/Inclusive)WithPhiDualRule:

Three similar critical pairs are identified by AGG for the rules *ParallelWith-PhiDualRule* (see Fig. 5.53), *ExclusiveWithPhiDualRule* (see Fig. 5.54), and *InclusiveWithPhiDualRule* (see Fig. 5.55). In all three cases, the gateways and the task are replaced by a deontically classified task.

The resulting graphs H_1 and H_2 are isomorphic. Thus, strict AC-confluence can be concluded based on the isomorphism and is shown in Fig. 5.56 for

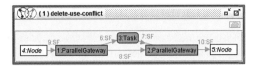

Figure 5.53: ParallelWithPhiDualRule/ParallelWithPhiDualRule

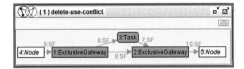

Figure 5.54: ExclusiveWithPhiDualRule/ExclusiveWithPhiDualRule

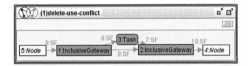

Figure 5.55: InclusiveWithPhiDualRule/InclusiveWithPhiDualRule

the rule *ParallelWithPhiDualRule*. The proof of strict AC-confluence for
the rules *ExclusiveWithPhiDualRule* and *InclusiveWithPhiDualRule* is similar; the only difference is that the resulting graphs H_1 and H_2 comprise a
permissible task.

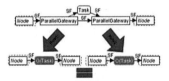

Figure 5.56: Strict AC-Confluence of CP shown in Fig. 5.53

ParallelRule/ParallelWithPhiDualRule:

Another critical pair is shown in Fig. 5.57 for the rules *ParallelRule* and
ParallelWithPhiDualRule. However, this critical pair is invalid, since the
rule *ParallelRule* defines the PAC *FurtherNode*, which only allows an application of the rule in case a further node exists. Since the critical pair does

not provide a further node, only the rule *ParallelWithPhiDualRule* may be applied.

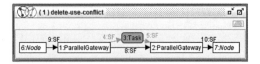

Figure 5.57: ParallelRule/ParallelWithPhiDualRule

The critical pair analysis of AGG currently only considers the NACs [31, p. 314]. Since PACs are not taken into account, the analysis may also provide invalid critical pairs.

(Exclusive/Inclusive)WithPhiRule/ (Exclusive/Inclusive)WithPhiDualRule:

The critical pairs identified for the rules *ExclusiveWithPhiRule* and *ExclusiveWithPhiDualRule* (see Fig. 5.58) as well as *InclusiveWithPhiRule* and *InclusiveWithPhiDualRule* (see Fig. 5.59) are also invalid due to the neglected PAC *FurtherNode*. In the described examples, only the rules *ExclusiveWithPhiDualRule* or *InclusiveWithPhiDualRule* may be applied.

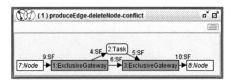

Figure 5.58: ExclusiveWithPhiRule/ExclusiveWithPhiDualRule

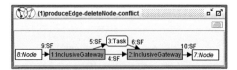

Figure 5.59: InclusiveWithPhiRule/InclusiveWithPhiDualRule

These two critical pairs are also the only conflicts that are not classified as *delete-use-conflict* but as *produceEdge-deleteNode-conflict*.

**(Parallel/ExclusiveWithoutPhi/InclusiveWithoutPhi)Rule/
(Parallel/ExclusiveWithoutPhi/InclusiveWithoutPhi)Rule:**

Three further CPs are provided for the rules *ParallelRule* (see Fig. 5.60), *ExclusiveWithoutPhiRule* (see Fig. 5.61), and *InclusiveWithoutPhiRule* (see Fig. 5.62). The critical pairs present two gateways with one task and one alternative node in between.

Figure 5.60: ParallelRule/ParallelRule

Figure 5.61: ExclusiveWithoutPhiRule/ExclusiveWithoutPhiRule

Figure 5.62: InclusiveWithoutPhiRule/InclusiveWithoutPhiRule

In all three cases, the two rules deontically classify the task leading to isomorphic graphs H_1 and H_2. Based on the isomorphism, all critical pairs are strictly AC-confluent as shown for the *ParallelRule* in Fig. 5.63.

**(Exclusive/Inclusive)WithPhiRule/
(Exclusive/Inclusive)WithPhiRule:**

Additional critical pairs are identified for the rules *ExclusiveWithPhiRule* (see Fig. 5.64) and *InclusiveWithPhiRule* (see Fig. 5.65) and present two gateways

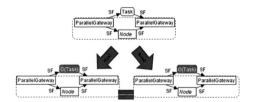

Figure 5.63: Strict AC-Confluence of CP shown in Fig. 5.60

with a task, a node, and two *Phi*-Paths in between. In fact, one of the two *Phi*-Paths should have been deleted in the first layer by the rule *SeveralPhiReductionRule*. All rules deontically classify the task as permissible.

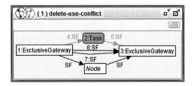

Figure 5.64: ExclusiveWithPhiRule/ExclusiveWithPhiRule

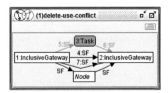

Figure 5.65: InclusiveWithPhiRule/InclusiveWithPhiRule

The resulting graphs H_1 and H_2 are isomorphic as shown in Fig. 5.66 for the exclusive gateway. Thus, both critical pairs are strictly AC-confluent as can be concluded from the isomorphism.

**(Parallel/ExclusiveWithPhi/InclusiveWithPhi)RuleFinish/
(Parallel/ExclusiveWithPhi/InclusiveWithPhi)RuleFinish:**

Considering the rules *ParallelRuleFinish*, *ExclusiveWithPhiRuleFinish*, and *InclusiveWithPhiRuleFinish*, seven critical pairs are identified for each of them. All critical pairs comprise exactly one *Phi*-Path. Furthermore, the

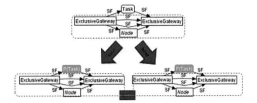

Figure 5.66: Strict AC-Confluence of CP shown in Fig. 5.64

first CP provides four deontically classified tasks, the four identical critical pairs 2-5 show three tasks, and the identical critical pairs 6-7 present two tasks. The three distinct critical pairs are shown in Fig. 5.67, 5.68, and 5.69.

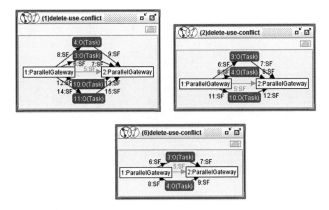

Figure 5.67: ParallelRuleFinish/ParallelRuleFinish

Since the corresponding *FinishRule* only removes the *Phi*-Path, the resulting graphs H_1 and H_2 of all critical pairs are isomorphic. Based on the isomorphism, all critical pairs are strictly AC-confluent as shown for the first critical pair of the rule *ParallelRuleFinish* in Fig. 5.70.

SequenceBpmnRulePragmatic/SequenceBpmnRulePragmatic:

The rule *SequenceBpmnRulePragmatic* is also parallel dependent as shown by the critical pair in Fig. 5.71. Both rules remove the precondition of the obligatory task leading to isomorphic graphs H_1 and H_2 as shown in Fig. 5.72. Since the two graphs are isomorphic, strict AC-confluence can be concluded.

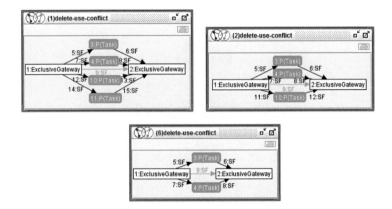

Figure 5.68: ExclusiveWithPhiRuleFinish/ExclusiveWithPhiRuleFinish

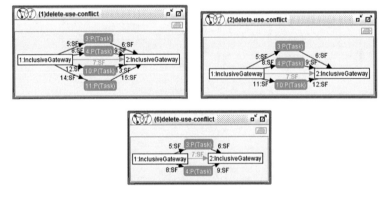

Figure 5.69: InclusiveWithPhiRuleFinish/InclusiveWithPhiRuleFinish

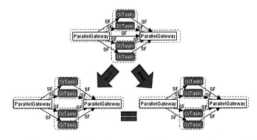

Figure 5.70: Strict AC-Confluence of first CP shown in Fig. 5.67

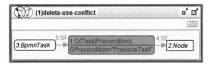

Figure 5.71: SequenceBpmnRulePragmatic/SequenceBpmnRulePragmatic

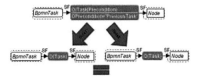

Figure 5.72: Strict AC-Confluence of CP shown in Fig. 5.71

SequenceDeonticRulePragmatic/SequenceBpmnRulePragmatic:

The rules *SequenceDeonticRulePragmatic* and *SequenceBpmnRulePragmatic* are also parallel dependent as shown by the critical pair in Fig. 5.73. In this case, the first rule considers *2:O(Task|Precondition)* whereas the second rule transforms *1:O(Task|Precondition)*.

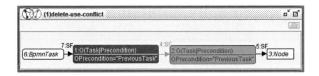

Figure 5.73: SequenceDeonticRulePragmatic/SequenceBpmnRulePragmatic

The resulting graphs H_1 and H_2 are different, but the respective other rule can be applied within the extended transformation resulting in graph X as shown in Fig. 5.74.

Considering AC-confluence, the three NACs (*NoFurtherGatewayFlow*, *NoFurtherDeonticTaskFlow*, and *NoFurtherBpmnTaskFlow*), which are equal for both rules, have to be taken into account. Since graph G must satisfy the three NACs in order to apply the first transformations and none of the two rules add a *Gateway*, *BpmnTask*, or *DeonticTask*, graphs H_1 and H_2 must also satisfy the NACs. In addition, the largest subgraph N of G, H_1, and H_2 comprises the *BpmnTask* and *Node* and is preserved by graph X. This critical pair is, therefore, strictly AC-confluent.

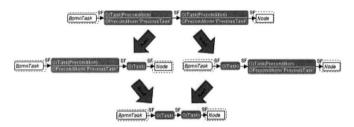

Figure 5.74: Strict AC-Confluence of CP shown in Fig. 5.73

SequenceDeonticRulePragmatic/SequenceDeonticRulePragmatic:

The last critical pair is identified for the rule *SequenceDeonticRulePragmatic* and shown in Fig. 5.75.

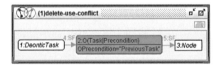

Figure 5.75: SequenceDeonticRulePragmatic/SequenceDeonticRule-
            Pragmatic

Both rules remove the precondition of the obligatory task and the resulting graphs H_1 and H_2 are isomorphic as shown in Fig. 5.76. Thus, the critical pair is strictly AC-confluent.

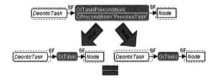

Figure 5.76: Strict AC-Confluence of CP shown in Fig. 5.75

Local Confluence: Since it has been proven that all CPs are strictly AC-confluent, it can be concluded that *DeonticBpmnGTS* is locally confluent.

5.5 Termination

In order to show confluence and consequently global determinism of a GTS, it is necessary to prove local confluence and termination. After an introduction to the foundations of termination and a description of the inheritance problem, this section provides a flattening algorithm to address the inheritance problem (first presented in [94]) and proves termination of *DeonticBpmnGTS*.

5.5.1 Foundations of Termination

A graph transformation $G \overset{*}{\Rightarrow} H$ is called terminating if no further transformation rule is applicable to H anymore, so that there is no infinite sequence of graph transformations [31, p. 59f].

In order to prove termination of DeonticBpmnGTS, the theorem for termination of layered typed graph grammars with the necessary layer conditions must be considered. The layers are divided into deletion and nondeletion layers. Every deletion layer deletes at least one element, whereas nondeletion layers do not delete anything, but provide NACs to prohibit an infinite application of the same rule (cf. for this paragraph [31, p. 63]).

Theorem 2. *Termination of Layered Typed Graph Grammars [31, p. 63f]:*

> *"Every layered typed graph grammar $GG = (TG, P, G_0)$ with injective matches terminates, provided that it is layered in the following sense:*
>
> 1. *P is layered, i.e. for each $p \in P$ there is a production layer $pl(p)$ with $0 \leq pl(p) \leq k_0$ $(pl(p), k_0 \in \mathbb{N})$, where $k_0 + 1$ is the number of layers of GG, and each typed graph production $p \in P$ has a set NAC_p of negative application conditions $NAC(n : L \to N)$ [...]; the latter is abbreviated as $n \in NAC_p$.*
>
> 2. *The type set $TYPE$ of GG is given by all graph nodes and edges of the type graph TG, i.e. $TYPE = V_{TG} \cup E_{TG}$.*
>
> 3. *GG is finite.*
>
> 4. *For each type $t \in TYPE$ there is a creation layer $cl(t) \in \mathbb{N}$ and a deletion layer $dl(t) \in \mathbb{N}$, and each production layer k is either a deletion layer or a nondeletion layer, satisfying the following layer conditions for all $p \in P_k$:" [see Tab. 5.3]*

Table 5.3: Layer Conditions (Source: [31, p. 64], slightly modified)

Deletion layer conditions	Nondeletion layer conditions
1. p deletes at least one item. 2. $0 \leq cl(t) \leq dl(t) \leq k_0 + 1$[1] for all $t \in TYPE$. 3. p deletes an item of type t $\Rightarrow dl(t) \leq pl(p)$. 4. p creates an item of type t $\Rightarrow cl(t) > pl(p)$.	1. p is nondeleting, i.e. $K = L$ such that p is given by $r : L \to R$ injective. 2. p has $n \in NAC_p$ with $n : L \to N$, and there is an injective $n' : N \to R$ with $n' \circ n = r$. 3. $x \in L$ with $type(x) = t$ $\Rightarrow cl(t) \leq pl(p)$. 4. p creates an item of type t $\Rightarrow cl(t) > pl(p)$.

[1] Corrected to $k_0 + 1$ (original: k_0), since the deletion layer of every not deleted type t is set to $k_0 + 1$ (according to the definition for layer assignments), which is always greater than the limit k_0. Thus, all graph transformation systems that do not delete items of every type would be classified as not terminating. Furthermore, a reduction to the essential part of the definition ($cl(t) \leq dl(t)$) is possible, since every creation layer is equal or greater than 0 ($0 \leq pl(p)$) and no deletion layer is greater than $k_0 + 1$ ($pl(p) \leq k_0$).

A layered graph grammar defines, for each rule r, a rule layer $rl(r) = k$ (also called production layer $pl(p)$) and for each type t, a creation layer $cl(t)$ and a deletion layer $dl(t)$ [3, p. 79]. The creation and deletion layer are calculated as follows:

Definition 9. *Layer Assignments [31, p. 253]:*

"Given a layered typed attributed graph grammar GG with a start graph G_0 and start types $T_0 \subseteq TYPE$, i.e. each typed item x in G_0 has $type(x) \in T_0$, then we can define for each $t \in TYPE$ the creation and deletion layers as follows:

$cl(t) =$ if $t \in T_0$ then 0 else $max\{pl(p)|p$ creates $t\} + 1$,
$dl(t) =$ if t is deleted by some p then $min\{pl(p)|p$ deletes $t\}$
            else $k_0 + 1$."

The termination of graph transformation systems is in general undecidable, but termination can be concluded if suitable termination criteria as described in the termination theorem are met [31, p. 318].

The tool AGG provides a termination analysis for layered graph transformation systems. The rule layers for the termination proof can either be set by the user or generated by AGG. Every rule within a deletion layer must decrease the number of graph items in general or the number of graph items of one special type. The creation and deletion layers for every node and edge type are then calculated by AGG so that the layer conditions are fulfilled if possible (cf. for this paragraph [31, p. 318]).

5.5.2 Inheritance Problem

AGG correctly proves termination for the included examples Pacman and Statecharts. However, considering DeonticBpmnGTS the creation and deletion layer of every type besides *MeasuredValues* is set to $k_0 + 1$ and the graph transformation system is classified to be terminating. This calculation is wrong, since it violates the third condition of deletion layers ($dl(l) \leq rl(r)$). Consider, for example, the rule *ParallelWithPhiDualRule*, which deletes items of the type *ParallelGateway*. Thus, the deletion layer of *ParallelGateway* must be equal or less than the rule layer.

DeonticBpmnGTS is also classified to be terminating even if a cyclic rule is included that leads to an infinite sequence of graph transformations. For example, the rule *CyclicRule* reverses the transformation of the rule *ExclusiveWithPhiRule* and is shown in Fig. 5.77.

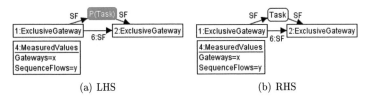

        (a) LHS   (b) RHS

Figure 5.77: CyclicRule

The reason for the incorrect termination proof of AGG is that DeonticBpmnGTS comprises abstract nodes and inheritance relationships within its type graph. This reduces the number of transformation rules, since several rules can be abstracted into one rule (cf. [12]). However, the termination criteria can only be used for GTSs with node type inheritance if the inheritance relationships are flattened (cf. [130]). Thus, the algebraic graph transformation approach provides a formal description for how to flatten the type graph as well as a definition of abstract and concrete rules.

The first definition defines the closure (or flattening) of ATGIs (see [31, p. 262f, Definition 13.4]). In a first step, all inheritance relationships are removed from the type graph and the edges and attributes of a parent node type are copied for every child node type. Thus, additional graph-, node attribute-, and edge attribute edges may be inserted in the type graph. The result is called the abstract closure (or abstract flattening) of the type graph. In a second step, all abstract nodes together with adjacent edges are removed from the type graph. This is called the concrete closure (or concrete flattening) of the type graph.

The second definition then defines abstract and concrete rules (or productions) (see [31, p. 272f, Definition 13.16]). An abstract rule typed over ATGI is given by $p = (L \xleftarrow{l} K \xrightarrow{r} R, type, NAC)$, where $type$ is a triple of typing morphisms, e.g. $type_L : L \to ATGI$, and NAC is a set of triples $(nac = (N, n, type_N))$ with an attributed graph N, a morphism $n : L \to N$ and a typing ATGI-clan morphism $type_N : N \to ATGI$, such that the following conditions hold: (i) types in K are equal with the morphism image types in L and R, (ii) all nodes that only exist in R must not be of an abstract type, and (iii) all nodes in a NAC have the same or a finer type as the morphism image in L. In a concrete rule $(p_t = (L \xleftarrow{l} K \xrightarrow{r} R, t, \overline{NAC}))$ again (i) the types in K are equal with the morphism image types in L and R, but (ii) the types can be equal or finer than in the abstract rule. Furthermore, (iii) all nodes that only exist in R must remain of the same type and (iv) all nodes in a NAC with a morphism image in L are flattened to the same type whereas nodes without a morphism image are flattened to all subtypes. Considering the last aspect, I suggest that the node type in the NAC should only be set to the same morphism image type if the original node types in L and NAC were equal (node type in a NAC might have been finer).

The flattening approach was extended in [24]. The main results of this publication show the equivalence of the abstract and the corresponding concrete transformation as well as the equivalence of attributed graph grammars with and without inheritance. Open issues of the flattening approach are changed attributes, dependency relationships with multiplicity, and edge inheritance (cf. [24]). The last two aspects were defined for graph transformations without attributes in [123].

However, I identified open issues in the definition of abstract and concrete rules. Thus, I will extend the definition to also consider vertices in NACs with finer types as well as PACs. Furthermore, I will prove the semantic equivalence of the original and the flattened graph transformation system. The suggested flattening algorithm was first presented in [94].

5.5.3 Flattening Algorithm

First of all, I provide some suggestions and extensions concerning the definition of abstract and concrete rules (see [31, p. 272f, Definition 13.16]). The fourth condition of concrete rules is adapted from:

- "for each $(N, n, type_N) \in NAC$, we have all $(N, n, t_N) \in \overline{NAC}$ for concrete ATGI-clan morphisms t_N satisfying $t_N \circ n = t_L$ and $t_N \leq type_N$."

to:

- for each $(N, n, type_N) \in NAC$, we have all $(N, n, t_N) \in \overline{NAC}$ for concrete ATGI-clan morphisms t_N satisfying $t_N \leq type_N$ and $\forall x \in L_{V_G}$:

  - if $(type_N \circ n)(x) = type_L(x)$ or $(type_N \circ n)(x) > t_L(x)$
    then $(t_N \circ n)(x) = t_L(x)$

  - else if $(type_N \circ n)(x) < type_L(x)$ and $(type_N \circ n)(x) \leq t_L(x)$
    then $t_N(x) = type_N(x)$

  - else $(N, n, t_N) \notin \overline{NAC}$

In the first case, $type_N$ and $type_L$ are equal or the flattened t_L is finer than $type_N$, thus the node in N is flattened to the same type as the node in L. In the second case, $type_N$ is finer than $type_L$ and finer or equal than the flattened t_L, so $type_N$ is not flattened. In the third case, however, the NAC is removed from the set of $\overline{NAC}$ of this rule. For example, if $type_L$ defines a *Node*, $type_N$ a *Gateway* and the node in L is flattened to an *Event* (t_L), then the NAC can be removed, since an *Event* cannot be replaced by a *Gateway*.

Furthermore, PACs have to be considered. The flattening of PACs is similar to that of NACs described in [31, p. 272f, Definition 13.16] and extended above. However, if a PAC comprises a refined node and the morphism image in L is flattened to a sibling, then the PAC must remain to ensure that the rule is never applied. Alternatively, the entire rule can be deleted.

In addition, there is a difference between flattening of NACs and PACs concerning nodes without morphism image in L. If a NAC has an abstract node without morphism image, then this node is flattened to all concrete nodes resulting in several flattened NACs for one rule. All NACs must be fulfilled in order to apply the rule. However, if a PAC has such an abstract node, then only one instance with a concrete node must be fulfilled. If, however, the PAC is flattened, then all flattened PACs must be satisfied in order to apply the rule. For example, if the original PAC defines that a node X must address an abstract node Y, and Y has no morphism image, then flattening this PAC means that node X must address all subnodes of Y, whereas the original definition states that only one subnode must be addressed. Thus, it is necessary to convert all flattened PACs to general application conditions (GACs) and to specify a formula. The formula defines which GACs must be fulfilled under which circumstances. For example, all flattened GACs of one abstract PAC are defined to be disjunctive (concatenated with $\vee$) and, thus, only one of the GACs must be fulfilled.

All other PACs which only comprise abstract nodes that have a morphism image in L are flattened together with the rule. These PACs can either remain as PAC or can also be transformed to a GAC. GACs that originate from different former PACs are concatenated with conjunction ($\wedge$). The two approaches are semantically equivalent. In the following, I will transform these PACs to GACs to be consistent with PACs that have abstract nodes without morphism image. Then I can generally define:

- $\overline{PAC}(x) \rightarrow \overline{GAC}(x)$;

- $PAC(x) \equiv \overline{GAC_1}(x) \vee ... \vee \overline{GAC_n}(x)$;

- $PAC(x) \wedge PAC(y) \equiv \overline{GAC}(x) \wedge \overline{GAC}(y)$

After defining the extensions, it must be proven that the original and the flattened GTS are still semantically equivalent. As already mentioned, the equivalence of abstract and corresponding concrete transformations as well as the equivalence of attributed graph grammars with and without inheritance is shown in [24] and [31, p. 275ff]. The theorem for equivalence of attributed graph grammars as well as the corresponding proof is not affected by the extensions (see Theorem 3 in [24]). However, the theorem for equivalence of transformations (see Theorem 2 in [24]) and the lemma for construction of concrete and abstract transformations (see Lemma 3 in [24]) must be adapted to also cover the proposed extensions.

Theorem 3. *Equivalence of Transformations (based on [24], slightly modified): Given an abstract production $p = (L \xleftarrow{l} K \xrightarrow{r} R, type, AC)$ over an attributed type graph ATGI with inheritance, a concrete typed attributed graph $(G, type_G)$ and a match morphism $m : L \rightarrow G$ (which satisfies the gluing condition w.r.t. the untyped production $L \leftarrow K \rightarrow R$). Then the following statements are equivalent, where $(H, type_H)$ is the same concrete typed graph in both cases:*

1. *$m : L \rightarrow G$ is a consistent match w.r.t. the abstract production p yielding an abstract direct transformation $(G, type_G) \overset{p,m}{\Rightarrow} (H, type_H)$.*

2. $m : L \to G$ is a consistent match w.r.t. the concrete production $p_t = (L \leftarrow K \to R, t, \overline{AC})$ with $p_t \in \widehat{p}$ and $t_L = type_G \circ m$ (where t_K, t_R and $\overline{AC}$ are uniquely defined by Lemma 1(1)) yielding a concrete direct transformation $(G, type_G) \overset{p_t, m}{\Rightarrow} (H, type_H)$.

Lemma 1. *Construction of Concrete and Abstract Transformations (based on [24], extended): Given an abstract production $p = (L \overset{l}{\leftarrow} K \overset{r}{\to} R, type, AC)$ with $AC = (NAC \cup PAC)$ ($NAC = \{(N_i, n_i, type_{N_i}) | i \in I\}$ and $PAC = \{(P_i, p_i, type_{P_i}) | i \in I\}$), a concrete typed attributed graph $(G, type_G : G \to ATGI)$ and a consistent match morphism $m : L \to G$ w.r.t. p and $(G, type_G)$, we have [...]:*

1. *There is a unique concrete production $p_t \in \widehat{p}$ with $p_t = (L \overset{l}{\leftarrow} K \overset{r}{\to} R, t, \overline{AC})$ and $t_L = type_G \circ m$. In this case, t_K, t_R and $\overline{AC}$ are defined by:*

   - $t_K = t_L \circ l$;
   - $t_{R,V_G}(x) = $ *if* $x = r_{V_G}(x')$ *then* $t_{K,V_G}(x')$ *else* $type_{R,V_G}(x)$ *for* $x \in R_{V_G}$;
   - $t_{R,X} = type_{R,X}$ *for* $X \in \{V_D, E_G, E_{NA}, E_{EA}, D\}$;
   - $\overline{AC} = (\overline{NAC} \cup \overline{GAC})$;
   - $\overline{NAC} = \bigcup_{i \in I}\{(N_i, n_i, t_{N_i}) | t_{N_i}$ *is a concrete ATGI-clan morphism with* $t_{N_i} \leq type_{N_i}$ *and* $\forall x \in L_{V_G}$:
     - *if* $(type_{N_i} \circ n_i)(x) = type_L(x)$ *or* $(type_{N_i} \circ n_i)(x) > t_L(x)$ *then* $(t_{N_i} \circ n_i)(x) = t_L(x)$
     - *else if* $(type_{N_i} \circ n_i)(x) < type_L(x)$ *and* $(type_{N_i} \circ n_i)(x) \leq t_L(x)$ *then* $t_{N_i}(x) = type_{N_i}(x)$
     - *else* $(N_i, n_i, t_{N_i}) \notin \overline{NAC}\}$;
   - $\overline{PAC} = \bigcup_{i \in I}\{(P_i, p_i, t_{P_i}) | t_{P_i}$ *is a concrete ATGI-clan morphism with* $t_{P_i} \leq type_{P_i}$ *and* $\forall x \in L_{V_G}$:
     - *if* $(type_{P_i} \circ p_i)(x) = type_L(x)$ *or* $(type_{P_i} \circ p_i)(x) > t_L(x)$ *then* $(t_{P_i} \circ p_i)(x) = t_L(x)$
     - *else if* $(type_{P_i} \circ p_i)(x) < type_L(x)$ *then* $t_{P_i}(x) = type_{P_i}(x)\}$;
   - $\overline{PAC}(x) \to \overline{GAC}(x)$;

   In addition, all $\overline{GAC}$ are concatenated by a formula as follows:

   - $PAC(x) \equiv \overline{GAC_1}(x) \vee ... \vee \overline{GAC_n}(x)$;
   - $PAC(x) \wedge PAC(y) \equiv \overline{GAC}(x) \wedge \overline{GAC}(y)$

[...]

The proof for the theorem is provided in [24] and can be extended from NAC to AC. Thus, it can be concluded that the original and the flattened graph transformation system are semantically equivalent and every concrete graph in a confluent graph transformation system is transformed to the same resulting graph independent of whether the GTS is flattened or not.

Afterwards the *Flattening Algorithm* is defined based on the extended definitions. The algorithm flattens the inheritance of a GTS in order to execute the termination analysis. It thereby considers abstract nodes, inheritance relationships, multiple inheritance, attributes and dependency relationships. A brief overview of the *Flattening Algorithm* is given below:

```
ReadXmlFile();
ReadNodeTypes();
FindAndOrderInheritancesBetweenNodes();
foreach (Inheritance in Inheritances)
    foreach (Rule in Rules)
        foreach (AC in Rule.ACs)
            foreach (Node in AC.Nodes)
                if (Node.Type == ParentType)
                    if (!HasMorphismNodeInLHS())
                        CloneAC();
                        ReplaceParentWithChildNodeInAC();
                        ChangeIds();
                        InsertACInDict();
    FindCombinationsOfNodeReplacementsInAC();
RemoveDuplicateACs();
InsertACs();
foreach (Inheritance in Inheritances)
    foreach (Rule in Rules)
        foreach (Node in Rule.LHS.Nodes)
            if (Node.Type == ParentType)
                CloneRule();
                ReplaceParentWithChildNodeInLHS();
                if (HasMorphismNodeInRHS())
                    rhsNode = GetMorphismNodeInRHS();
                    ReplaceParentWithChildNodeInRHS(rhsNode);
                foreach (AC in Rule.ACs)
                    acNode = GetMorphismNodeInAC();
                    ReplaceParentWithChildNodeInAC(acNode);
                ChangeIds();
```

```
        InsertRuleInDict();
    FindCombinationsOfNodeReplacementsInRule();
    RemoveInheritanceBetweenNodes();
RemoveDuplicateRules();
InsertRules();
if (userChoice == concreteFlattening)
    RemoveAbstractNodes();
SaveXmlFile();
```

First of all, the user provides the AGG-file (XML) and a boolean parameter, which defines whether an abstract or concrete flattening should be executed. The *Flattening Algorithm* starts with reading in the XML-file and the node types together with their hierarchy. Then, all inheritance relationships are identified and ordered starting with those relationships where the parent node is not derived from any further node. The ordering is necessary, since a node Z may be derived from a node Y which is in turn derived from a node X that defines an attribute *name*. If the inheritance relationship between Z and Y is considered first, then no attribute is taken over from Y to Z. Thus, it is necessary to first flatten the inheritance relationship between Y and X thereby taking the attribute *name* over to Y, followed by the flattening of Z and Y.

Then, all inheritance relationships are iterated and the ACs of all rules are taken into account. For every node that has the same type as the parent node type and no morphism image on the LHS of the rule, the AC is duplicated and the parent node type is replaced by the child node type. If the child node type has an additional attribute, then this attribute remains unspecified due to the missing value. Attributes do not affect the termination analysis, but default values may be considered within further work. Then the IDs within the new AC are changed and the AC is inserted in a dictionary. Afterwards, possible combinations of replacements are identified. This is necessary in case an AC comprises two or more abstract nodes. For every combination a new AC is created, the nodes are replaced, IDs changed and the AC is inserted in the dictionary. Since the calculation of combinations may also lead to duplicate ACs, all generated ACs are iterated and the duplicate ACs are removed. Afterwards the remaining ACs are inserted in the XML-structure.

Similarly, all inheritance relationships are iterated again to consider the rules. Whenever a node in the LHS of a rule corresponds to the parent node type, the rule is duplicated and the node is replaced by the child node type. Morphism nodes on the RHS or within ACs (except finer types) are replaced by the same child node type. Further nodes on the RHS that are equivalent with the parent node type but not a morphism image are not replaced, since exactly this node type should be created in the host graph. Then the IDs within the rule are changed and the rule is inserted in a dictionary. Again all combinations of replacements are identified and further rules generated.

Afterwards, all attributes as well as the dependency and inheritance relationships of the parent node type are copied for the child node type and the inheritance relationship between the two of them is deleted from the type graph (abstract closure). Then the duplicate rules within the dictionary are removed and the remaining rules are inserted in the XML-structure.

Depending on the user's choice, the abstract node types together with adjacent edges as well as all rules and ACs with abstract nodes are deleted afterwards (concrete closure). Finally, the XML-file with the flattened hierarchy is saved and can be opened with AGG.

Based on the flattening algorithm, a concrete prototype was developed using the programming language C# and is presented in appendix B. This prototype is used to flatten DeonticBpmnGTS resulting in 822 rules and 10.170 ACs (concrete closure). For example, the flattening of the rule *SeveralPhiReductionRule* leads to nine concrete rules in which the two abstract nodes *Gateway* are replaced in any combination. The LHS of the nine generated rules without the *MeasuredValues* element is shown in Fig. 5.78.

Figure 5.78: Flattened SeveralPhiReductionRule (LHS)

Inheritance relationships between concrete nodes have been flattened, for example, within the rule *ParallelRuleFinish*. The two concrete nodes *O(Task)* can be replaced by two more concretely nodes *O(Task|Precondition)* and *P(Task)&O(Task|Precondition)* resulting in nine combinations. The LHS of the generated rules without the *MeasuredValues* element is shown in Fig. 5.79.

The abstract flattening of the type graph of DeonticBpmnGTS (abstract closure) is shown in Fig. 5.80. All inheritance relationships have been removed from the type graph and the attributes and dependency relationships have been copied, e.g., *P(Task)&O(Task|Precondition)* provides the attribute

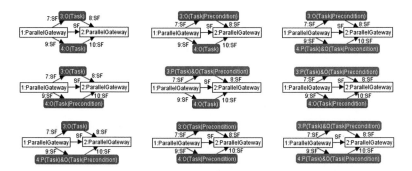

Figure 5.79: Flattened ParallelRuleFinish (LHS)

OPrecondition and specifies all incoming and outgoing sequence flows by itself. The multiplicity of the dependency relationships is either taken from
the current node, if this node specified an edge of the same type between the
source and target node, or otherwise inherited from the parent node type.
The abstract flattening of DeonticBpmnGTS with the flattening prototype
results in 1.471 rules and 24.942 ACs (414 GACs and 24.528 NACs).

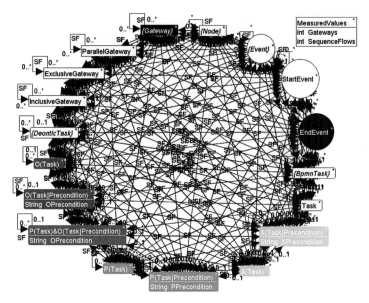

Figure 5.80: Abstract Flattening of Type Graph of *DeonticBpmnGTS*

Furthermore, the concrete flattening of the type graph of DeonticBpmnGTS (concrete closure) is shown in Fig. 5.81. In this case, also the abstract nodes have been removed from the type graph and all rules and ACs with abstract nodes have been deleted. The concrete flattening of DeonticBpmnGTS with the flattening prototype results in 822 rules and 10.170 ACs (234 GACs and 9.936 NACs).

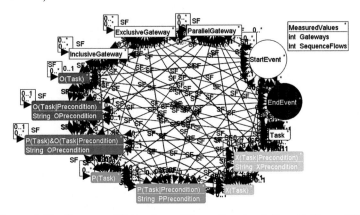

Figure 5.81: Concrete Flattening of Type Graph of *DeonticBpmnGTS*

The flattening of DeonticBpmnGTS resulted in 1.147 abstract and 822 concrete rules which corresponds to the calculations in Tab. 5.4. For example, the rule *ParallelWithPhiDualRule* comprises two abstract *Nodes* that can be replaced by 18 node types (*Node* and 17 subnodes) of which 13 are concrete. Thus, $18 \times 18 = 324$ abstract and $13 \times 13 = 169$ concrete rules are generated.

Furthermore, the flattening of DeonticBpmnGTS resulted in 24.942 abstract and 10.170 concrete ACs (see Tab. 5.5). Every node that has no morphism image on the LHS of the rule leads to additional ACs that must then be multiplied with the number of rules. For example, the rule *ParallelWithPhiDualRule* includes the NAC *NoFurtherNode*, which comprises one abstract *Node* without morphism image on the LHS of the rule. Thus, the flattening of the NAC leads to $18 \times 324 = 5.832$ abstract and $13 \times 169 = 2.197$ concrete NACs.

The correspondence of the flattening results and the calculated numbers allows to assume a correct flattening. Duplicate rules and ACs can be ruled out due to the algorithm (see methods *RemoveDuplicateRules* and *RemoveDuplicateACs*) and a manual check.

However, the flattening of DeonticBpmnGTS reveals a minor open issue concerning restricted dependency relationships of subtypes. If the flattening of

Table 5.4: Flattening of DeonticBpmnGTS: Transformation Rules

Rule	Description	Abstract	Concrete
1	Gateway x Gateway	16	9
2		1	1
3	Node	18	13
4	Node x O(Task|Precondition)	36	26
5	Node x O(Task|Precondition)	36	26
6	Node x Node	324	169
7		1	1
8	O(Task) x O(Task)	9	9
9	Node x Node	324	169
10		1	1
11	P(Task) x P(Task)	9	9
12		1	1
13	Node x Node	324	169
14		1	1
15	P(Task) x P(Task)	9	9
16		1	1
17	BpmnTask x O(Task|Precondition) x Node	72	26
18	DeonticTask x O(Task|Precondition) x Node	288	182
		1.471	822

Rule Numbers:

[1] SeveralPhiReductionRule
[2] IterationRepeatUntilRule
[3] SequenceRuleBase
[4] SequenceRuleExtended
[5] SequenceRuleFinish
[6] ParallelWithPhiDualRule
[7] ParallelRule
[8] ParallelRuleFinish
[9] ExclusiveWithPhiDualRule
[10] ExclusiveWithPhiRule
[11] ExclusiveWithPhiRuleFinish
[12] ExclusiveWithoutPhiRule
[13] InclusiveWithPhiDualRule
[14] InclusiveWithPhiRule
[15] InclusiveWithPhiRuleFinish
[16] InclusiveWithoutPhiRule
[17] SequenceBpmnRulePragmatic
[18] SequenceDeonticRulePragmatic

the type graph results in two dependency relationships of the same type being specified between a source and target node, then the restricted dependency relationship of the subtype is taken. However, during the flattening, every node is replaced by all subnodes without considering restricted multiplicities of dependency relationships. Thus, the flattening algorithm may provide invalid rules and ACs. For example, a *Node* may have several incoming and outgoing sequence flows, which is necessary for *Gateways*, but some subtypes are restricted to at most one incoming or one outgoing sequence flow. Thus, a *Node* with two incoming sequence flows should not be replaced by all sub-

Table 5.5: Flattening of DeonticBpmnGTS: Application Conditions

Rule	AC	Description	Abstract	Concrete
2	NoPhiPath		1	1
	NoMixedStartGateway	Node	18	13
	IncomingOutgoingSF	Node x Node	324	169
5	NoSplittingNode	Node	648	338
6	NoFurtherNode	Node	5.832	2.197
7	FurtherNode	Node	18	13
8	NoFurtherTask		9	9
9	NoFurtherNode	Node	5.832	2.197
10	FurtherNode	Node	18	13
11	NoFurtherTask		9	9
12	NoPhiPath		1	1
	NoMixedStartGateway	Node x Node	324	169
	NoMixedEndGateway	Node x Node	324	169
	FurtherNode	Node	18	13
13	NoFurtherNode	Node	5.832	2.197
14	FurtherNode	Node	18	13
15	NoFurtherTask		9	9
16	NoPhiPath		1	1
	NoMixedStartGateway	Node x Node	324	169
	NoMixedEndGateway	Node x Node	324	169
	FurtherNode	Node	18	13
17	NoFurtherGatewayFlow	Gateway	288	78
	NoFurtherDeonticTaskFlow	DeonticTask	576	182
	NoFurtherBpmnTaskFlow	BpmnTask	144	26
18	NoFurtherGatewayFlow	Gateway	1.152	546
	NoFurtherDeonticTaskFlow	DeonticTask	2.304	1.274
	NoFurtherBpmnTaskFlow	BpmnTask	576	182
			24.942	10.170

Rule Numbers:

[1] SeveralPhiReductionRule
[2] IterationRepeatUntilRule
[3] SequenceRuleBase
[4] SequenceRuleExtended
[5] SequenceRuleFinish
[6] ParallelWithPhiDualRule
[7] ParallelRule
[8] ParallelRuleFinish
[9] ExclusiveWithPhiDualRule
[10] ExclusiveWithPhiRule

[11] ExclusiveWithPhiRuleFinish
[12] ExclusiveWithoutPhiRule
[13] InclusiveWithPhiDualRule
[14] InclusiveWithPhiRule
[15] InclusiveWithPhiRuleFinish
[16] InclusiveWithoutPhiRule
[17] SequenceBpmnRulePragmatic
[18] SequenceDeonticRulePragmatic

types. The invalid rules and ACs are highlighted by the tool AGG and can be easily disabled or removed.

In general, it can be said that invalid ACs do not affect the termination analysis, since invalid NACs are redundant and PACs are not used for the termination proof. Concerning the flattening of rules, three cases are distinguished. If (i) a node is created and, thus, only part of the RHS, then this node is not flattened. Hence, no invalid rules may emerge in this case. If (ii) the node is defined on the LHS and has a morphism image on the RHS, then the node is neither created nor deleted. An invalid rule may emerge but does not affect the termination analysis. If (iii), a node is defined on the LHS but not on the RHS, then this node is deleted. In this case, invalid rules that affect the termination analysis may occur.

In DeonticBpmnGTS, only some invalid NACs are produced and the flattened type graph is enabled without considering the minimum and maximum cardinality. However, NACs specify graphs that must not be part of the match in graph G. When the replacement has also been forbidden by restricted dependency relationships, then this definition is redundant. Furthermore, NACs are only necessary for the termination analysis of nondeletion layers. Since all layers in DeonticBpmnGTS are classified as deletion layers, the termination analysis of DeonticBpmnGTS is not affected by invalid NACs.

Finally, the flattening of DeonticBpmnGTS also increases the size of the XML-file. The original file including 18 rules and 27 ACs requires 0,27MB. After a concrete flattening the XML-file demands 37MB (concrete closure). However, if the abstract nodes remain (abstract closure), then the resulting XML-file has a size of 89,6MB. The tool AGG still supports working with the flattened GTS, but loading the GTS requires more time.

5.5.4 Proof: Termination

After flattening DeonticBpmnGTS, the termination analysis (TA) is executed by the tool AGG. In case of nondeletion layers, the comprised rules only create items and $r : L \rightarrow R$ must be total and injective [3, p. 80]. Since every rule of DeonticBpmnGTS deletes at least one node or edge, all layers are classified as deletion layer.

In a first step, the termination analysis computes layers for the rules as shown in Tab. 5.6. In a deletion layer, each rule must decrease the number of graph items in general or of one special type [3, p. 80]. For example, in the first layer, the rule *SeveralPhiReductionRule* decreases the number of graph items in general whereas the rules *IterationRepeatUntilRule* and *SequenceRuleBase* decrease the number of items of the type *Task*. However, a minor issue of the layer calculation is that too many layers are calculated, e.g., flattened rules of *SequenceRuleBase* are either part of the first or the second layer although they all delete nodes of type *Task*. Flattened rules of one former rule may only span several layers if a deleted item has an inheritance relationship.

Table 5.6: TA of DeonticBpmnGTS: Rule Layers

Rule	Layer
SeveralPhiReductionRule	0
IterationRepeatUntilRule	0
SequenceRuleBase	0-1
SequenceRuleExtended	2
SequenceRuleFinish	2-3
ParallelWithPhiDualRule	3-8
ParallelRule	8
ParallelRuleFinish	8
ExclusiveWithPhiDualRule	8-12
ExclusiveWithPhiRule	12
ExclusiveWithPhiRuleFinish	12
ExclusiveWithoutPhiRule	12
InclusiveWithPhiDualRule	12-15
InclusiveWithPhiRule	15
InclusiveWithPhiRuleFinish	15
InclusiveWithoutPhiRule	15
SequenceBpmnRulePragmatic	15-16
SequenceDeonticRulePragmatic	16-24

Afterwards, the creation and deletion layer of the node types are calculated as shown in Tab. 5.7. The item *O(Task|Precondition)* is, for example, lastly created in the rule *SequenceRuleExtended* within layer 2 ($cl(O(Task|Precondition)) = 2 + 1 = 3$) and for the first time deleted in *SequenceBpmnRulePragmatic* within layer 15 ($dl(O(Task|Precondition)) = 15$).

The deletion layer of the node type *P(Task)&O(Task|Precondition)* ($dl(t) = 16$) might be confusing, since this node type is derived from *O(Task|Precondition)* and, thus, also deleted within the rules *SequenceBpmnRulePragmatic* and *SequenceDeonticRulePragmatic*. Although the rule *SequenceBpmnRule-Pragmatic* ranges from layer 15 to 16, layer 15 only comprises one flattened rule that deletes a node of type *O(Task|Precondition)*, so that the deletion layer of *P(Task)&O(Task|Precondition)* is correctly set to 16.

Table 5.7: TA of DeonticBpmnGTS: Node Types

Type	cl(t)	dl(t)
ParallelGateway	0	3
ExclusiveGateway	0	8
InclusiveGateway	0	12
O(Task)	25	25
O(Task|Precondition)	3	15
X(Task)	13	13
X(Task|Precondition)	0	0
P(Task)	16	16
P(Task|Precondition)	0	0
P(Task)&O(Task|Precondition)	16	16
Task	0	1
StartEvent	0	0
EndEvent	0	0
MeasuredValues	0	0

Although all creation and deletion layers calculated for node types fulfill the deletion layer conditions described in Tab. 5.3, a minor issue is that the calculation of the creation and deletion layers is not conform to the calculation suggested in [31, p. 253]. For example, node types that are nowhere deleted like *X(Task)* or *StartEvent* should have a deletion layer of $k_0 + 1$, but are instead set to the same layer as the creation layer.

In order to determine the creation and deletion layer of edge types, the termination analysis considers all combinations of source and target nodes with an edge in between as shown in Tab. 5.8. For example, a sequence flow between a *ParallelGateway* and a *Task* $(1 - SF - 11)$ is nowhere created $(cl(1 - SF - 11) = 0)$, but deleted within the rule *ParallelWithPhiDualRule* $(dl(1 - SF - 11) = 3)$.

The termination analysis for all combinations of edges with source and target nodes (i.e. edge types) is very extensive but not necessary for DeonticBpmn-GTS, because termination can be concluded based on the fact that all edge types referencing *BpmnTasks* are replaced by edge types referencing *DeonticTasks*. Only the two pragmatic rules delete edge types referencing *DeonticTasks*, but also in this case the termination criteria are fulfilled, since the edge types are first created and then deleted. Thus, it is sufficient for DeonticBpmnGTS to consider the edge label *SF* and to show a general reduction of sequence flows.

Table 5.8: TA of DeonticBpmnGTS: Edge Types

Type	cl(t)	dl(t)	Type	cl(t)	dl(t)	Type	cl(t)	dl(t)
1–SF–1	0	3	5–SF–6	3	15	9–SF–11	0	2
1–SF–2	0	4	5–SF–7	3	16	9–SF–12	0	0
1–SF–3	0	4	5–SF–8	16	16	9–SF–13	0	0
1–SF–4	9	9	5–SF–9	3	16	10–SF–1	0	4
1–SF–5	0	4	5–SF–10	1	16	10–SF–2	0	10
1–SF–6	0	3	5–SF–11	3	3	10–SF–3	16	16
1–SF–7	0	3	5–SF–12	1	16	10–SF–4	20	22
1–SF–8	16	16	5–SF–13	3	16	10–SF–5	3	16
1–SF–9	0	3	6–SF–1	0	3	10–SF–6	0	16
1–SF–10	0	3	6–SF–2	3	8	10–SF–7	0	16
1–SF–11	0	3	6–SF–3	0	12	10–SF–8	16	16
1–SF–12	0	4	6–SF–4	17	17	10–SF–9	0	16
1–SF–13	0	4	6–SF–5	0	16	10–SF–10	0	16
2–SF–1	0	8	6–SF–6	0	0	10–SF–11	0	2
2–SF–2	0	8	6–SF–7	0	0	10–SF–12	0	16
2–SF–3	0	9	6–SF–8	16	16	10–SF–13	0	16
2–SF–4	9	9	6–SF–9	0	0	11–SF–1	0	1
2–SF–5	0	9	6–SF–10	0	16	11–SF–2	0	1
2–SF–6	13	13	6–SF–11	0	2	11–SF–3	0	1
2–SF–7	0	8	6–SF–12	0	0	11–SF–4	17	17
2–SF–8	16	16	6–SF–13	0	0	11–SF–5	2	2
2–SF–9	0	8	7–SF–1	0	3	11–SF–6	0	1
2–SF–10	0	8	7–SF–2	0	8	11–SF–7	0	2
2–SF–11	0	3	7–SF–3	0	12	11–SF–8	16	16
2–SF–12	0	9	7–SF–4	14	14	11–SF–9	0	2
2–SF–13	0	9	7–SF–5	0	16	11–SF–10	0	2
3–SF–1	0	7	7–SF–6	0	0	11–SF–11	0	1
3–SF–2	0	11	7–SF–7	0	0	11–SF–12	0	1
3–SF–3	0	12	7–SF–8	16	16	11–SF–13	0	1
3–SF–4	9	14	7–SF–9	0	0	12–SF–1	0	6
3–SF–5	0	14	7–SF–10	0	16	12–SF–2	0	11
3–SF–6	0	12	7–SF–11	0	2	12–SF–3	0	12
3–SF–7	0	12	7–SF–12	0	0	12–SF–4	7	7
3–SF–8	16	16	7–SF–13	0	0	12–SF–5	0	0
3–SF–9	0	13	8–SF–1	15	15	12–SF–6	0	0
3–SF–10	16	16	8–SF–2	16	16	12–SF–7	0	0
3–SF–11	0	3	8–SF–3	15	15	12–SF–8	16	16
3–SF–12	0	14	8–SF–4	15	15	12–SF–9	0	0
3–SF–13	0	14	8–SF–5	15	16	12–SF–10	0	0
4–SF–1	25	25	8–SF–6	13	13	12–SF–11	0	3
4–SF–2	20	20	8–SF–7	13	13	12–SF–12	0	0
4–SF–3	25	25	8–SF–8	16	16	12–SF–13	0	0
4–SF–4	25	25	8–SF–9	15	15	13–SF–1	0	6
4–SF–5	24	24	8–SF–10	15	16	13–SF–2	0	11
4–SF–6	21	21	8–SF–11	16	16	13–SF–3	0	12
4–SF–7	21	21	8–SF–12	15	15	13–SF–4	7	7
4–SF–8	23	23	8–SF–13	15	15	13–SF–5	0	0
4–SF–9	17	17	9–SF–1	0	4	13–SF–6	0	0
4–SF–10	23	23	9–SF–2	0	10	13–SF–7	0	0
4–SF–11	25	25	9–SF–3	0	12	13–SF–8	16	16
4–SF–12	25	25	9–SF–4	20	20	13–SF–9	0	0
4–SF–13	25	25	9–SF–5	0	16	13–SF–10	0	0
5–SF–1	1	5	9–SF–6	0	0	13–SF–11	0	3
5–SF–2	3	11	9–SF–7	0	0	13–SF–12	0	0
5–SF–3	3	12	9–SF–8	16	16	13–SF–13	0	0
5–SF–4	24	24	9–SF–9	0	0			
5–SF–5	3	16	9–SF–10	0	16			

Node Numbers:

[1] ParallelGateway
[2] ExclusiveGateway
[3] InclusiveGateway
[4] O(Task)
[5] O(Task|Precondition)
[6] X(Task)
[7] X(Task|Precondition)
[8] P(Task)
[9] P(Task|Precondition)
[10] P(Task)&O(Task|Precondition)
[11] Task
[12] StartEvent
[13] EndEvent

Furthermore, if the whole edge type ($Source - Edge - Target$) is taken into account, then the termination analysis of DeonticBpmnGTS is in some cases incorrect. Consider, for example, the edge type ($ParallelGateway - SF - ParallelGateway$), which is deleted in the rule $SeveralPhiReductionRule$ ($rl(r) = 0$). Thus, the deletion layer must be set to layer 0, but is in fact $dl(1 - SF - 1) = 3$, which violates the third condition of deletion layers ($dl(t) \leq rl(r)$).

All in all, AGG classifies DeonticBpmnGTS as terminating. The termination analysis is largely correct, however, some issues emerged:

- Too many different layers are calculated, although the rules can be comprised in less layers.

- The calculation of creation and deletion layers for node types is not conform to the calculation suggested in [31, p. 253].

- All combinations of edges with source and target nodes (i.e. edge types) are considered but not required for DeonticBpmnGTS.

- The calculation of creation and deletion layers for edge types is in some cases incorrect.

Due to the mentioned problems, the termination of DeonticBpmnGTS is also proven manually and presented in the subsequent paragraphs.

In a first step the rule layers are revised and shown in Tab. 5.9. The layers are based on the ordering described in section 5.2 and refined to fulfill the termination criteria. The rules $SequenceBpmnRulePragmatic$ and $SequenceDeonticRulePragmatic$ span two layers (3-4), since the flattened rules defined within layer 3 delete a node of type $O(Task/Precondition)$ whereas the rules in layer 4 delete a node of the sub-type $P(Task)\&O(Task/Precondition)$. The third column of Tab. 5.9 specifies the type of the reduction, since each rule in a deletion layer must decrease the number of graph items in general or of one special type.

Afterwards the creation and deletion layers for all node types and for the edge label are calculated and presented in Tab. 5.10. The adapted second deletion layer condition ($0 \leq cl(l) \leq dl(l) \leq k_0 + 1$) is fulfilled by all node types and by the edge label as can be seen in the table.

The remaining deletion layer conditions (1, 3-4) are proven within the corresponding rules.

Table 5.9: Manual TA of DeonticBpmnGTS: Rule Layers

Rule	Layer	Reduction
SeveralPhiReductionRule	0	General Reduction
IterationRepeatUntilRule	0	Reduction of *Tasks*
SequenceRuleBase	0	Reduction of *Tasks*
SequenceRuleExtended	0	Reduction of *Tasks*
SequenceRuleFinish	1	Reduction of *Tasks*
ParallelWithPhiDualRule	2	General Reduction
ParallelRule	2	Reduction of *Tasks*
ParallelRuleFinish	2	General Reduction
ExclusiveWithPhiDualRule	2	General Reduction
ExclusiveWithPhiRule	2	Reduction of *Tasks*
ExclusiveWithPhiRuleFinish	2	General Reduction
ExclusiveWithoutPhiRule	2	Reduction of *Tasks*
InclusiveWithPhiDualRule	2	General Reduction
InclusiveWithPhiRule	2	Reduction of *Tasks*
InclusiveWithPhiRuleFinish	2	General Reduction
InclusiveWithoutPhiRule	2	Reduction of *Tasks*
SequenceBpmnRulePragmatic	3	Reduction of *O(Task/Precondition)*
	4	and *P(Task)&O(Task/Precondition)*
SequenceDeonticRulePragmatic	3	Reduction of *O(Task/Precondition)*
	4	and *P(Task)&O(Task/Precondition)*

SeveralPhiReductionRule (Layer 0):

1. The rule deletes one edge of type *SF*.

3. $dl(SF) = 0 \leq rl(SeveralPhiReductionRule) = 0$

4. No item created!

IterationRepeatUntilRule (Layer 0):

1. The rule deletes one node of type *Task*.

3. $dl(Task) = 0 \leq rl(IterationRepeatUntilRule) = 0$

4. $cl(O(Task)) = 5 > rl(IterationRepeatUntilRule) = 0$

Table 5.10: Manual TA of DeonticBpmnGTS: Node Types & Edge Label

Type	cl(t)	dl(t)
ParallelGateway	0	2
ExclusiveGateway	0	2
InclusiveGateway	0	2
O(Task)	5	5
O(Task|Precondition)	1	3
X(Task)	3	5
X(Task|Precondition)	0	5
P(Task)	3	5
P(Task|Precondition)	0	5
P(Task)&O(Task|Precondition)	3	4
Task	0	0
StartEvent	0	5
EndEvent	0	5
MeasuredValues	0	5
SF	0	0

SequenceRuleBase (Layer 0):

1. The rule deletes one node of type *Task*.

3. $dl(Task) = 0 \leq rl(SequenceRuleBase) = 0$

4. $cl(O(Task|Precondition)) = 1 > rl(SequenceRuleBase) = 0$

SequenceRuleExtended (Layer 0):

1. The rule deletes one node of type *Task*.

3. $dl(Task) = 0 \leq rl(SequenceRuleExtended) = 0$

4. $cl(O(Task|Precondition)) = 1 > rl(SequenceRuleExtended) = 0$

SequenceRuleFinish (Layer 1):

1. The rule deletes one node of type *Task*.

3. $dl(Task) = 0 \leq rl(SequenceRuleFinish) = 1$

4. $cl(O(Task)) = 5 > rl(SequenceRuleFinish) = 1$

ParallelWithPhiDualRule (Layer 2):

1. The rule deletes one node of type *Task*, two nodes of type *ParallelGateway* and three edges of type *SF*.

3. $dl(Task) = 0 \leq rl(ParallelWithPhiDualRule) = 2$
   $dl(ParallelGateway) = 2 \leq rl(ParallelWithPhiDualRule) = 2$
   $dl(SF) = 0 \leq rl(ParallelWithPhiDualRule) = 2$

4. $cl(O(Task)) = 5 > rl(ParallelWithPhiDualRule) = 2$

ParallelRule (Layer 2):

1. The rule deletes one node of type *Task*.

3. $dl(Task) = 0 \leq rl(ParallelRule) = 2$

4. $cl(O(Task)) = 5 > rl(ParallelRule) = 2$

ParallelRuleFinish (Layer 2):

1. The rule deletes one edge of type *SF*.

3. $dl(SF) = 0 \leq rl(ParallelRuleFinish) = 2$

4. No item created!

ExclusiveWithPhiDualRule (Layer 2):

1. The rule deletes one node of type *Task*, two nodes of type *ExclusiveGateway* and three edges of type *SF*.

3. $dl(Task) = 0 \leq rl(ExclusiveWithPhiDualRule) = 2$
   $dl(ExclusiveGateway) = 2 \leq rl(ExclusiveWithPhiDualRule) = 2$
   $dl(SF) = 0 \leq rl(ExclusiveWithPhiDualRule) = 2$

4. $cl(P(Task)) = 3 > rl(ExclusiveWithPhiDualRule) = 2$

ExclusiveWithPhiRule (Layer 2):

1. The rule deletes one node of type *Task*.

3. $dl(Task) = 0 \leq rl(ExclusiveWithPhiRule) = 2$

4. $cl(P(Task)) = 3 > rl(ExclusiveWithPhiRule) = 2$

ExclusiveWithPhiRuleFinish (Layer 2):

1. The rule deletes one edge of type *SF*.

3. $dl(SF) = 0 \leq rl(ExclusiveWithPhiRuleFinish) = 2$

4. No item created!

ExclusiveWithoutPhiRule (Layer 2):

1. The rule deletes one node of type *Task*.

3. $dl(Task) = 0 \leq rl(ExclusiveWithoutPhiRule) = 2$

4. $cl(X(Task)) = 3 > rl(ExclusiveWithoutPhiRule) = 2$

InclusiveWithPhiDualRule (Layer 2):

1. The rule deletes one node of type *Task*, two nodes of type *Inclusive-Gateway* and three edges of type *SF*.

3. $dl(Task) = 0 \leq rl(InclusiveWithPhiDualRule) = 2$
   $dl(InclusiveGateway) = 2 \leq rl(InclusiveWithPhiDualRule) = 2$
   $dl(SF) = 0 \leq rl(InclusiveWithPhiDualRule) = 2$

4. $cl(P(Task)) = 3 > rl(InclusiveWithPhiDualRule) = 2$

InclusiveWithPhiRule (Layer 2):

1. The rule deletes one node of type *Task*.

3. $dl(Task) = 0 \leq rl(InclusiveWithPhiRule) = 2$

4. $cl(P(Task)) = 3 > rl(InclusiveWithPhiRule) = 2$

InclusiveWithPhiRuleFinish (Layer 2):

1. The rule deletes one edge of type *SF*.

3. $dl(SF) = 0 \leq rl(InclusiveWithPhiRuleFinish) = 2$

4. No item created!

InclusiveWithoutPhiRule (Layer 2):

1. The rule deletes one node of type *Task*.

3. $dl(Task) = 0 \leq rl(InclusiveWithoutPhiRule) = 2$

4. $cl(P(Task)\&O(Task|Precondition)) = 3 > rl(InclusiveWithoutPhiRule) = 2$

SequenceBpmnRulePragmatic (Layer 3-4):

1. The rule deletes one node of type *O(Task|Precondition)* in layer 3 and one node of type *P(Task)&O(Task|Precondition)* in layer 4.

3. $dl(O(Task|Precondition)) = 3 \leq$
   $rl(SequenceBpmnRulePragmatic) = 3$
   $dl(P(Task)\&O(Task|Precondition)) = 4 \leq$
   $rl(SequenceBpmnRulePragmatic) = 4$

4. $cl(O(Task)) = 5 > rl(SequenceBpmnRulePragmatic) = 3 - 4$

SequenceDeonticRulePragmatic (Layer 3-4):

1. The rule deletes one node of type *O(Task|Precondition)* in layer 3 and one node of type *P(Task)&O(Task|Precondition)* in layer 4.

3. $dl(O(Task|Precondition)) = 3 \leq$
   $rl(SequenceDeonticRulePragmatic) = 3$
   $dl(P(Task)\&O(Task|Precondition)) = 4 \leq$
   $rl(SequenceDeonticRulePragmatic) = 4$

4. $cl(O(Task)) = 5 > rl(SequenceDeonticRulePragmatic) = 3 - 4$

Since all deletion layer conditions and consequently the termination criteria are fulfilled, it is proven that DeonticBpmnGTS is terminating.

5.6 Discussion

After proving that DeonticBpmnGTS is locally confluent and terminating, further results and conclusions are presented in this section. Although the transformation from BPMN to Deontic BPMN is unique, the opposite direction may be ambiguous. Nevertheless, it can be concluded that Deontic-BpmnGTS is globally deterministic, which allows to validate Hypothesis 3. In addition, Hypothesis 1 is approved and it can be confirmed that BPMN and Deontic BPMN are semantically equivalent.

5.6.1 Unidirectional Uniqueness

The transformation from BPMN to Deontic BPMN is locally confluent and terminating, thus, the result is unique. However, transforming in the other direction from Deontic BPMN to BPMN might be ambiguous, since the two rules *ExclusiveWithPhiDualRule* (Fig. 5.14) and *InclusiveWithPhiDualRule* (Fig. 5.19) transform to the same RHS. Thus, whenever a permissible task is part of the main flow, the transformation to BPMN can either result in surrounding exclusive or inclusive gateways.

5.6.2 Global Determinism

DeonticBpmnGTS is locally nondeterministic, since several rules might be applicable to a given graph and for a given rule several matches might be possible. Nevertheless, DeonticBpmnGTS is globally deterministic, since the proven local confluence and termination imply confluence, which in turn allows to conclude global determinism. This means that for each pair of terminating graph transformations $G \overset{*}{\Rightarrow} H_1$ and $G \overset{*}{\Rightarrow} H_2$, the resulting graphs H_1 and H_2 are isomorphic, so the overall result of the graph transformation is unique (cf. for this paragraph [31, p. 59-62]).

5.6.3 Validation of Hypotheses

Hypothesis 1 states that the transformation from BPMN to Deontic BPMN leads to equally many or fewer gateways and sequence flows. This hypothesis can be validated for that part of the transformation that is described by DeonticBpmnGTS. Every rule in DeonticBpmnGTS comprises a *Measured-Values* element, which counts the number of gateways and sequence flows.

Since every rule leads to equally many or fewer gateways and sequence flows, it can be concluded that the entire transformation results in equally many or fewer gateways and sequence flows.

Concerning the extended version of DeonticBpmnGTS, the rule *ExclusiveReplaceGatewayRuleBase* increases the number of gateways and sequence flows; however, the rule is only applied once per conditional gateway and the corresponding rule *ExclusiveReplaceGatewayRuleFinish* will in any case be executed afterwards and decreases the number of gateways and sequence flows by the same amount. Thus, the two rules together lead to equally many gateways and sequence flows.

Hypothesis 3 states that the transformation from BPMN to Deontic BPMN defined by the graph transformation system DeonticBpmnGTS is globally deterministic. This hypothesis can be validated, since the local confluence of DeonticBpmnGTS was proven in section 5.4 followed by the termination proof in section 5.5. Based on these proofs, global determinism of DeonticBpmnGTS can be concluded.

5.6.4   Semantic Equivalence

The semantic equivalence of BPMN and Deontic BPMN is proven in [93]. Although the combination of deontic logic and BPMN changes the display format, the meaning and behavior of the flow remains the same. Furthermore, the cyclomatic complexity according to McCabe, which measures the complexity of a model's decision structure [78], is unaffected, since even if a task is permissible, the user must decide whether to execute the task or not.

According to Varró et al., the most important correctness properties of a trusted model transformation are termination, uniqueness (confluence), and behavior preservation [130]. All three properties have been proven for DeonticBpmnGTS, so that the transformation from BPMN to Deontic BPMN can be called a trusted model transformation.

Chapter 6

Conclusion

This chapter provides the conclusion and is sub-divided into a summary of
the results, a final discussion of the three hypotheses and optional activities,
as well as a description of future work.

6.1 Summary

The goals of this thesis were to provide a formal definition of the BPMN syntax and to extend BPMN with deontic logic in order to highlight the modality
of activities and support actor modeling. These goals were addressed by the
following three contributions:

1. Definition of a BPMN Ontology

2. Extension of BPMLs with Deontic Logic

3. Graph Transformation from BPMN to Deontic BPMN

The first contribution is given by the definition of an ontology that formally
represents the syntactical definitions of BPMN based on description logic and
is called the *BPMN 2.0 Ontology*. The *BPMN 2.0 Ontology* comprises the
syntactical restrictions from the BPMN metamodel and the natural text of
the specification and revealed several contradictions (see appendix A.2). In
addition, the ontology can be used as a knowledge base to familiarize with
the BPMN elements and for syntax checking to identify correct, incorrect
and incomplete BPMN models. The *BPMN 2.0 Ontology* is available under

the creative commons license (CC BY-NC-SA 3.0) and can be downloaded from the SCCH website[1]. Until now (May 2012), the ontology was downloaded more than fifty times and several interesting discussions with other researchers arose.

The second contribution was the extension of BPMLs in general and BPMN in particular with deontic concepts to highlight modalities and specify the decisions directly within the corresponding activities. After an overview of possible deontic classifications and a discussion to which extent deontic logic should be used in process flows, the *Control-Flow Patterns* were extended with deontic concepts. The Control-Flow Patterns are part of the *Workflow Patterns* provided by van der Aalst et al. (see [129]) and specify the requirements for the process flow based on patterns for branching, synchronizing, multiple instances, etc. A major advantage of the Workflow Patterns is that they are independent of concrete BPMLs and, thus, the deontic extensions can be easily adapted for most concrete BPMLs including BPMN, UML ADs, and EPCs. Afterwards, the deontic extension was applied to BPMN and the result called *Deontic BPMN*. The deontic analysis is supported by a path exploration approach and the benefits of Deontic BPMN were demonstrated by a case study and a preliminary survey. Another issue addressed in this work was the limited support for actor modeling in BPMN. A new approach including deontic logic and speech act theory was proposed and evaluated based on the resource perspective of the Workflow Patterns.

The third contribution of this thesis was the definition of a graph transformation system that transforms models from a subset of BPMN to Deontic BPMN, called *DeonticBpmnGTS*. DeonticBpmnGTS is based on the algebraic graph transformation approach and consists of an attributed type graph with inheritance and eighteen transformation rules with positive and negative application conditions distributed across four layers. In order to show that the transformation from BPMN to Deontic BPMN is globally deterministic, it was proven that DeonticBpmnGTS is strictly AC-confluent (i.e. the resulting graph is unique) and terminating. The termination proof was complicated by inheritance relationships in the type graph, so a flattening algorithm was proposed and a flattening prototype developed. Upon request, the flattening prototype together with DeonticBpmnGTS were then sent to the AGG tool developers. Furthermore, the semantic equivalence of BPMN and Deontic BPMN is proven in [93], so DeonticBpmnGTS fulfills the most important correctness properties of a trusted model transformation.

---

[1]BPMN 2.0 Ontology: `http://www.scch.at/en/zugang-download-ontologie`

6.2 Discussion of Results

In this section, the three initially presented hypotheses are discussed and validated, and suggestions regarding optional activities are given.

6.2.1 Validation of Hypotheses

The first hypothesis claimed that the structural complexity of a process flow expressed in Deontic BPMN is equal to or lower than the BPMN equivalent (see Hypothesis 1 in section 1.3). This hypothesis is confirmed for several BPMLs including BPMN by the extension of the Control-Flow Patterns with deontic logic (see section 4.2.2). The extension with deontic logic never increases the number of elements but in several cases allows to remove surrounding gateways and alternative paths. The reduction of structural complexity is further demonstrated by a case study in section 4.3.3. Note that the extent to which the structural complexity can be reduced depends on the extent to which deontic logic is used (see section 4.1.6). Moreover, the approach for actor modeling in Deontic BPMN replaces pools and lanes by a task-based deontic classification. Due to this classification, it is sometimes possible to unify activities, providing the possibility to reduce the number of elements, but in seldom cases requiring additional gateways and sequence flows (see section 4.4.3). However, the unification of activities is optional and, thus, there is at least one transformation from Deontic BPMN to Deontic BPMN with actor modeling with an equal or reduced structural complexity.

In addition, the first hypothesis is also confirmed for the subset of BPMN models which are transformed to Deontic BPMN by DeonticBpmnGTS. Every transformation rule in DeonticBpmnGTS defines a *MeasuredValues* element, which counts the number of gateways and sequence flows. Since every rule leads to equally many or fewer gateways and sequence flows (see section 5.3.2), it can be concluded that the entire transformation results in an equal or smaller number of gateways and sequence flows. Regarding the extended version of DeonticBpmnGTS (see section 5.3.3), the replacement of, e.g., an exclusive gateway with a parallel gateway requires three consecutively executed rules. Although the first rule increases the number of gateways and sequence flows, the rule can only be applied once and the corresponding third rule decreases the number of gateways and sequence flows by the same amount. So all in all, the structural complexity of a process flow expressed in BPMN and Deontic BPMN is either the same or lower in the deontic extension.

The second hypothesis claimed that the extension of Deontic BPMN with actor modeling is more expressive than the *Swimlane* concept provided by standard BPMN (see Hypothesis 2 in section 1.3). This hypothesis is confirmed by a comparison of BPMN and Deontic BPMN with actor modeling based on the Workflow Resource Patterns (see section 4.4.4). BPMN only supports 8 out of 43 Resource Patterns, whereas Deontic BPMN with actor modeling provides full support for 15 patterns and partial or enhanced support for 4 further patterns. In addition, the possibility to increase the expressiveness was confirmed by a case study (see section 4.4.3).

Finally, the third hypothesis claimed that the transformation from BPMN to Deontic BPMN defined by the graph transformation system DeonticBpmn-GTS is globally deterministic (see Hypothesis 3 in section 1.3). This hypothesis is confirmed by the local confluence proof in section 5.4 and the termination proof in section 5.5. Based on these proofs, global determinism of DeonticBpmnGTS can be concluded.

6.2.2 Optional Activity

A drawback of many business process modeling languages is that modalities are implicitly expressed through the structure of the process flow (e.g., see [97, p. 253] for UML ADs). All activities are implicitly mandatory, and whenever something should be optional, the process flow is split to offer the possibility to execute the activity or to do nothing. This implies that the decision whether to execute one or more activities is described within another element, e.g. a gateway. Thus, the main idea of this thesis is to support explicitly optional activities in business process modeling languages like BPMN, UML ADs, and EPCs. An explicitly optional activity is deemed to be more intuitive and also positively affects the structural complexity and the understandability of the process flow. In the current work, optional activities were expressed based on the deontic concept of permission ($P(x)$) to provide a formal basis and support further concepts like pre- and postconditions as well as actor modeling.

However, the main recommendation for the common business process modeler is to use optional activities independently of a formal basis. The graphical representation of an optional activity should conform to the concrete BPML. For example, three possible representations of an optional BPMN activity, which are conform to the permitted extensions of BPMN diagrams (see [99]), are shown in Fig. 6.1. In Fig. 6.1(a), an activity is marked as optional by an additional marker that corresponds to the modal operator of possibility ($\Diamond$). The advantage of this representation is that markers are a well-known concept in BPMN and easy to understand; however, since activities may comprise several markers, a further marker can result in an overcrowded representation. Thus, another possibility is to define a different background color for an optional activity, e.g. green (see Fig. 6.1(b)). The advantage of this representation is that it is supported by most modeling tools; however, it requires diagrams to be colored. The last suggestion is shown in Fig. 6.1(c) and uses a dashed line to highlight an optional activity. This representation is easy to understand and presentable by several modeling tools. Note that the dashed line style does not conflict with the dotted line style of an event sub-process.

(a) Marker   (b) Color   (c) Line Style

Figure 6.1: Possible Representations of Optional Activities in BPMN

In summary, an explicitly optional activity reduces the structural complexity and increases the understandability of a process flow. Thus, optional activities should be supported in business process modeling languages like BPMN, UML ADs, and EPCs.

6.3 Future Work

Further goals are distinguished based on the three main contributions of this thesis. Considering the *BPMN 2.0 Ontology*, the first goal is to automatically generate the basic structure of the ontology from the XML schema of the BPMN specification. In addition, syntax checking currently requires the manual definition of concrete models, so only simple models were defined until now. Thus, another goal is to extend the syntax checker with a graphical tool (e.g., BPMN Modeler for Eclipse [30]), and to automatically validate the models against the ontology. For this purpose, the Jena Semantic Web framework can be used as suggested in [54]. Furthermore, the idea of using the ontology to query concrete BPMN diagrams, e.g. to count the number of activities with a given attribute set to true, arose in an industrial project. Finally, it is planned to provide a combined list of contradictions in the BPMN specification together with other researchers.

Considering *Deontic BPMN*, the preliminary survey showed problems with preconditions, especially in combination with multiple deontic classifications. Hence, the notation of preconditions should be revised within further work. In addition, a more comprehensive survey is necessary to confirm that optional activities increase the understandability. Furthermore, only activities were deontically classified or assigned to actors so far. Thus, another goal is to extend Deontic BPMN to also classify further elements like events and gateways. Finally, the approach for actor modeling in Deontic BPMN must be studied in more detail.

Considering *DeonticBpmnGTS*, the graph transformation is currently limited to structured diagrams, a basic set of BPMN elements, and one task per path. Thus, a further goal is to address these restrictions. The most challenging issue will be the transformation of unstructured diagrams. In addition, an extension of DeonticBpmnGTS that transforms conditional gateways to parallel gateways was presented in section 5.3.3. The transformation rules are currently restricted to complete and distinct decisions and neither confluence nor termination were proven. These issues should be addressed within further work to simplify the execution of business processes by a process engine. Finally, regarding the flattening algorithm, restricted dependency relationships of subtypes must be considered and the size of the resulting graph transformation system can be reduced by deleting unnecessary application conditions.

In summary, several open issues were identified and will be addressed within the *Vertical Model Integration* (VMI) research project. The two most important issues are the extension of the *BPMN 2.0 Ontology* with a graphical tool for syntax checking and a detailed evaluation of the approach for actor modeling in Deontic BPMN.

Acknowledgement: The thesis was carried out in the frame of the *Vertical Model Integration* (VMI) research project. The project *Vertical Model Integration* is supported within the program "Regionale Wettbewerbsfähigkeit OÖ 2007-2013" by the European Fund for Regional Development as well as the State of Upper Austria.

Appendix A

BPMN 2.0 Ontology

The *BPMN 2.0 Ontology* is based on the BPMN 2.0 specification [99] and developed using the *Web Ontology Language* (OWL) and the open source ontology editor Protégé (see [120]). The *BPMN 2.0 Ontology* is divided in two sub-ontologies; the first is called *bpmn20base* and contains the specifications taken from the BPMN metamodel including all class diagrams, the tables specifying the attributes and model associations, as well as the XML schemas. The second sub-ontology is called *bpmn20* and derived from the first ontology. The *bpmn20* ontology provides an extension and contains almost all further syntactical requirements taken from the natural text of the BPMN specification. Together, the two ontologies build the *BPMN 2.0 Ontology*.

The primary goal of the *BPMN 2.0 Ontology* is to provide a knowledge base that can be used to familiarize with BPMN. In addition, the ontology can be used as a syntax checker, which detects correct, incorrect, and incomplete models. A major advantage of syntax checking based on an ontology is the possibility to draw conclusions.

A short description of the *BPMN 2.0 Ontology* is provided in chapter 3 and includes the motivation and an evaluation of the ontology. However, only an overview of the classes and extracts of the object and data properties were presented. Furthermore, only a small number of contradictions in the BPMN specification were described. Thus, in the following a more detailed description of the *BPMN 2.0 Ontology* is provided (see section A.1) and further contradictions are listed in section A.2. Since the *BPMN 2.0 Ontology* can be downloaded for free, some installation guidelines are finally presented in section A.3.

A.1   Description

The *BPMN 2.0 Ontology* provides a formal description of the syntactical
definitions of BPMN resulting in about 18.800 lines of code (text format).
Furthermore, the ontology consists of 256 classes; the class hierarchy is shown
in Fig. 3.4 and further information is provided in Tab. A.1. In the first column
the name of the class is given and the second column provides a list of all
superclasses. Moreover, the number of restrictions in the base (NoRB) and in
the extended (NoRE) ontology are presented in the third and fourth column.
The last column then specifies whether the given class is a primitive or a
defined class (DC), i.e. whether it specifies only necessary or also sufficient
conditions. The list starts with all classes from the base ontology followed
by the classes from the extended ontology.

Table A.1: Classes of *BPMN 2.0 Ontology*

Name	Superclasses	NoRB	NoRE	DC
Base Ontology				
BaseElement	Thing	4	0	
Artifact	BaseElement	0	5	
Association	Artifact	3	0	
Group	Artifact	1	0	
TextAnnotation	Artifact	2	0	
Assignment	BaseElement	2	0	
Auditing	BaseElement	0	0	
CategoryValue	BaseElement	3	0	
ComplexBehaviorDefinition	BaseElement	2	0	
ConversationAssociation	BaseElement	2	0	
ConversationLink	BaseElement	3	1	
ConversationNode	BaseElement and InteractionNode	4	0	
CallConversation	ConversationNode	2	2	
Conversation	ConversationNode	0	0	
SubConversation	ConversationNode	1	1	
CorrelationKey	BaseElement	2	0	
CorrelationPropertyBinding	BaseElement	2	0	
CorrelationPropertyRetrieval-Expression	BaseElement	2	0	
CorrelationSubscription	BaseElement	2	0	
DataAssociation	BaseElement	4	2	
DataInputAssociation	DataAssociation	0	0	
DataOutputAssociation	DataAssociation	0	0	
DataState	BaseElement	1	0	
Definitions	BaseElement	11	0	
Documentation	BaseElement	2	0	
Expression	BaseElement	0	0	
FormalExpression	Expression	3	0	
FlowElement	BaseElement	4	0	
DataObject	FlowElement and ItemAwareElement	1	2	
DataObjectReference	FlowElement and ItemAwareElement	1	1	
DataStoreReference	FlowElement and ItemAwareElement	1	0	
FlowNode	FlowElement	2	0	

Name	Superclasses	NoRB	NoRE	DC
Activity	FlowNode	12	2	
CallActivity	Activity	1	0	
SubProcess	Activity and FlowElementsContainer	2	17	
AdHocSubProcess	SubProcess	3	17	✓
Transaction	SubProcess	2	6	
Task	Activity and InteractionNode	0	4	
BusinessRuleTask	Task	1	0	
ManualTask	Task	0	0	
ReceiveTask	Task	4	1	
ScriptTask	Task	2	1	
SendTask	Task	3	0	
ServiceTask	Task	2	0	
UserTask	Task	4	0	
ChoreographyActivity	FlowNode	4	1	
CallChoreography	ChoreographyActivity	2	0	
ChoreographyTask	ChoreographyActivity	1	1	
SubChoreography	ChoreographyActivity and FlowElementsContainer	1	14	
Event	FlowNode and InteractionNode	1	6	
CatchEvent	Event	6	1	
BoundaryEvent	CatchEvent	2	9	
IntermediateCatchEvent	CatchEvent	0	7	
StartEvent	CatchEvent	1	8	
ThrowEvent	Event	5	2	
EndEvent	ThrowEvent	0	7	
ImplicitThrowEvent	ThrowEvent	0	0	
IntermediateThrowEvent	ThrowEvent	0	6	
Gateway	FlowNode	1	2	
ComplexGateway	Gateway	4	0	
EventBasedGateway	Gateway	2	7	
ExclusiveGateway	Gateway	1	0	
InclusiveGateway	Gateway	1	0	
ParallelGateway	Gateway	0	0	
SequenceFlow	FlowElement	4	5	
FlowElementsContainer	BaseElement	2	6	
Choreography	FlowElementsContainer and Collaboration	0	20	
GlobalChoreographyTask	Choreography	1	1	
Process	FlowElementsContainer and CallableElement	12	10	
InputOutputBinding	BaseElement	3	0	
InputOutputSpecification	BaseElement	4	0	
InputSet	BaseElement	5	0	
InteractionNode	BaseElement	0	0	
Participant	InteractionNode and BaseElement	7	0	
ItemAwareElement	BaseElement	2	0	
DataInput	ItemAwareElement	5	2	
DataOutput	ItemAwareElement	5	2	
DataStore	ItemAwareElement and RootElement	3	0	
Property	ItemAwareElement	1	1	
Lane	BaseElement	5	0	
LaneSet	BaseElement	4	0	
LoopCharacteristics	BaseElement	1	0	
MultiInstanceLoopCharacteristics	LoopCharacteristics	16	3	
StandardLoopCharacteristics	LoopCharacteristics	3	0	
MessageFlow	BaseElement	4	3	
MessageFlowAssociation	BaseElement	2	0	

Name	Superclasses	NoRB	NoRE	DC
Monitoring	BaseElement	0	0	
Operation	BaseElement	5	0	
OutputSet	BaseElement	5	0	
ParticipantAssociation	BaseElement	2	0	
ParticipantMultiplicity	BaseElement	3	0	
Relationship	BaseElement	4	0	
Rendering	BaseElement	0	0	
ResourceAssignmentExpression	BaseElement	1	0	
ResourceParameterBinding	BaseElement	2	0	
ResourceRole	BaseElement	4	0	
Performer	ResourceRole	0	0	
HumanPerformer	Performer	0	0	
PotentialOwner	HumanPerformer	0	0	
RootElement	BaseElement	0	0	
CallableElement	RootElement	4	0	
GlobalTask	CallableElement	1	0	
GlobalBusinessRuleTask	GlobalTask	1	0	
GlobalManualTask	GlobalTask	0	0	
GlobalScriptTask	GlobalTask	2	0	
GlobalUserTask	GlobalTask	2	0	
Category	RootElement	2	0	
Collaboration	RootElement	12	0	
GlobalConversation	Collaboration	0	6	
CorrelationProperty	RootElement	3	0	
EndPoint	RootElement	0	0	
Error	RootElement	3	0	
Escalation	RootElement	3	0	
EventDefinition	RootElement	0	0	
CancelEventDefinition	EventDefinition	0	0	
CompensationEventDefinition	EventDefinition	2	0	
ConditionalEventDefinition	EventDefinition	1	0	
ErrorEventDefinition	EventDefinition	1	0	
EscalationEventDefinition	EventDefinition	1	0	
LinkEventDefinition	EventDefinition	3	0	
MessageEventDefinition	EventDefinition	2	0	
SignalEventDefinition	EventDefinition	1	0	
TerminateEventDefinition	EventDefinition	0	0	
TimerEventDefinition	EventDefinition	3	0	
Interface	RootElement	4	0	
ItemDefinition	RootElement	4	0	
Message	RootElement	2	0	
PartnerEntity	RootElement	2	0	
PartnerRole	RootElement	2	0	
Resource	RootElement	2	0	
ResourceParameter	RootElement	3	0	
Signal	RootElement	2	0	
DIDiagram	Thing	0	0	
BPMNDiagram	DIDiagram	0	0	
Element	Thing	0	0	
Enumerations	Thing	0	0	
AdHocOrderingEnumeration	Enumerations	2	0	✓
Parallel	AdHocOrderingEnumeration and EventBasedGatewayTypeEnumeration	0	0	
Sequential	AdHocOrderingEnumeration	0	0	
AssociationDirectionEnumeration	Enumerations	2	0	✓
Both	AssociationDirectionEnumeration and RelationshipDirectionEnumeration	0	0	

Name	Superclasses	NoRB	NoRE	DC
None	AssociationDirectionEnumeration and ChoreographyLoopTypeEnumeration and MultiInstanceBehaviorEnumeration and ProcessTypeEnumeration and RelationshipDirectionEnumeration	0	0	
One	AssociationDirectionEnumeration and MultiInstanceBehaviorEnumeration	0	0	
ChoreographyLoopTypeEnumeration	Enumerations	2	0	✓
MultiInstanceParallel	ChoreographyLoopTypeEnumeration	0	0	
MultiInstanceSequential	ChoreographyLoopTypeEnumeration	0	0	
Standard	ChoreographyLoopTypeEnumeration	0	0	
EventBasedGatewayTypeEnumeration	Enumerations	2	0	✓
Exclusive	EventBasedGatewayTypeEnumeration	0	0	
GatewayDirectionEnumeration	Enumerations	2	0	✓
Converging	GatewayDirectionEnumeration	0	0	
Diverging	GatewayDirectionEnumeration	0	0	
Mixed	GatewayDirectionEnumeration	0	0	
Unspecified	GatewayDirectionEnumeration	0	0	
ItemKindEnumeration	Enumerations	2	0	✓
Information	ItemKindEnumeration	0	0	
Physical	ItemKindEnumeration	0	0	
MultiInstanceBehaviorEnumeration	Enumerations	2	0	✓
All	MultiInstanceBehaviorEnumeration	0	0	
Complex	MultiInstanceBehaviorEnumeration	0	0	
ProcessTypeEnumeration	Enumerations	2	0	✓
Private	ProcessTypeEnumeration	0	0	
Public	ProcessTypeEnumeration	0	0	
RelationshipDirectionEnumeration	Enumerations	2	0	✓
Backward	RelationshipDirectionEnumeration	0	0	
Forward	RelationshipDirectionEnumeration	0	0	
Extension	Thing	2	0	
ExtensionAttributeDefinition	Thing	3	0	
ExtensionAttributeValue	Thing	3	0	
ExtensionDefinition	Thing	2	0	
Import.	Thing	3	0	
Extended Ontology				
CollapsedSubConversation	SubConversation		2	✓
ExpandedSubConversation	SubConversation		2	✓
CollapsedSubProcess	SubProcess		2	✓
EmbeddedSubProcess	SubProcess		5	
EventSubProcess	SubProcess		9	✓
ExpandedSubProcess	SubProcess		2	✓
AbstractTask	Task		0	
CollapsedSubChoreography	SubChoreography		2	✓
ExpandedSubChoreography	SubChoreography		2	✓
StartEventEventSubProcess	StartEvent		3	✓
StartEventNotEventSubProcess	StartEvent		3	✓
CancelEvent	Event		7	✓
CancelEventInterrupting	CancelEvent		3	✓
CompensationEvent	Event		7	✓
CompensationEventInterrupting	CompensationEvent		3	✓
ConditionalEvent	Event		7	✓

Name	Superclasses	NoRB	NoRE	DC
ConditionalEventInterrupting	ConditionalEvent		3	✓
ConditionalEventNonInterrupting	ConditionalEvent		3	✓
ErrorEvent	Event		7	✓
ErrorEventInterrupting	ErrorEvent		3	✓
EscalationEvent	Event		7	✓
EscalationEventInterrupting	EscalationEvent		3	✓
EscalationEventNonInterrupting	EscalationEvent		3	✓
LinkEvent	Event		7	✓
LinkEventInterrupting	LinkEvent		4	✓
MessageEvent	Event		8	✓
MessageEventInterrupting	MessageEvent		3	✓
MessageEventNonInterrupting	MessageEvent		3	✓
MultipleEvent	Event		6	✓
MultipleEventInterrupting	MultipleEvent		3	✓
MultipleEventNonInterrupting	MultipleEvent		3	✓
NoneEvent	Event		7	✓
NoneEventInterrupting	NoneEvent		3	✓
ParallelMultipleEvent	Event		5	✓
ParallelMultipleEventInterrupting	ParallelMultipleEvent		3	✓
ParallelMultipleEventNonInterrupting	ParallelMultipleEvent		3	✓
SignalEvent	Event		7	✓
SignalEventInterrupting	SignalEvent		3	✓
SignalEventNonInterrupting	SignalEvent		3	✓
TerminateEvent	Event		7	✓
TerminateEventInterrupting	TerminateEvent		3	✓
TimerEvent	Event		7	✓
TimerEventInterrupting	TimerEvent		3	✓
TimerEventNonInterrupting	TimerEvent		3	✓
ExclusiveEventBasedGateway	EventBasedGateway		2	✓
ParallelEventBasedGateway	EventBasedGateway		3	✓
GatewayDirectionConverging	Gateway		4	✓
GatewayDirectionDiverging	Gateway		4	✓
GatewayDirectionMixed	Gateway		4	✓
GatewayDirectionUnspecified	Gateway		2	✓
SequenceFlowConditional	SequenceFlow		4	✓
SequenceFlowDefault	SequenceFlow		2	
SequenceFlowNormal	SequenceFlow		0	
PrivateProcess	Process		2	✓
PrivateExecutableProcess	PrivateProcess		2	✓
PrivateNonExecutableProcess	PrivateProcess		2	✓
PublicProcess	Process		3	✓
EventMarkerEnumeration	Enumerations		1	✓
CancelEventMarker	EventMarkerEnumeration		0	
CompensationEventMarker	EventMarkerEnumeration		0	
ConditionalEventMarker	EventMarkerEnumeration		0	
ErrorEventMarker	EventMarkerEnumeration		0	
EscalationEventMarker	EventMarkerEnumeration		0	
LinkEventMarker	EventMarkerEnumeration		0	
MessageEventMarker	EventMarkerEnumeration		0	
MultipleEventMarker	EventMarkerEnumeration		0	
NoneEventMarker	EventMarkerEnumeration		0	
ParallelMultipleEventMarker	EventMarkerEnumeration		0	
SignalEventMarker	EventMarkerEnumeration		0	
TerminateEventMarker	EventMarkerEnumeration		0	

Name	Superclasses	NoRB	NoRE	DC
TimerEventMarker	EventMarkerEnumeration		0	
MarkerEnumeration	Enumerations		1	✓
AdHocMarker	MarkerEnumeration		0	
CollapsedMarker	MarkerEnumeration		0	
CompensationMarker	MarkerEnumeration		0	
LoopMarker	MarkerEnumeration		1	✓
MultiInstanceLoopMarker	LoopMarker		0	
StandardLoopMarker	LoopMarker		0	
MultiInstanceMarker	MarkerEnumeration		1	✓
ParallelMultiInstanceMarker	MultiInstanceMarker		0	
SequentialMultiInstanceMarker	MultiInstanceMarker		0	
TransactionResultEnumeration	Enumerations		1	✓
FailedCompletion	TransactionResultEnumeration		0	
Hazard	TransactionResultEnumeration		0	
SuccessfulCompletion	TransactionResultEnumeration		0	

The 178 object properties are presented in detail in Tab. A.2. For each object property the domain and range are specified in the second and third column. For example, the object property *artifacts* may be defined for *Processes, Sub-Processes, Collaborations,* or *SubChoreographies* and may reference *Artifacts*. In addition, the fourth column defines whether the object property is functional (FCN). If a property is functional, then an individual of the domain can reference at most one individual of the range.

Table A.2: Object Properties of *BPMN 2.0 Ontology*

Name	Domain	Range	FCN
	Base Ontology		
activationCondition	ComplexGateway	Expression	✓
activityRef	CompensationEventDefinition	Activity	✓
artifacts	Collaboration or Process or SubChoreography or SubProcess	Artifact	
assignment	DataAssociation	Assignment	
associationDirection	Association	AssociationDirectionEnumeration	✓
attachedTo	BoundaryEvent	Activity	✓
auditing	FlowElement or Process	Auditing	✓
behavior	MultiInstanceLoopCharacteristics	MultiInstanceBehaviorEnumeration	✓
body	Expression	Element	✓
boundaryEventRefs	Activity	BoundaryEvent	
callableElements	Interface	CallableElement	
calledChoreographyRef	CallChoreography	CallableElement	✓
calledCollaborationRef	CallConversation	Collaboration	✓
calledElement	CallActivity	CallableElement	✓
categorizedFlowElements	CategoryValue	FlowElement	
category	CategoryValue	Category	✓

Name	Domain	Range	FCN
categoryValue	Category	CategoryValue	
categoryValueRef	FlowElement or Group	CategoryValue	
childLaneSet	Lane	LaneSet	✓
choreographyRef	Collaboration	Choreography	
completionCondition	AdHocSubProcess or MultiInstanceLoopCharacteristics	Expression	✓
complexBehaviorDefinition	MultiInstanceLoopCharacteristics	ComplexBehaviorDefinition	
condition	ComplexBehaviorDefinition or ConditionalEventDefinition	Expression or FormalExpression	✓
conditionExpression	SequenceFlow	Expression	✓
conversationAssociations	Collaboration	ConversationAssociation	
conversationLinks	Collaboration	ConversationLink	
conversationNodes	SubConversation	ConversationNode	
conversations	Collaboration	ConversationNode	
correlationKeyRef	CorrelationSubscription	CorrelationKey	✓
correlationKeys	ChoreographyActivity or Collaboration or ConversationNode	CorrelationKey	
correlationPropertyBinding	CollaborationSubscription	CorrelationPropertyBinding	
correlationPropertyRef	CollaborationKey or CorrelationPropertyBinding	CorrelationProperty	
correlationPropertyRetrievalExpression	CorrelationProperty	CorrelationPropertyRetrievalExpression	
correlationSubscriptions	Process	CorrelationSubscription	
dataInputAssociations	Activity or ThrowEvent	DataInputAssociation	
dataInputRefs	InputSet	DataInput	
dataInputs	InputOutputSpecification or ThrowEvent	DataInput	
dataObjectRef	DataObjectReference	DataObject	✓
dataOutputAssociations	Activity or CatchEvent	DataOutputAssociation	
dataOutputRefs	OutputSet	DataOutput	
dataOutputs	CatchEvent or InputOutputSpecification	DataOutput	
dataPath	CorrelationPropertyBinding	FormalExpression	✓
dataState	ItemAwareElement	DataState	✓
dataStoreRef	DataStoreReference	DataStore	✓
default	Activity or Gateway	SequenceFlow	✓
definition	Extension	ExtensionDefinition	✓
definitionalCollaborationRef	Process	Collaboration	✓
diagrams	Definitions	BPMNDiagram	
direction	Relationship	RelationshipDirectionEnumeration	✓
documentation	BaseElement	Documentation	
endPointRefs	Participant	EndPoint	
error	ErrorEventDefinition	Error	✓
errorRef	Operation	Error	
escalationRef	EscalationEventDefinition	Escalation	✓
escalationToTypeRef	FormalExpression	ItemDefinition	✓
event	ComplexBehaviorDefinition	ImplicitThrowEvent	✓
eventDefinitionRefs	Event	EventDefinition	
eventDefinitions	Event	EventDefinition	
eventGatewayType	EventBasedGateway	EventBasedGatewayTypeEnumeration	✓

Name	Domain	Range	FCN
expression	ResourceAssignmentExpression or ResourceParameterBinding	Expression	✓
extensionAttributeDefinition	ExtensionAttributeValue	ExtensionAttributeDefinition	✓
extensionAttributeDefinitions	ExtensionDefinition	ExtensionAttributeDefinition	
extensionDefinitions	BaseElement	ExtensionDefinition	
extensionValues	BaseElement	ExtensionAttributeValue	
extensions	Definitions	Extension	
flowElements	FlowElementsContainer	FlowElement	
flowNodeRefs	Lane	FlowNode	
from	Assignment	Expression	✓
gatewayDirection	Gateway	GatewayDirectionEnumeration	✓
implementationRef	Interface or Operation	Element	✓
import	ItemDefinition	Import.	✓
imports	Definitions	Import.	
inMessageRef	Operation	Message	✓
incoming	FlowNode	SequenceFlow	
initiatingParticipantRef	ChoreographyActivity or GlobalChoreographyTask	Participant	✓
innerConversationNodeRef	ConversationAssociation	ConversationNode	✓
innerMessageFlowRef	MessageFlowAssociation	MessageFlow	✓
innerParticipantRef	ParticipantAssociation	Participant	✓
inputDataItem	MultiInstanceLoopCharacteristics	DataInput	✓
inputDataRef	InputOutputBinding	DataInput	✓
inputSet	ThrowEvent	InputSet	✓
inputSetRefs	DataInput or OutputSet	InputSet	
inputSetWithOptional	DataInput	InputSet	
inputSetWithWhileExecuting	DataInput	InputSet	
inputSets	InputOutputSpecification	InputSet	
interfaceRef	Participant or Process	Interface	
ioBinding	CallableElement	InputOutputBinding	
ioSpecification	Activity or CallableElement	InputOutputSpecification	✓
itemKind	ItemDefinition	ItemKindEnumeration	✓
itemRef	Message	ItemDefinition	✓
itemSubjectRef	ItemAwareElement	ItemDefinition	✓
laneSets	FlowElementsContainer	LaneSet	
lanes	LaneSet	Lane	
loopCardinality	MultiInstanceLoopCharacteristics	Expression	✓
loopCharacteristics	Activity	LoopCharacteristics	✓
loopCondition	StandardLoopCharacteristics	Expression	✓
loopDataInputRef	MultiInstanceLoopCharacteristics	ItemAwareElement	✓
loopDataOutputRef	MultiInstanceLoopCharacteristics	ItemAwareElement	✓
loopType	ChoreographyActivity	ChoreographyLoopTypeEnumeration	✓
messageFlowAssociations	Collaboration	MessageFlowAssociation	
messageFlowRef	ChoreographyTask	MessageFlow	
messageFlowRefs	ConversationNode	MessageFlow	
messageFlows	Collaboration	MessageFlow	

Name	Domain	Range	FCN
messagePath	CorrelationPropertyRetrieval-Expression	FormalExpression	✓
messageRef	CorrelationPropertyRetrieval-Expression or Event or MessageEventDefinition or MessageFlow or Task	Message	✓
monitoring	FlowElement or Process	Monitoring	✓
noneBehaviorEventRef	MultiInstanceLoopCharacter-istics	EventDefinition	✓
oneBehaviorEventRef	MultiInstanceLoopCharacter-istics	EventDefinition	✓
operationRef	InputOutputBinding or MessageEventDefinition or Task	Operation	✓
operations	Interface	Operation	
optionalInputRefs	InputSet	DataInput	
optionalOutputRefs	OutputSet	DataOutput	
ordering	AdHocSubProcess	AdHocOrderingEnumeration	✓
outMessageRef	Operation	Message	✓
outerConversationNode-Ref	ConversationAssociation	ConversationNode	
outerMessageFlowRef	MessageFlowAssociation	MessageFlow	✓
outerParticipantRef	ParticipantAssociation	Participant	✓
outgoing	FlowNode	SequenceFlow	
outputDataItem	MultiInstanceLoopCharacter-istics	DataOutput	✓
outputDataRef	InputOutputBinding	DataOutput	✓
outputSet	CatchEvent	OutputSet	✓
outputSetRefs	DataOutput or InputSet	OutputSet	
outputSetWithOptional	DataOutput	OutputSet	
outputSetWithWhile-Executing	DataOutput	OutputSet	
outputSets	InputOutputSpecification	OutputSet	
parameterRef	ResourceParameterBinding	ResourceParameter	✓
parentLane	LaneSet	Lane	✓
participantAssociations	CallChoreography or CallConversation or Collaboration	ParticipantAssociation	
participantMultiplicity-Ref	Participant	ParticipantMultiplicity	✓
participantRef	PartnerEntity or PartnerRole	Participant	
participantRefs	ChoreographyActivity or ConversationNode	Participant	
participants	Collaboration	Participant	
partitionElement	Lane	BaseElement	✓
partitionElementRef	Lane	BaseElement	✓
partnerEntityRef	Participant	PartnerEntity	✓
partnerRoleRef	Participant	PartnerRole	✓
process	LaneSet	Process	✓
processRef	Participant	Process	✓
processType	Process	ProcessTypeEnumeration	✓
properties	Activity or Event or Process	Property	
relationships	Definitions	Relationship	
renderings	GlobalUserTask or UserTask	Rendering	
resourceAssignmentEx-pression	ResourceRole	ResourceAssignmentExpres-sion	✓
resourceParameterBind-ings	ResourceRole	ResourceParameterBinding	
resourceParameters	Resource	ResourceParameter	

Name	Domain	Range	FCN
resourceRef	ResourceRole	Resource	✓
resources	Activity or GlobalTask or Process	ResourceRole	
rootElements	Definitions	RootElement	
signalRef	SignalEventDefinition	Signal	✓
sourceRef	Association or ConversationLink or DataAssociation or MessageFlow or SequenceFlow	BaseElement or FlowNode or InteractionNode or ItemAwareElement	
sources	LinkEventDefinition or Relationship	Element or LinkEventDefinition	
structureRef	Error or Escalation or ItemDefinition	Element or ItemDefinition	✓
supportedInterfaceRefs	CallableElement	Interface	
supports	Process	Process	
target	LinkEventDefinition	LinkEventDefinition	✓
targetRef	Association or ConversationLink or DataAssociation or MessageFlow or SequenceFlow	BaseElement or FlowNode or InteractionNode or ItemAwareElement	
targets	Relationship	Element	
timeCycle	TimerEventDefinition	Expression	✓
timeDate	TimerEventDefinition	Expression	✓
timeDuration	TimerEventDefinition	Expression	✓
to	Assignment	Expression	✓
transformation	DataAssociation	Expression	✓
type.	CorrelationProperty or ResourceParameter	ItemDefinition	✓
value(.)	ExtensionAttributeValue	Element	✓
valueRef	ExtensionAttributeValue	Element	✓
whileExecutingInput-Refs	InputSet	DataInput	
whileExecutingOutput-Refs	OutputSet	DataOutput	
Extended Ontology			
hasElement	Thing	Thing	
hasEventMarker	Thing	EventMarkerEnumeration	✓
hasMarker	Thing	MarkerEnumeration	
hasResult	Thing	TransactionResultEnumeration	✓
incomingDataAssociation	Thing	DataAssociation	
incomingMsgFlow	Thing	MessageFlow	
isElementOf	Thing	Thing	
outgoingAssociation	Thing	Association	
outgoingDataAssociation	Thing	DataAssociation	
outgoingMsgFlow	Thing	MessageFlow	
usedAs	Cancel- or Compensation- or Conditional- or Error- or Escalation- or Link- or Message- or Multiple- or None- or ParallelMultiple- or Signal- or Terminate- or TimerEvent	CatchEvent or ThrowEvent	

The 59 data properties of the *BPMN 2.0 Ontology* are presented in Tab. A.3. The domain and data type of each property are specified in the second and third column. Again, the fourth column defines whether the data property is functional or not; however, in our case every property may have at most one value so all data properties are functional.

Table A.3: Data Properties of *BPMN 2.0 Ontology*

Name	Domain	Type	FCN
Base Ontology			
activationCount	ComplexGateway	integer	✓
actualOwner	UserTask	string	✓
cancelActivity	BoundaryEvent	boolean	✓
cancelRemainingInstances	AdHocSubProcess	boolean	✓
capacity	DataStore	integer	✓
completionQuantity	Activity	integer	✓
errorCode	Error	string	✓
escalationCode	Escalation	string	✓
exporter	Definitions	string	✓
exporterVersion	Definitions	string	✓
expressionLanguage	Definitions	string	✓
id	BaseElement	string	✓
implementation	GlobalTask or Task	string	✓
importType	Import.	string	✓
instantiate	EventBasedGateway or ReceiveTask	boolean	✓
isClosed	Collaboration or Process	boolean	✓
isCollection	ItemAwareElement or ItemDefinition	boolean	✓
isExecutable	Process	boolean	✓
isForCompentsation	Activity	boolean	✓
isImmediate	SequenceFlow	boolean	✓
isInterrupting	BaseElement	boolean	✓
isReference	ExtensionAttributeDefinition	boolean	✓
isRequired	ResourceParameter	boolean	✓
isSequential	MultiInstanceLoopCharacteristics	boolean	✓
isUnlimited	DataStore	boolean	✓
language.	FormalExpression	string	✓
location	Import.	string	✓
loopCounter	LoopCharacteristics	integer	✓
loopMaximum	StandardLoopCharacteristics	integer	✓
maximum	ParticipantMultiplicity	integer	✓
method	Transaction	string	✓
minimum	ParticipantMultiplicity	integer	✓
mustUnderstand	Extension	boolean	✓
name	Thing	string	✓
namespace	Import.	string	✓
numParticipants	ParticipantMultiplicity	integer	✓
numberOfActiveInstances	MultiInstanceLoopCharacteristics	integer	✓
numberOfCompletedInstances	MultiInstanceLoopCharacteristics	integer	✓
numberOfInstances	MultiInstanceLoopCharacteristics	integer	✓
numberOfTerminatedInstances	MultiInstanceLoopCharacteristics	integer	✓
parallelMultiple	CatchEvent	boolean	✓
protocol	Transaction	string	✓
script	GlobalScriptTask or ScriptTask	string	✓

Name	Domain	Type	FCN
scriptFormat	ScriptTask	string	✓
scriptLanguage	GlobalScriptTask	string	✓
startQuantity	Activity	integer	✓
state	Activity or Process	string	✓
targetNamespace	Definitions	string	✓
taskPriority	UserTask	integer	✓
testBefore	StandardLoopCharacteristics	boolean	✓
text	Documentation or TextAnnotation	string	✓
textFormat	Documentation or TextAnnotation	string	✓
triggeredByEvent	SubProcess	boolean	✓
type.	ExtensionAttributeDefinition or Relationship	string	✓
typeLanguage	Definitions	string	✓
value(.)	CategoryValue	string	✓
waitForCompletion	CompensationEventDefinition	boolean	✓
waitingForStart	ComplexGateway	boolean	✓
	Extended Ontology		
isAttachedToBoundary	EndEvent or StartEvent	boolean	✓

A.2 Contradictions

During the definition of the *BPMN 2.0 Ontology*, several contradictions within the BPMN specification were identified. The following contradictions were reported to the OMG (see [100]):

- *IntermediateEvent* with *NoneEventMarker*: According to [99, p. 272], a *NoneEventMarker* can only be used for *StartEvent*, *Intermediate-CatchEvent*, and *EndEvent*. However, Table 10.89 in [99, p. 251] and Table 10.93 in [99, p. 261] define that an *IntermediateThrowEvent*, but not an *IntermediateCatchEvent*, may have a *NoneEventMarker* (Issue 15687).

- Relationship *calledChoreographyRef* of *CallChoreography*: According to the class diagram of *CallChoreography* ([99, p. 334]), the relationship *calledChoreographyRef* references *Choreography*. However, according to the description of model associations in Table 11.4 ([99, p. 335]), *calledChoreographyRef* references *CallableElement* (Issue 15807).

- Outgoing Paths after *InclusiveGateway*: According to [99, p. 38] and [99, p. 292], after an *InclusiveGateway* all combinations of paths may be taken, from zero to all. However, in [99, p. 352] it is defined that one or more alternative branches are chosen (Issue 15808).

- Cardinality of relationship *category* of *CategoryValue*: According to the class diagram in [99, p. 70], *CategoryValue* references exactly one *Category* (name of relationship not defined). However, according to Table 8.23 in [99, p. 71], the relationship *category* references *Category* with a cardinality of (0, 1) (Issue 15814).

- Attributes of *Transaction*: According to the class diagram, *Transaction* specifies two attributes, *protocol* and *method*, both of type string [99, p. 176], but in the corresponding description only *method* is mentioned and defined to be of type *TransactionMethod* [99, p. 180] (Issue 15815).

- Relationship *loopMaximum* of *StandardLoopCharacteristics*: According to the class diagram in [99, p. 189], the relationship *loopMaximum* of *StandardLoopCharacteristics* references an *Expression*. However, according to Table 10.28 in [99, p. 191], *loopMaximum* is of type integer (Issue 15816).

- Connection Rules for *MessageFlow*: According to Table 7.4 in [99, p. 44], *MessageFlows* can only connect to *Events* with *MessageEventMarker*. However, according to [99, p. 249], an *EndEvent* must be set to *MessageEventMarker* or *MultipleEventMarker* if there are any outgoing *MessageFlows* (Issue 15817).

- Attributes of *GlobalScriptTask*: The BPMN specification does not specify a table containing the attributes and model associations of *GlobalScriptTask*. However, according to the class diagram of *GlobalTask* ([99, p. 188]) and the XML schema ([99, p. 198]), *GlobalScriptTask* specifies two attributes, *script* and *scriptLanguage*, both of type string. The first contradiction is that according to the class diagram, the attribute *script* has a cardinality of (1, 1) whereas the XML schema specifies the cardinality (0, 1). Furthermore, it is assumed that the attributes of *ScriptTask* and *GlobalScriptTask* should correspond to each other. However, according to the class diagram ([99, p. 157]), *ScriptTask* has two attributes, *script* and *scriptFormat*, both of type string with cardinality (1, 1). This contradicts with Table 10.12 in [99, p. 165], which defines that the cardinality of *script* and *scriptFormat* is (0, 1). Furthermore, *scriptFormat* of *ScriptTask* contradicts with *scriptLanguage* of *GlobalScriptTask*. Moreover, also the attributes of *GlobalUserTask* differ from that of *UserTask* (Issue 15818).

- Element *Repository*: The natural text of the BPMN specification mentions an element *Repository* (see [99, p. 349]), which is not described in the BPMN metamodel and nowhere else mentioned (Issue 15819).

- Attributes of *ResourceRole*: According to the class diagram of *Resources* in [99, p. 154], *ResourceRole* has an attribute *name* of type string. However, in Table 10.5 in [99, p. 155] only three relationships but no attribute is mentioned (Issue 15891).

- Attributes of *CorrelationProperty*: According to the class diagram in [99, p. 76], *CorrelationProperty* has a relationship *type* with cardinality (0, 1) to *ItemDefinition*. However, in Table 8.32 in [99, p. 77], *type* is defined to be an attribute of type string (Issue 15893).

- Relationships of *Event*: According to [99, p. 84], the element *Event* inherits the attributes and model associations of *FlowElement* (should be *FlowNode*), but adds no additional attributes or model associations. However, according to the class diagram of *Event* (see [99, p. 84]), *Event* has one model association to *Property* with the name *properties* and the cardinality (0, *) (Issue 15894).

- Superclass of *ResourceParameter*: According to the class diagram ([99, p. 96]) and XML schema ([99, p. 103]), *ResourceParameter* inherits from *BaseElement* and has a relationship *type* with cardinality (0, 1) to *ItemDefinition*. However, according to the last paragraph in [99, p. 96], the *ResourceParameter* element inherits the attributes and model associations of *BaseElement* through its relationship to *RootElement*. The phrase "through its relationship to" is also used within other element descriptions and means that the described element is derived from the specified element. So the natural text defines that the element *ResourceParameter* is derived from *RootElement*. Furthermore, Table 8.50 in [99, p. 97] specifies no cardinality for the relationship *type* and, thus, leads to the assumption that the cardinality is (1, 1) (Issue 15900).

- Subclasses of *InteractionNode*: The contradiction concerning the subclasses of *InteractionNode* is described in section 3.3.4 (Issue 15901).

- Relationship from *Choreography* to *Artifacts*: According to the class diagram of *Artifacts* ([99, p. 66]), *Collaboration*, *Process*, *SubProcess*, and *SubChoreography* have a relationship to *Artifacts*, but *Choreography* is not mentioned. However, the natural text specifies that when an *Artifact* is defined it is contained within a *Collaboration* or a *FlowElementsContainer* (a *Process* or *Choreography*) [99, p. 66]. In addition, it is not consistent if only a *SubChoreography* but not a *Choreography* may reference an *Artifact*. Furthermore, in [99, p. 321] it is defined that *Artifacts* can be used within *Choreographies* (Issue 15973).

- Cardinality of relationship *id* of *BaseElement*: According to Table 8.5 in [99, p. 56], the attribute *id* is of type string and, since no cardinality is specified, the cardinality is assumed to be (1, 1). However, according to the corresponding textual description, the *id* may be omitted. Thus, the cardinality should be (0, 1) (Issue 15974).

- Furthermore, some mistakes in form and content were reported (Issue 15666, 15667, 15679, 15681, 15682, 15686, 15806, 15809, 15810, 15811, 15812, 15817, 15839, 15883, 15892, 16003).

In addition, some further unpublished issues are described shortly:

- 42 attributes described in Table 2.1-2.4 (see [99, p. 3ff]) are not conform to the defined class diagrams of the BPMN metamodel.

- A *Choreography* consists of *ChoreographyActivities* but not of *Activities* as defined in [99, p. 25].

- In the class diagram of *FlowElement* (see [99, p. 87]), the also derived element *DataObjectReference* is missing.

- According to the natural text of the BPMN specification, the *Flow-Node* element does not inherit from any other BPMN element [99, p. 99]. However, according to the class diagram in [99, p. 87] and the XML schema in [99, p. 101], the *FlowNode* element is derived from *FlowElement*.

- In the class diagram of *Collaboration* (see [99, p. 109]), the relationship from *SubConversation* to *ConversationNode* is called *subConversation* but in the corresponding table the same relationship is called *conversationNodes*. In addition, the relationship *conversationAssociations* has according to the class diagram a cardinality of (1, 1) but the corresponding table specifies a cardinality of (0, *) [99, p. 110].

- According to the natural text of the BPMN specification, *PartnerRole* is derived from *BaseElement* [99, p. 117]. However, the class diagram of *Participant* specifies that *PartnerRole* inherits from *RootElement* [99, p. 115].

- According to the class diagram of *MessageFlow* ([99, p. 122]) and the XML schema in [99, p. 365], *ChoreographyTask* has a relationship *messageFlowRef* with cardinality (1, 2). However, the corresponding table ([99, p. 328]) defines a cardinality of (1, *).

- According to the *ConversationAssociation* class diagram ([99, p. 136]), the relationships *innerConversationNodeRef* and *outerConversation- NodeRef* define a cardinality of (1, 1). However, according to the corresponding table, *innerConversationNodeRef* has a cardinality of (0, 1) and *outerConversationNodeRef* a cardinality of (0, *) [99, p. 136].

- According to the class diagrams of *Artifacts* [99, p. 66] and *Process* [99, p. 147], the relationship *artifact* to *Artifact* has a cardinality of (0, 1). However, the corresponding table defines the slightly different name *artifacts* and a cardinality of (0, *) [99, p. 148].

- The elements *Activity* and *Event* are derived from *FlowNode* but not from *FlowElement* as stated in the natural text of the BPMN specification (see [99, p. 151] and [99, p. 235]).

- The elements *ServiceTask*, *SendTask*, *ReceiveTask*, *BusinessRuleTask*, *ScriptTask*, *ManualTask*, and *UserTask* are derived from *Task* and not from *Activity* as stated in the natural text of the BPMN specification (see [99, p. 159ff]).

- According to the class diagram in [99, p. 160], *SendTask* and *Receive- Task* define a relationship *operationRef* with cardinality (0, 1). However, the corresponding tables [99, p. 161f] specify the cardinality (1, 1).

- According to the natural text of the BPMN specification [99, p. 177], *StartEvent* may have the *EventMarkers Message, Error, Escalation, Compensation, Conditional, Signal,* and *Multiple*. However, Table 10.93 in [99, p. 261f] specifies two further *EventMarkers: Timer* and *Paral- lelMultiple*.

- According to the class diagram of *ItemAwareElement* [99, p. 204], the relationship *dataStoreRef* of *DataStoreReference* has a cardinality of (0, 1). However, the corresponding table defines a cardinality of (1, 1) [99, p. 210].

- According to the natural text of the BPMN specification, the attribute *optional* defines whether a *DataInput* is valid [99, p. 214]. However, this attribute is nowhere else mentioned.

- Since all subclasses of *Event* (*CatchEvent* and *ThrowEvent*) specify the same two relationships, *eventDefinitions* and *eventDefinitionRefs* (see [99, p. 234]), a suggestion is to define the relationships once within the superclass *Event*.

- According to the class diagram of *EventDefinition* [99, p. 262], the relationship *target* of *LinkEventDefinition* has a cardinality of (0, 1). However, the corresponding table explicitly defines a cardinality of (1, 1) [99, p. 270].

- According to the natural text of the BPMN specification, *SubProcess* has an attribute *compensable* [99, p. 304]. However, this attribute is nowhere else defined.

- Furthermore, several relationships in the class diagrams are named and sometimes specify a cardinality, but the model association is neither defined within the corresponding table nor within the XML schema. Concerned are, for example, the class diagrams of the core BPMN elements, *Definitions, Correlation, FlowElement, Gateway, SequenceFlow, Collaboration, Participant, ParticipantAssociation, ConversationAssociation, Resources, Event, Gateway,* and *Choreography.*

- In addition, there are several further XML schemas that do not correspond to the class diagram or the table specifying the attributes and model associations. Concerned are, for example, the XML schemas of *Extension, CategoryValue, TextAnnotation, CorrelationSubscription, FormalExpression, ItemDefinition, Interface, ConversationNode, MessageFlow, Participant, PartnerEntity, HumanPerformer, PartnerRole, Activity, AdHocSubProcess, ScriptTask, StandardLoopCharacteristics, SubProcess, DataInput, DataObject, DataOutput, Property, CompensateEventDefinition, ErrorEventDefinition, EscalationEventDefinition, Event, EventDefinition, LinkEventDefinition, MessageEventDefinition, Signal, SignalEventDefinition, ComplexGateway, Process, Lane, LaneSet, ChoreographyTask,* and *SubChoreography.*

A.3   Installation Guidelines

The *BPMN 2.0 Ontology* is available under the creative commons license (CC BY-NC-SA 3.0) (see http://creativecommons.org/licenses/by-nc-sa/3.0) and can be downloaded from:
http://www.scch.at/en/zugang-download-ontologie

In order to use the *BPMN 2.0 Ontology*, the open source ontology editor Protégé [120] must be installed. Download the current version of Protégé (in our case Protégé 4.1 (Build 239)) and install it on your computer. Save the two ontologies (bpmn20base.owl and bpmn20.owl) in the same folder and open the *bpmn20* ontology with Protégé. You can now switch between the two ontologies (see Fig. A.3).

The current version of Protégé provides the reasoners HermiT 1.3.4 and FaCT++. In addition, the Pellet reasoner can be installed manually. Open Protégé and select "File" → "Check for plugins..." and choose the Pellet Reasoner Plug-in (see Fig. A.1). Furthermore, you may want to update HermiT to version 1.3.5.

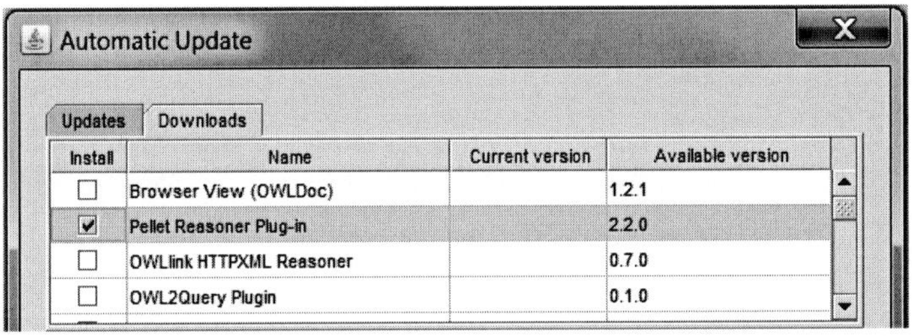

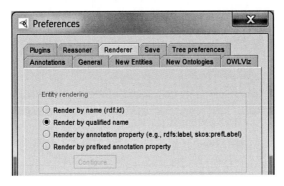

Figure A.1: Pellet Reasoner Plug-in

Afterwards, in order to display the prefixes, select "File" → "Preferences..." and switch to the tab "Renderer". Ensure that "Render by qualified name" is selected (see Fig. A.2). Afterwards, select the tab "Active Ontology" in the main window and switch to "Ontology Prefixes" (see Fig. A.3). It is recommended to use the prefix "base" for the *bpmn20base* ontology and the prefix "ext" for the *bpmn20* ontology.

Figure A.2: Render by qualified name

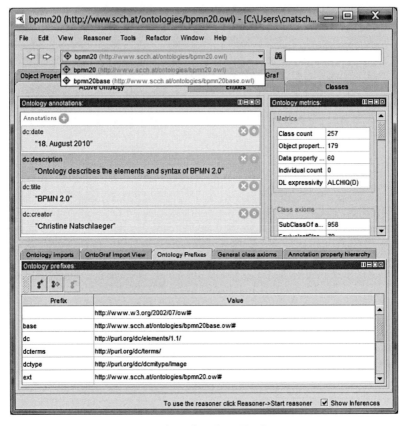

Figure A.3: Ontology Prefixes

Appendix B

Flattening Prototype

The termination proof executed by the tool AGG is limited to graph transformation systems without inheritance in the type graph. Since DeonticBpmn-GTS comprises abstract nodes and inheritance relationships, a flattening of the type graph is necessary. Thus, I defined the *Flattening Algorithm* (see section 5.5.3), which removes the inheritance relationships and abstract nodes from the type graph and thereby flattens the hierarchy of the GTS.

A prototype of the *Flattening Algorithm* is provided in the programming language C#. The `Main` method takes the XML-file generated by the tool AGG (.ggx) as input and asks the user whether an abstract or concrete flattening of the GTS should be executed. Afterwards, the method `FlattenHierarchyOf-GTS` is called in order to parse the XML-file and flatten the hierarchy.

```
static void Main(string[] args)
{
    Console.Out.Write("Insert File: ");
    string filename = Console.In.ReadLine();
    if (String.IsNullOrEmpty(filename))
    {
        filename = "C:\\tmp\\DeonticBPMN.ggx";
    }
    Console.Out.Write(
        "Abstract (1) or Concrete (2) Flattening: ");
    string abstractOrConcrete = Console.In.ReadLine();
    bool concrete = false;
    if (!String.IsNullOrEmpty(abstractOrConcrete) &&
        abstractOrConcrete.Equals("2"))
```

```
    {
        concrete = true;
    }
    FlattenHierarchy fh = new FlattenHierarchy();
    fh.FlattenHierarchyOfGTS(filename, concrete);
    Console.In.Read();
}
```

The class NodeType is defined in order to generate an object for each node
of the type graph. Every object provides three auto-implemented properties
to get and set the ID, a boolean field IsAbstract that defines whether the
node is abstract or not, and a list of ParentIDs, since algebraic graph transformation supports multiple inheritance. All three fields may be set by the
constructor. In addition, the method HasParents returns the value true if
the current node inherits from another node.

```
public class NodeType
{
    public string ID { get; set; }
    public bool IsAbstract { get; set; }
    public List<string> ParentIDs { get; set; }

    public NodeType(string id, bool isAbstr, List<string> pIDs)
    {
        ID = id;
        IsAbstract = isAbstr;
        ParentIDs = pIDs;
    }

    public bool HasParents()
    {
        return (ParentIDs != null && ParentIDs.Count != 0);
    }
}
```

The main class of the *Flattening Prototype* is called FlattenHierarchy and
defines four private fields to store the XmlDocument (doc), two dictionaries
of all nodes specified within the type graph (nodeDict, and origNodeDict),
and an integer field (idCounter) that provides the new IDs and is initialized
with the value 3000. Furthermore, a static field RuleNameAppendix defines

a string that is used to extend the new rule names. The constructor of this class is empty.

```
private XmlDocument doc = new XmlDocument();
private Dictionary<string, NodeType> nodeDict =
    new Dictionary<string, NodeType>();
private Dictionary<string, NodeType> origNodeDict =
    new Dictionary<string, NodeType>();
private int idCounter = 3000;
private static string RuleNameAppendix = "-";
```

The method `FlattenHierarchyOfGTS` is called by the `Main` method and loads the XmlDocument. The node types of the type graph are then read in and saved in the dictionaries `nodeDict` and `origNodeDict`. The method `ConsoleWriteNodeTypes` only informs the user of the node hierarchy and will not be shown in detail. Afterwards an abstract flattening of the type graph and all rules is executed in the private method `FlattenHierarchyOfGTS`. If the user chose a concrete flattening, then the abstract nodes are removed from the type graph and all rules with abstract nodes are deleted in the method `RemoveAbstractNodes`. In a last step, all flattened PACs are transformed to GACs and a boolean formula is defined in the method `ChangePacsToGacs`. The number of rules, PACs, and NACs in the flattened file are then provided by the method `ConsoleWriteResults` (not shown in detail).

```
public void FlattenHierarchyOfGTS(string filename,
    bool concrete)
{
    doc.Load(filename);
    ReadNodeTypes();
    ConsoleWriteNodeTypes();
    FlattenHierarchyOfGTS();
    if (concrete)
    {
        RemoveAbstractNodes();
    }
    ChangePacsToGacs();
    doc.Save("C:\\tmp\\DeonticBPMN-Flattened.ggx");
    ConsoleWriteResults();
    Console.Out.WriteLine(filename);
}
```

The method `ReadNodeTypes` extracts all node types from the XmlDocument
and creates an object containing the ID, a boolean field whether the node is
abstract, and a list of parent IDs. The objects are saved in the dictionaries
`nodeDict` and `origNodeDict`.

```
private void ReadNodeTypes()
{
    XmlNodeList list = doc.GetElementsByTagName("NodeType");
    foreach (XmlNode node in list)
    {
        string key = node.Attributes.GetNamedItem("ID").Value;
        bool isAbstract = Convert.ToBoolean(
            node.Attributes.GetNamedItem("abstract").Value);
        List<string> parentIDs = new List<string>();
        foreach (XmlNode child in node)
        {
            if (child.Name.Equals("Parent"))
            {
                parentIDs.Add(child.Attributes.
                    GetNamedItem("pID").Value);
            }
        }
        nodeDict.Add(key, new NodeType(key, isAbstract,
            parentIDs));
        origNodeDict.Add(key, new NodeType(key, isAbstract,
            parentIDs));
    }
}
```

The method `FlattenHierarchyOfGTS` is called once and provides an abstract
flattening of the GTS. The ordered inheritance relationships are iterated and
all rules, application conditions, and the type graph are considered.

In a first step all ACs are taken into account in the method `FlattenHierar-
chyOfGTSAcHelperOuter` and for every parent node type without morphisms,
the AC is duplicated and the node replaced by the child node type. Afterwards every generated AC in the `duplAcList` is again considered and
further nodes are replaced for as long as possible. These further ACs are
necessary to support combinations of child nodes. For example, if a NAC
consists of two nodes *X(Task)* without morphisms, then one NAC is generated with the node *X(Task/Precondition)* as first node and another NAC with

X(Task/Precondition) as second node. If those ACs are again considered in further calculations, then also the combination with *X(Task/Precondition)* as first and second node is identified. This approach may also lead to duplicate ACs. Thus, it is necessary to iterate all ACs and remove identical ones before inserting the remaining ACs in the XML-structure.

In a second step all rules are taken into account in the method `FlattenHierarchyOfGTSRuleHelper` and for every node that corresponds to the parent node type, the rule is duplicated and the node replaced by the child node type. Again the generated rules are taken as basic rules for further calculations to identify combinations. Afterwards the inheritance relationship between the parent and child node is deleted from the type graph and the child node receives the attributes as well as the dependency and inheritance relationships of its former parent node in the method `RemoveInheritanceBetweenNodes`. After all rules and inheritance relationships have been considered, the identical rules are deleted and the remaining ones inserted in the XML-structure.

```
private void FlattenHierarchyOfGTS()
{
    Dictionary<XmlNode, Dictionary<XmlNode, XmlNode>>
        duplAcDict = new Dictionary<XmlNode,
        Dictionary<XmlNode, XmlNode>>();
    Dictionary<XmlNode, XmlNode> duplRuleList =
        new Dictionary<XmlNode, XmlNode>();
    XmlNode parent = null;
    XmlNodeList ruleList = doc.GetElementsByTagName("Rule");
    List<KeyValuePair<string, string>> parentChildList =
        FindAllInheritancesBetweenNodes();
    foreach(KeyValuePair<string, string> parentChild
        in parentChildList)
    {
        foreach (XmlNode rule in ruleList)
        {
            parent = rule.ParentNode;
            if (!duplAcDict.ContainsKey(rule))
            {
                duplAcDict.Add(rule,
                    new Dictionary<XmlNode, XmlNode>());
            }
            Dictionary<XmlNode, XmlNode> duplAcList =
                duplAcDict[rule];
```

```
            duplAcList = FlattenHierarchyOfGTSAcHelperOuter(
                rule, parentChild, duplAcList);
            duplAcDict[rule] = duplAcList;
        }
        foreach (KeyValuePair<XmlNode,Dictionary<XmlNode,
            XmlNode>> duplAcListKvp in duplAcDict)
        {
            Dictionary<XmlNode, XmlNode> furtherAcList =
                FlattenFurtherHierarchyOfGTSAcHelper(
                duplAcListKvp.Value, parentChild);
            Dictionary<XmlNode, XmlNode> furtherfurtherAcList =
                furtherAcList;
            while (furtherfurtherAcList.Count > 0)
            {
                furtherfurtherAcList =
                    FlattenFurtherHierarchyOfGTSAcHelper
                    (furtherfurtherAcList, parentChild);
                foreach (KeyValuePair<XmlNode, XmlNode> duplAc
                    in furtherfurtherAcList)
                {
                    furtherAcList.Add(duplAc.Key,
                        duplAc.Value);
                }
            }
            foreach (KeyValuePair<XmlNode, XmlNode> duplAc
                in furtherAcList)
            {
                duplAcListKvp.Value.Add(duplAc.Key,
                    duplAc.Value);
            }
        }
    }
    foreach (KeyValuePair<XmlNode, Dictionary<XmlNode,
        XmlNode>> acKvp in duplAcDict)
    {
        Dictionary<XmlNode, XmlNode> acDict = acKvp.Value;
        acDict = RemoveIdenticACs(acDict);
        foreach (KeyValuePair<XmlNode, XmlNode> kvp in acDict)
        {
            kvp.Value.ParentNode.InsertAfter(kvp.Key,
                kvp.Value);
```

```
        }
    }
    foreach (KeyValuePair<string, string> parentChild
        in parentChildList)
    {
        foreach (XmlNode rule in ruleList)
        {
            parent = rule.ParentNode;
            duplRuleList = FlattenHierarchyOfGTSRuleHelper(
                rule, parentChild, duplRuleList);
        }
        Dictionary<XmlNode, XmlNode> furtherRuleList =
            FlattenFurtherHierarchyOfGTSRuleHelper(
            duplRuleList, parentChild);
        Dictionary<XmlNode, XmlNode> furtherfurtherRuleList =
            furtherRuleList;
        while (furtherfurtherRuleList.Count > 0)
        {
            furtherfurtherRuleList =
                FlattenFurtherHierarchyOfGTSRuleHelper(
                furtherfurtherRuleList, parentChild);
            foreach (KeyValuePair<XmlNode, XmlNode> duplRule
                in furtherfurtherRuleList)
            {
                furtherRuleList.Add(duplRule.Key,
                    duplRule.Value);
            }
        }
        foreach (KeyValuePair<XmlNode, XmlNode> duplRule
            in furtherRuleList)
        {
            duplRuleList.Add(duplRule.Key, duplRule.Value);
        }
        Console.Out.WriteLine("Parent: " + parentChild.Key +
            " Child: " + parentChild.Value);
        RemoveInheritanceBetweenNodes(parentChild);
    }
    duplRuleList = RemoveRulesWithIdenticNodesOnLhs(
        duplRuleList);
    foreach (KeyValuePair<XmlNode, XmlNode> duplRule
        in duplRuleList)
```

```
    {
        if (duplRule.Value.ParentNode != null)
        {
            parent.InsertAfter(duplRule.Key, duplRule.Value);
        }
        else
        {
            parent.AppendChild(duplRule.Key);
        }
    }
}
```

The method `FlattenHierarchyOfGTSAcHelperOuter` identifies all ACs of a transformation rule and calls the method `FlattenHierarchyOfGTSAcHelperInner` to consider the inheritance relationship of every single AC.

```
private Dictionary<XmlNode, XmlNode>
    FlattenHierarchyOfGTSAcHelperOuter(XmlNode rule,
    KeyValuePair<string, string> parentChild,
    Dictionary<XmlNode, XmlNode> duplAcList)
{
    XmlNode applCondition = null;
    foreach (XmlNode child in rule)
    {
        if (child.Name.Equals("ApplCondition"))
        {
            applCondition = child;
            break;
        }
    }
    if (applCondition != null)
    {
        foreach (XmlNode applChild in applCondition)
        {
            duplAcList = FlattenHierarchyOfGTSAcHelperInner(
                applChild, parentChild, duplAcList);
        }
    }
    return duplAcList;
}
```

The method `FlattenHierarchyOfGTSAcHelperInner` receives an AC, an inheritance relationship between two node types, and a list of the already generated ACs as input. For every node that has the same type as the parent node type and no morphism node in the LHS, the AC is duplicated and the child node type replaces the parent node type. Subsequently the IDs of the duplicated AC are updated and the AC is added to the list of generated ACs.

```
private Dictionary<XmlNode, XmlNode>
    FlattenHierarchyOfGTSAcHelperInner(XmlNode
    applChild, KeyValuePair<string, string> parentChild,
    Dictionary<XmlNode, XmlNode> duplAcList)
{
    if (applChild.Name.Equals("NAC") ||
        applChild.Name.Equals("PAC"))
    {
        XmlNode applGraph = null;
        XmlNode acMorphism = null;
        foreach (XmlNode acChild in applChild)
        {
            if (acChild.Name.Equals("Graph"))
            {
                applGraph = acChild;
            }
            if (acChild.Name.Equals("Morphism"))
            {
                acMorphism = acChild;
            }
        }
        foreach (XmlNode applGraphChild in applGraph)
        {
            if (applGraphChild.Name.Equals("Node"))
            {
                if (applGraphChild.Attributes.GetNamedItem(
                    "type").Value.Equals(parentChild.Key))
                {
                    string nodeId = applGraphChild.Attributes.
                        GetNamedItem("ID").Value;
                    string morphismNodeId = GetOriginalNode(
                        acMorphism, nodeId);
                    if (morphismNodeId == null)
```

```
                {
                    XmlNode duplAC = applChild.CloneNode(
                        true);
                    ReplaceNodeWithChild(duplAC,
                        applChild.Name, nodeId,
                        nodeDict[parentChild.Value]);
                    duplAC = ChangeIdsOfAC(duplAC);
                    duplAcList.Add(duplAC, applChild);
                }
            }
        }
    }
}
    return duplAcList;
}
```

The transformation rules are flattened by the method `FlattenHierarchy-OfGTSRuleHelper`. In a first step, the LHS, RHS, and morphism section of the rule are extracted. Subsequently the rule is duplicated for every node in the LHS that corresponds to the parent node type and the node is replaced by the child node type. If a morphism node exists in the RHS or in an AC, then this node is also replaced by the child node type. The RHS of a rule cannot comprise abstract nodes without morphisms, since all created nodes must have a concrete type according to the rules of algebraic graph transformation [31, p. 271]. Furthermore, the type of a created concrete node in the RHS remains the same. In a last step, the IDs of the duplicated rule are updated and the rule is added to the list of generated rules.

```
private Dictionary<XmlNode, XmlNode>
    FlattenHierarchyOfGTSRuleHelper(XmlNode rule,
    KeyValuePair<string, string> parentChild,
    Dictionary<XmlNode, XmlNode> duplRuleList)
{
    XmlNode lhs = null, rhs = null, morphism = null;
    foreach (XmlNode child in rule)
    {
        if (child.Name.Equals("Graph"))
        {
            if (child.Attributes.GetNamedItem("kind").
                Value.Equals("LHS"))
            {
```

```
            lhs = child;
        }
        else if (child.Attributes.GetNamedItem("kind").
            Value.Equals("RHS"))
        {
            rhs = child;
        }
    }
    if (child.Name.Equals("Morphism"))
    {
        morphism = child;
    }
}
foreach (XmlNode lhsChild in lhs)
{
    if (lhsChild.Name.Equals("Node") &&
        lhsChild.Attributes.GetNamedItem("type").Value.
        Equals(parentChild.Key))
    {
        string nodeId = lhsChild.Attributes.
            GetNamedItem("ID").Value;
        string rhsMorphismNodeId = GetMorphismNode(
            morphism, nodeId);
        XmlNode duplRule = rule.CloneNode(true);
        ReplaceNodeWithChild(duplRule, "LHS", nodeId,
            nodeDict[parentChild.Value]);
        if (!String.IsNullOrEmpty(rhsMorphismNodeId))
        {
            ReplaceNodeWithChild(duplRule, "RHS",
                rhsMorphismNodeId, nodeDict[parentChild.
                Value]);
        }
        ReplaceNodeInACsWithChild(duplRule, nodeId,
            nodeDict[parentChild.Value]);
        duplRule = ChangeIdsOfRule(duplRule);
        duplRuleList.Add(duplRule, rule);
    }
}
return duplRuleList;
}
```

The method `FlattenFurtherHierarchyOfGTSAcHelper` calls the method `FlattenHierarchyOfGTSAcHelperInner` for all generated ACs in order to identify combinations of derived nodes. Identical ACs are then removed and the list of distinct ACs is returned.

```
private Dictionary<XmlNode, XmlNode>
    FlattenFurtherHierarchyOfGTSAcHelper(
    Dictionary<XmlNode, XmlNode> duplAcList,
    KeyValuePair<string, string> parentChild)
{
    Dictionary<XmlNode, XmlNode> furtherAcList =
        new Dictionary<XmlNode, XmlNode>();
    foreach (KeyValuePair<XmlNode, XmlNode> duplAc
        in duplAcList)
    {
        furtherAcList = FlattenHierarchyOfGTSAcHelperInner(
            duplAc.Key, parentChild, furtherAcList);
    }
    return RemoveIdenticACs(furtherAcList);
}
```

The method `FlattenFurtherHierarchyOfGTSRuleHelper` is similar; it calls the method `FlattenHierarchyOfGTSRuleHelper` for all generated rules to identify combinations of derived nodes. It then deletes identical rules.

```
private Dictionary<XmlNode, XmlNode>
    FlattenFurtherHierarchyOfGTSRuleHelper(
    Dictionary<XmlNode, XmlNode> duplRuleList,
    KeyValuePair<string, string> parentChild)
{
    Dictionary<XmlNode, XmlNode> furtherRuleList =
        new Dictionary<XmlNode, XmlNode>();
    foreach (KeyValuePair<XmlNode, XmlNode> duplRule
        in duplRuleList)
    {
        furtherRuleList = FlattenHierarchyOfGTSRuleHelper(
            duplRule.Key, parentChild, furtherRuleList);
    }
    return RemoveRulesWithIdenticNodesOnLhs(
        furtherRuleList);
}
```

Inheritance relationships between node types are identified and ordered by the method `FindAllInheritancesBetweenNodes`. The inheritance relationships are ordered based on the number of steps that are necessary to reach the farthest root node with the smallest number (i.e., the root nodes) being inserted first. The maximum number of steps for reaching the root node are recursively determined.

Without an ordering a transformation rule might comprise a node of type *O(Task)* and if the inheritance relationship between *O(Task/Precondition)* and *P(Task)&O(Task/Precondition)* is considered before the relationship between *O(Task)* and *O(Task/Precondition)*, then no rule is generated with *P(Task)&O(Task/Precondition)*.

```
private List<KeyValuePair<string, string>>
    FindAllInheritancesBetweenNodes()
{
    List<KeyValuePair<string, string>> inheritanceList =
        new List<KeyValuePair<string, string>>();
    List<KeyValuePair<string, string>> nodes =
        new List<KeyValuePair<string, string>>();
    Dictionary<int, List<KeyValuePair<string, string>>>
        orderList = new Dictionary<int,
        List<KeyValuePair<string, string>>>();
    foreach (KeyValuePair<string, NodeType> kvp in nodeDict)
    {
        if (kvp.Value.HasParents())
        {
            foreach (string parentId in kvp.Value.ParentIDs)
            {
                if (!nodeDict[parentId].IsAbstract)
                {
                    nodes.Add(new KeyValuePair<string,
                        string>(parentId, kvp.Key));
                }
            }
        }
    }
    foreach (KeyValuePair<string, string> kvp in nodes)
    {
        int abstractionLevel = StepsOfInheritance(kvp);
        if (orderList.ContainsKey(abstractionLevel))
```

```
    {
        orderList[abstractionLevel].Add(kvp);
    }
    else
    {
        List<KeyValuePair<string, string>> list =
            new List<KeyValuePair<string, string>>();
        list.Add(kvp);
        orderList.Add(abstractionLevel, list);
    }
}
while (orderList.Count > 0)
{
    int minimum = orderList.Keys.Min();
    foreach (KeyValuePair<string, string> kvp
        in orderList[minimum])
    {
        inheritanceList.Add(kvp);
    }
    orderList.Remove(minimum);
}
return inheritanceList;
}
```

The method `StepsOfInheritance` calls for each parent node the recursive method `StepsOfInheritanceRecursive` to calculate the number of steps to a root node. Root nodes themselves return zero as the number of steps and are arranged first. The maximum function is necessary in case of multiple inheritance, since the longest path must be taken.

```
private int StepsOfInheritance(
    KeyValuePair<string, string> kvp)
{
    string parentId = kvp.Key;
    int level = 0;
    foreach (string grandparentId
        in nodeDict[parentId].ParentIDs)
    {
        int helperLevel = StepsOfInheritanceRecursive(0, 0,
            grandparentId);
        level = Math.Max(helperLevel, level);
```

```
    }
    return level;
}
```

The recursive method StepsOfInheritanceRecursive is used to determine the number of steps from a given node to a root node. The additional parameter startLevel is necessary in case of multiple inheritance to reset the parameter level.

```
private int StepsOfInheritanceRecursive(int level,
    int startLevel, string parentId)
{
    level++;
    startLevel++;
    if (startLevel < level)
    {
        level = startLevel;
    }
    foreach (string grandparentId
        in nodeDict[parentId].ParentIDs)
    {
        int helperLevel = StepsOfInheritanceRecursive(
            level, startLevel, grandparentId);
        level = Math.Max(helperLevel, level);
    }
    return level;
}
```

The method RemoveInheritanceBetweenNodes removes the inheritance relationship between a given parent and child node type. After extracting the two node types, all attributes as well as the dependency and inheritance relationships of the parent node type are copied for the child node type. Then the inheritance relationship is deleted.

For example, the node type *P(Task)&O(Task|Precondition)* is derived from *P(Task)* and *O(Task|Precondition)* (multiple inheritance). If the inheritance relationship between *O(Task|Precondition)* and *P(Task)&O(Task|Precondition)* is removed, then the attribute *OPrecondition* as well as the dependency and inheritance relationships must be taken over. Thus, the node type *P(Task)&O(Task|Precondition)* is then derived from *P(Task)* and from all parents of *O(Task|Precondition)*.

```
private void RemoveInheritanceBetweenNodes(KeyValuePair<string,
    string> parentChild)
{
    XmlNode parentNode = null;
    XmlNodeList list = doc.GetElementsByTagName("NodeType");
    foreach (XmlNode node in list)
    {
        if (node.Attributes.GetNamedItem("ID").Value.Equals(
            parentChild.Key))
        {
            parentNode = node;
            break;
        }
    }
    foreach (XmlNode node in list)
    {
        if (node.Attributes.GetNamedItem("ID").Value.Equals(
            parentChild.Value))
        {
            foreach (XmlNode child in node)
            {
                if (child.Name.Equals("Parent") &&
                    child.Attributes.GetNamedItem("pID").Value.
                    Equals(parentChild.Key))
                {
                    foreach (XmlNode parentChildNode
                        in parentNode)
                    {
                        if (parentChildNode.Name.
                            Equals("Parent"))
                        {
                            string parentId = parentChildNode.
                                Attributes.GetNamedItem("pID").
                                Value;
                            if (!nodeDict[parentChild.Value].
                                ParentIDs.Contains(parentId))
                            {
                                nodeDict[parentChild.Value].
                                    ParentIDs.Add(parentId);
                                XmlNode duplNode =
                                    parentChildNode.
```

```
                        CloneNode(true);
                    node.AppendChild(duplNode);
                }
            }
            else if (parentChildNode.Name.
                Equals("AttrType"))
            {
                XmlNode duplNode = parentChildNode.
                    CloneNode(true);
                duplNode.Attributes.GetNamedItem(
                    "ID").Value = NextId();
                node.AppendChild(duplNode);
            }
            else
            {
                XmlNode duplNode = parentChildNode.
                    CloneNode(true);
                node.AppendChild(duplNode);
            }
        }
        CopyEdges(parentChild);
        nodeDict[parentChild.Value].ParentIDs.
            Remove(parentChild.Key);
        node.RemoveChild(child);
        return;
    }
}
}
}
```

The method CopyEdges copies all dependency relationships of the parent node for the child node. After identifying all nodes and edges in the type graph, the dependency relationships where either the source or the target is the parent node are copied. The source or target is then set to the child node and it is checked whether the dependency relationship already exists. If this is not the case, then it is inserted in the type graph. A special case are all those dependency relationships where both, the source and the target, references the parent node. In this case, additional dependency relationships referencing the parent, children, and siblings of the child node are necessary.

```
private void CopyEdges(KeyValuePair<string, string>
    parentChild)
{
    XmlNode typeGraph = null;
    XmlNodeList graphList = doc.GetElementsByTagName("Graph");
    foreach (XmlNode graph in graphList)
    {
        if (graph.Attributes.GetNamedItem("name").Value.Equals
            ("TypeGraph"))
        {
            typeGraph = graph;
            break;
        }
    }
    List<XmlNode> edgeList = new List<XmlNode>();
    Dictionary<string, XmlNode> idNodeDict =
        new Dictionary<string, XmlNode>();
    Dictionary<string, List<XmlNode>> typeNodeDict =
        new Dictionary<string, List<XmlNode>>();
    Dictionary<KeyValuePair<string, string>, XmlNode> edgeDict
        = new Dictionary<KeyValuePair<string, string>,
        XmlNode>();
    foreach (XmlNode tg in typeGraph)
    {
        if (tg.Name.Equals("Node"))
        {
            idNodeDict.Add(tg.Attributes.GetNamedItem("ID").
                Value, tg);
            string type = tg.Attributes.GetNamedItem("type").
                Value;
            if (!typeNodeDict.ContainsKey(type))
            {
                typeNodeDict.Add(type, new List<XmlNode>());
            }
            typeNodeDict[type].Add(tg);
        }
        if (tg.Name.Equals("Edge"))
        {
            string s, t;
            s = tg.Attributes.GetNamedItem("source").Value;
            t = tg.Attributes.GetNamedItem("target").Value;
```

```
            edgeDict.Add(new KeyValuePair<string, string>(
                s, t), tg);
            edgeList.Add(tg);
        }
    }
    List<XmlNode> duplEdgeList = new List<XmlNode>();
    foreach (XmlNode edge in edgeList)
    {
        string sourceType = idNodeDict[edge.Attributes.
            GetNamedItem("source").Value].Attributes.
            GetNamedItem("type").Value;
        string targetType = idNodeDict[edge.Attributes.
            GetNamedItem("target").Value].Attributes.
            GetNamedItem("type").Value;
        if (parentChild.Key.Equals(sourceType)
            || parentChild.Key.Equals(targetType))
        {
            foreach (XmlNode childNode in
                typeNodeDict[parentChild.Value])
            {
                string childId = childNode.Attributes.
                    GetNamedItem("ID").Value;
                if (sourceType.Equals(parentChild.Key) &&
                    targetType.Equals(parentChild.Key))
                {
                    List<XmlNode> scList = new List<XmlNode>();
                    foreach (KeyValuePair<string, NodeType> kvp
                        in nodeDict)
                    {
                        if (kvp.Key.Equals(parentChild.Key))
                        {
                            scList.AddRange(
                                typeNodeDict[kvp.Key]);
                        }
                        else
                        {
                            foreach (string parentId in
                                kvp.Value.ParentIDs)
                            {
                                if (parentId.Equals(parentChild
                                    .Key) || parentId.Equals(
```

```
                parentChild.Value))
          {
                scList.AddRange(
                    typeNodeDict[kvp.Key]);
          }
       }
    }
}
foreach (XmlNode sc in scList)
{
    string scId = sc.Attributes.
        GetNamedItem("ID").Value;
    XmlNode scEdge1 = edge.CloneNode(true);
    XmlNode scEdge2 = edge.CloneNode(true);
    scEdge1.Attributes.GetNamedItem(
        "source").Value = childId;
    scEdge1.Attributes.GetNamedItem(
        "target").Value = scId;
    scEdge2.Attributes.GetNamedItem(
        "source").Value = scId;
    scEdge2.Attributes.GetNamedItem(
        "target").Value = childId;
    KeyValuePair<string, string> pair =
        new KeyValuePair<string, string>
        (childId, scId);
    if (!edgeDict.ContainsKey(pair))
    {
        edgeDict.Add(pair, scEdge1);
        scEdge1.Attributes.GetNamedItem(
            "ID").Value = NextId();
        duplEdgeList.Add(scEdge1);
    }
    pair = new KeyValuePair<string,
        string>(scId, childId);
    if (!edgeDict.ContainsKey(pair))
    {
        edgeDict.Add(pair, scEdge2);
        scEdge2.Attributes.GetNamedItem(
            "ID").Value = NextId();
        duplEdgeList.Add(scEdge2);
    }
```

```
            }
        }
        XmlNode duplEdge = edge.CloneNode(true);
        if (sourceType.Equals(parentChild.Key))
        {
            duplEdge.Attributes.GetNamedItem("source").
                Value = childId;
        }
        if (targetType.Equals(parentChild.Key))
        {
            duplEdge.Attributes.GetNamedItem("target").
                Value = childId;
        }
        string s = duplEdge.Attributes.
            GetNamedItem("source").Value;
        string t = duplEdge.Attributes.
            GetNamedItem("target").Value;
        KeyValuePair<string, string> st =
            new KeyValuePair<string, string>(s, t);
        if (!edgeDict.ContainsKey(st))
        {
            edgeDict.Add(st, duplEdge);
            duplEdge.Attributes.GetNamedItem("ID").
                Value = NextId();
            duplEdgeList.Add(duplEdge);
        }
    }
    }
    }
    foreach (XmlNode duplEdge in duplEdgeList)
    {
        typeGraph.AppendChild(duplEdge);
    }
}
```

The method RemoveAbstractNodes deletes all transformation rules and application conditions with abstract node types. In addition, it further removes the abstract node types with addressed dependency relationships from the type graph. The result is called the concrete flattening of the graph transformation system.

```
private void RemoveAbstractNodes()
{
    XmlNodeList ruleList = doc.GetElementsByTagName("Rule");
    List<XmlNode> delList = new List<XmlNode>();
    foreach (XmlNode rule in ruleList)
    {
        if (HasAbstractNodes(rule))
        {
            delList.Add(rule);
        }
    }
    foreach (XmlNode rule in delList)
    {
        rule.ParentNode.RemoveChild(rule);
    }
    XmlNodeList nacList = doc.GetElementsByTagName("NAC");
    XmlNodeList pacList = doc.GetElementsByTagName("PAC");
    delList = new List<XmlNode>();
    foreach (XmlNode nac in nacList)
    {
        if (HasAbstractNodes(nac))
        {
            delList.Add(nac);
        }
    }
    foreach (XmlNode pac in pacList)
    {
        if (HasAbstractNodes(pac))
        {
            delList.Add(pac);
        }
    }
    foreach (XmlNode ac in delList)
    {
        ac.ParentNode.RemoveChild(ac);
    }
    List<XmlNode> abstractNodes = new List<XmlNode>();
    XmlNodeList list = doc.GetElementsByTagName("Types");
    foreach (XmlNode node in list[0].ChildNodes)
    {
        if (node.Name.Equals("NodeType"))
```

```
    {
        if (Convert.ToBoolean(node.Attributes.
            GetNamedItem("abstract").Value))
        {
            abstractNodes.Add(node);
        }
    }
}
List<string> abstractIds = new List<string>();
foreach (XmlNode node in abstractNodes)
{
    abstractIds.Add(node.Attributes.GetNamedItem("ID").
        Value);
    list[0].RemoveChild(node);
}
XmlNode typeGraph = null;
XmlNodeList gList = doc.GetElementsByTagName("Graph");
foreach (XmlNode graph in gList)
{
    if (graph.Attributes.GetNamedItem("name").Value.
        Equals("TypeGraph"))
    {
        typeGraph = graph;
        break;
    }
}
List<XmlNode> tgList = new List<XmlNode>();
List<string> tgNodeIds = new List<string>();
foreach (XmlNode tgn in typeGraph)
{
    if (tgn.Name.Equals("Node") && abstractIds.Contains(
        tgn.Attributes.GetNamedItem("type").Value))
    {
        tgNodeIds.Add(tgn.Attributes.GetNamedItem("ID").
            Value);
        tgList.Add(tgn);
    }
}
foreach (XmlNode tgn in typeGraph)
{
    if (tgn.Name.Equals("Edge") && (tgNodeIds.Contains
```

```
                (tgn.Attributes.GetNamedItem("source").Value) ||
                tgNodeIds.Contains(tgn.Attributes.GetNamedItem(
                "target").Value)))
        {
            tgList.Add(tgn);
        }
    }
    foreach (XmlNode tgn in tgList)
    {
        typeGraph.RemoveChild(tgn);
    }
}
```

The method `ChangePacsToGacs` transforms every PAC to a GAC (i.e., a `NestedAC`). The method `RenameNode` only renames the XmlNode and will not be shown in detail. Furthermore, this method defines a boolean formula that concatenates all GACs of a rule. GACs originating from one former PAC are concatenated with **or** ($\vee$), whereas GACs from different PACs are concatenated with **and** ($\wedge$).

```
private void ChangePacsToGacs()
{
    XmlNodeList pacList = doc.GetElementsByTagName("PAC");
    Dictionary<XmlNode, List<XmlNode>> gacDict =
        new Dictionary<XmlNode, List<XmlNode>>();
    List<XmlNode> pacCopy = new List<XmlNode>();
    foreach (XmlNode pac in pacList)
    {
        pacCopy.Add(pac);
    }
    foreach (XmlNode pac in pacCopy)
    {
        XmlNode gac = RenameNode(pac, "NestedAC");
        if (!gacDict.ContainsKey(gac.ParentNode))
        {
            gacDict[gac.ParentNode] = new List<XmlNode>();
        }
        gacDict[gac.ParentNode].Add(gac);
    }
    foreach (KeyValuePair<XmlNode, List<XmlNode>> kvp
        in gacDict)
```

```
{
    Dictionary<string, List<XmlNode>> dict =
        new Dictionary<string,List<XmlNode>>();
    foreach (XmlNode gac in kvp.Value)
    {
        string name = GetOriginalAcName(gac);
        if (!dict.ContainsKey(name))
        {
            dict[name] = new List<XmlNode>();
        }
        dict[name].Add(gac);
    }
    int counter = 1;
    string f1 = string.Empty, f2 = string.Empty;
    for (int i = 1; i < dict.Keys.Count; i++)
    {
        f1 += "( "; f2 += "( ";
    }
    bool outerFirst = true;
    foreach (KeyValuePair<string, List<XmlNode>> gacType
        in dict)
    {
        bool first = true;
        foreach (XmlNode gac in gacType.Value)
        {
            if (first)
            {
                for (int i = 1; i < gacType.Value.Count;
                    i++)
                {
                    f1 += "( "; f2 += "( ";
                }
                f1 += counter++.ToString();
                f2 += gac.FirstChild.Attributes.
                    GetNamedItem("name").Value;
                first = false;
            }
            else
            {
                f1 += " | "; f2 += " | ";
                f1 += counter++.ToString();
```

```
                    f2 += gac.FirstChild.Attributes.
                    GetNamedItem("name").Value;
                    f1 += " )"; f2 += " )";
                }
            }
            if (outerFirst)
            {
                f1 += " & "; f2 += " & ";
                outerFirst = false;
            }
            else
            {
                f1 += " ) & "; f2 += " & ";
            }
        }
        f1 = f1.Substring(0, f1.Length - 3);
        f2 = f2.Substring(0, f2.Length - 3);
        XmlNode rule = kvp.Key.ParentNode;
        rule.Attributes.GetNamedItem("formula").Value = f1;
        foreach (XmlNode rChild in rule)
        {
            if (rChild.Name.Equals("Morphism"))
            {
                rChild.Attributes.GetNamedItem("comment").Value
                    = "Formula: " + f2;
                break;
            }
        }
    }
}
```

The method `ChangeIdsOfRule` changes the ID and name of a given rule. Further IDs within the rule and in the application conditions are replaced by the method `ChangeIdsOfGraphsAndMorphism`. The replaced IDs are saved in a dictionary and required for the update of edges and mappings. The new IDs are provided by the method `NextId` (not shown in detail) based on the global field `idCounter`. Since all IDs created by AGG have the prefix "I", the same prefix is also used for the new IDs.

```
private XmlNode ChangeIdsOfRule(XmlNode duplRule)
{
```

```
Dictionary<string, string> replacedNodeIds =
    new Dictionary<string, string>();
string ruleId = NextId();
duplRule.Attributes.GetNamedItem("ID").Value = ruleId;
duplRule.Attributes.GetNamedItem("name").Value +=
    RuleNameAppendix + ruleId;
XmlNodeList children = duplRule.ChildNodes;
replacedNodeIds = ChangeIdsOfGraphsAndMorphism(
    replacedNodeIds, children, ruleId, false);
foreach (XmlNode child in children)
{
    if (child.Name.Equals("ApplCondition"))
    {
        foreach (XmlNode grandchild in child)
        {
            replacedNodeIds = ChangeIdsOfGraphsAndMorphism(
                replacedNodeIds, grandchild.ChildNodes,
                ruleId, false);
        }
        break;
    }
}
return duplRule;
}
```

The method `ChangeIdsOfAC` is used to change the IDs within an AC and further calls the method `ChangeIdsOfGraphsAndMorphism`. The replaced IDs are saved in a dictionary and required for the update of edges and mappings.

```
private XmlNode ChangeIdsOfAC(XmlNode duplAC)
{
    Dictionary<string, string> replacedNodeIds =
        new Dictionary<string, string>();
    replacedNodeIds = ChangeIdsOfGraphsAndMorphism(
        replacedNodeIds, duplAC.ChildNodes, NextId(), true);
    return duplAC;
}
```

The method `ChangeIdsOfGraphsAndMorphism` changes the IDs and names within graphs and morphisms of rules and ACs. In a first step, all graphs (LHS, RHS, NAC, and PAC) are considered and the ID and name is changed.

Afterwards every node and edge defined within the graph receives a new ID and the source and target nodes of all edges are actualized. Furthermore, the morphism node receives a new name and every mapping is updated.

```
private Dictionary<string, string>
    ChangeIdsOfGraphsAndMorphism(Dictionary<string, string>
    replacedNodeIds, XmlNodeList children, string ruleId,
    bool isOnlyAC)
{
    foreach (XmlNode child in children)
    {
        if (child.Name.Equals("Graph"))
        {
            child.Attributes.GetNamedItem("ID").Value =
                NextId();
            child.Attributes.GetNamedItem("name").Value +=
                RuleNameAppendix + ruleId;
            foreach (XmlNode grandchild in child)
            {
                if (grandchild.Name.Equals("Node"))
                {
                    string oldValue = grandchild.Attributes.
                        GetNamedItem("ID").Value;
                    string newValue = NextId();
                    replacedNodeIds.Add(oldValue, newValue);
                    grandchild.Attributes.GetNamedItem("ID").
                        Value = newValue;
                }
                else if (grandchild.Name.Equals("Edge"))
                {
                    string oldValue = grandchild.Attributes.
                        GetNamedItem("ID").Value;
                    string newValue = NextId();
                    replacedNodeIds.Add(oldValue, newValue);
                    grandchild.Attributes.GetNamedItem("ID").
                        Value = newValue;
                    grandchild.Attributes.GetNamedItem(
                        "source").Value = replacedNodeIds[
                        grandchild.Attributes.GetNamedItem(
                        "source").Value];
                    grandchild.Attributes.GetNamedItem(
```

```
                        "target").Value = replacedNodeIds[
                        grandchild.Attributes.GetNamedItem(
                        "target").Value];
                }
            }
        }
        else if (child.Name.Equals("Morphism"))
        {
            child.Attributes.GetNamedItem("name").Value +=
                RuleNameAppendix + ruleId;
            foreach (XmlNode grandchild in child)
            {
                if (grandchild.Name.Equals("Mapping"))
                {
                    grandchild.Attributes.GetNamedItem(
                        "image").Value = replacedNodeIds[
                        grandchild.Attributes.GetNamedItem(
                        "image").Value];
                    if (!isOnlyAC)
                    {
                        grandchild.Attributes.GetNamedItem(
                            "orig").Value = replacedNodeIds[
                            grandchild.Attributes.GetNamedItem(
                            "orig").Value];
                    }
                }
            }
        }
    }
    return replacedNodeIds;
}
```

The method `ReplaceNodeWithChild` calls the method `GetParentNode` and replaces the parent node type by the child node type.

```
private void ReplaceNodeWithChild(XmlNode node, string kind,
    string id, NodeType child)
{
    XmlNode parent = GetParentNode(node, kind, id);
    if (parent != null)
    {
```

```
        parent.Attributes.GetNamedItem("type").Value =
            child.ID;
    }
}
```

The method `GetParentNode` takes an XmlNode that comprises a rule or AC, the kind of the graph (LHS, RHS, NAC, or PAC), and the ID of the parent node. After the graph has been identified, the parent node is returned.

```
private XmlNode GetParentNode(XmlNode node,
    string kind, string id)
{
    XmlNode graph = null;
    foreach (XmlNode nodeChild in node)
    {
        if (nodeChild.Name.Equals("Graph"))
        {
            if (nodeChild.Attributes.GetNamedItem("kind").
                Value.Equals(kind))
            {
                graph = nodeChild;
                break;
            }
        }
    }
    foreach (XmlNode nodeChild in graph)
    {
        if (nodeChild.Name.Equals("Node") && nodeChild.
            Attributes.GetNamedItem("ID").Value.Equals(id))
        {
            return nodeChild;
        }
    }
    return null;
}
```

The method `ReplaceNodeInACsWithChild` is used to replace the parent node within all ACs of a rule. The ACs are iterated and for every AC the graph and the morphism sections are identified. Since the parameter `id` describes the ID of the parent node in the LHS of the rule, it is necessary to determine the mapped node within the AC. Afterwards the method `GetParentNode` is called for every AC. Since the mapped node within an AC may also be of a finer type, the node type is only replaced if it is a parent of the given child node type. Furthermore, if the node type is neither a parent nor a child node type (e.g., a sibling) and it is a NAC, then the whole NAC is removed.

```
private void ReplaceNodeInACsWithChild(XmlNode node, string id,
    NodeType child)
{
    foreach (XmlNode nodeChild in node)
    {
        if (nodeChild.Name.Equals("ApplCondition"))
        {
            List<XmlNode> delList = new List<XmlNode>();
            foreach (XmlNode applChild in nodeChild)
            {
                if (applChild.Name.Equals("NAC") ||
                    applChild.Name.Equals("PAC"))
                {
                    XmlNode graph = null, morphism = null;
                    foreach (XmlNode acChild in applChild)
                    {
                        if (acChild.Name.Equals("Graph"))
                        {
                            graph = acChild;
                        }
                        if (acChild.Name.Equals("Morphism"))
                        {
                            morphism = acChild;
                        }
                    }
                    string morphismId = GetMorphismNode(
                        morphism, id);
                    XmlNode parent = GetParentNode(applChild,
                        applChild.Name, morphismId, child);
                    if (parent != null)
                    {
                        string lType = child.ID;
                        string nType = parent.Attributes.
                            GetNamedItem("type").Value;
                        if (lType.Equals(nType) || IsParent
                            (origNodeDict, nType, lType))
```

```
                    {
                        parent.Attributes.GetNamedItem(
                            "type").Value = lType;
                    }
                    else if (!IsParent(origNodeDict, lType,
                        nType) && applChild.Name.
                        Equals("NAC"))
                    {
                        delList.Add(applChild);
                    }
                }
            }
        }
        foreach (XmlNode delNode in delList)
        {
            nodeChild.RemoveChild(delNode);
        }
    }
}
}
```

The method `GetMorphismNode` takes the morphism section and a node ID and returns the mapped node.

```
private string GetMorphismNode(XmlNode morphism, string nodeId)
{
    foreach (XmlNode morphismChild in morphism)
    {
        if (morphismChild.Name.Equals("Mapping") &&
            morphismChild.Attributes.GetNamedItem("orig").
            Value.Equals(nodeId))
        {
            return morphismChild.Attributes.GetNamedItem(
                "image").Value;
        }
    }
    return null;
}
```

The method `GetOriginalNode` takes the morphism section and the mapped node and returns the original node.

```
private string GetOriginalNode(XmlNode morphism,
    string nodeId)
{
    foreach (XmlNode morphismChild in morphism)
    {
        if (morphismChild.Name.Equals("Mapping") &&
            morphismChild.Attributes.GetNamedItem("image").
            Value.Equals(nodeId))
        {
            return morphismChild.Attributes.GetNamedItem(
                "orig").Value;
        }
    }
    return null;
}
```

The method RemoveRulesWithIdenticNodesOnLhs receives a collection of generated rules and removes the identical ones. The dictionary ruleList comprises all generated rules as key and the original rules as value. All rules are iterated within two nested loops and whenever two rules have the same basic name, all nodes of the LHS are compared in the method HasNodeListIdenticTypes. Afterwards a collection of distinct rules is returned.

```
private Dictionary<XmlNode, XmlNode>
    RemoveRulesWithIdenticNodesOnLhs(
    Dictionary<XmlNode, XmlNode> ruleList)
{
    Dictionary<XmlNode, XmlNode> helperList =
        new Dictionary<XmlNode, XmlNode>();
    if (ruleList == null || ruleList.Count == 0)
    {
        return helperList;
    }
    foreach (KeyValuePair<XmlNode, XmlNode> kvp1 in ruleList)
    {
        bool found = false;
        List<XmlNode> nodeList1 = GetNodesOfXmlNode(kvp1.Key,
            "LHS");
        foreach (KeyValuePair<XmlNode, XmlNode> kvp2
            in helperList)
```

```
        {
            string rulename1 = GetOriginalRuleName(kvp1.Key.
                Attributes.GetNamedItem("name").Value);
            string rulename2 = GetOriginalRuleName(kvp2.Key.
                Attributes.GetNamedItem("name").Value);
            if (rulename1 == rulename2)
            {
                List<XmlNode> nodeList2 = GetNodesOfXmlNode(
                    kvp2.Key, "LHS");
                if (HasNodeListIdenticTypes(nodeList1,
                    nodeList2))
                {
                    found = true;
                    break;
                }
            }
        }
        if (!found)
        {
            helperList.Add(kvp1.Key, kvp1.Value);
        }
    }
    return helperList;
}
```

The method `RemoveIdenticACs` is similar to the former method and removes
the identical ACs from a dictionary containing all generated ACs. If the basic
names of two ACs are equal, then all nodes within the ACs are compared.
Afterwards a collection of distinct ACs is returned.

```
private Dictionary<XmlNode, XmlNode> RemoveIdenticACs(
    Dictionary<XmlNode, XmlNode> acList)
{
    Dictionary<XmlNode, XmlNode> helperList =
        new Dictionary<XmlNode, XmlNode>();
    if (acList == null || acList.Count == 0)
    {
        return helperList;
    }
    foreach (KeyValuePair<XmlNode, XmlNode> kvp1 in acList)
    {
```

```
    bool found = false;
    List<XmlNode> nodeList1 = GetNodesOfXmlNode(
        kvp1.Key, kvp1.Key.Name);
    foreach (KeyValuePair<XmlNode, XmlNode> kvp2
        in helperList)
    {
        string acname1 = GetOriginalAcName(kvp1.Key);
        string acname2 = GetOriginalAcName(kvp2.Key);
        if (acname1 == acname2)
        {
            List<XmlNode> nodeList2 = GetNodesOfXmlNode(
                kvp2.Key, kvp2.Key.Name);
            if (HasNodeListIdenticTypes(nodeList1,
                nodeList2))
            {
                found = true;
                break;
            }
        }
    }
    if (!found)
    {
        helperList.Add(kvp1.Key, kvp1.Value);
    }
}
return helperList;
}
```

The nodes of two rules or application conditions are compared within the method `HasNodeListIdenticTypes`. Since identical rules and ACs must have the same node order, node types at the same position can directly be compared.

```
private bool HasNodeListIdenticTypes(List<XmlNode> listA,
    List<XmlNode> listB)
{
    if (listA.Count != listB.Count)
    {
        return false;
    }
    for (int i = 0; i < listA.Count; i++)
```

```
    {
        XmlNode nodeA = listA[i];
        XmlNode nodeB = listB[i];
        string typeA =
            nodeA.Attributes.GetNamedItem("type").Value;
        string typeB =
            nodeB.Attributes.GetNamedItem("type").Value;
        if (typeA != typeB)
        {
            return false;
        }
    }
    return true;
}
```

The method `GetNodesOfXmlNode` gets an XmlNode that comprises a rule or AC and returns a list of all nodes defined within the graph of that XmlNode.

```
private List<XmlNode> GetNodesOfXmlNode(XmlNode node,
    string kind)
{
    List<XmlNode> nodeList = new List<XmlNode>();
    foreach (XmlNode nodeChild in node)
    {
        if (nodeChild.Name.Equals("Graph") && nodeChild.
            Attributes.GetNamedItem("kind").Value.Equals(kind))
        {
            foreach (XmlNode graphChild in nodeChild)
            {
                if (graphChild.Name.Equals("Node"))
                {
                    nodeList.Add(graphChild);
                }
            }
        }
    }
    return nodeList;
}
```

The method `HasAbstractNodes` checks whether a given rule or AC comprises any abstract nodes.

```
private bool HasAbstractNodes(XmlNode node)
{
    string kind = node.Name;
    List<XmlNode> nList = new List<XmlNode>();
    if (kind.Equals("Rule"))
    {
        nList = GetNodesOfXmlNode(node, "LHS");
        nList.AddRange(GetNodesOfXmlNode(node, "RHS"));
    }
    else
    {
        nList = GetNodesOfXmlNode(node, kind);
    }
    foreach (XmlNode n in nList)
    {
        string type = n.Attributes.GetNamedItem("type").Value;
        if (nodeDict[type].IsAbstract)
        {
            return true;
        }
    }
    return false;
}
```

The method IsParent takes a dictionary (either nodeDict or origNodeDict) and two node types and checks whether the first node type is a parent of the second node type.

```
private bool IsParent(Dictionary<string, NodeType> dict,
    string pType, string cType)
{
    List<string> pList = dict[cType].ParentIDs.ToList();
    List<string> cList = dict[cType].ParentIDs.ToList();
    while (pList.Count > 0)
    {
        foreach (string id in pList)
        {
            if (id.Equals(pType))
            {
                return true;
            }
```

```
            cList.Remove(id);
            cList.AddRange(dict[id].ParentIDs);
        }
        pList = cList.ToList();
    }
    return false;
}
```

The method `GetOriginalRuleName` receives a rule name that may have been extended in case of a generated rule. The original rule name is extracted by creating a substring until the first occurrence of `RuleNameAppendix`. A similar method is defined for ACs and called `GetOriginalAcName`.

```
private string GetOriginalRuleName(string rulename)
{
    if (rulename.Contains(RuleNameAppendix))
    {
        return rulename.Substring(0,
            rulename.IndexOf(RuleNameAppendix));
    }
    return rulename;
}
```

This prototype is used to flatten the hierarchy of DeonticBpmnGTS. The abstract flattening leads to 1.471 rules with 24.942 ACs, whereas the concrete flattening results in 822 rules with 10.170 ACs. However, it should be mentioned that the current prototype implementation of the flattening algorithm does not provide for exception handling. Furthermore, during the parsing of the XML-file, the encoding is changed and automatically extended with a byte order mark (BOM). Thus, the encoding must be set to UTF-8 without BOM, for example with Notepad++, before opening the resulting XML-file with AGG.

The prototype can also be used to flatten other graph transformation systems with abstract nodes and (multiple) inheritance. The only open issue is the validation of the generated rules and ACs based on restrictions of the dependency relationships. For example, the flattening may replace an abstract node with two outgoing edges with a concrete subnode, even if this subnode is only allowed to have a maximum of one outgoing edge.

Bibliography

[1] Witold Abramowicz, Monika Kaczmarek, Tomasz Kaczmarek, and Agata Filipowska. Semantically enhanced business process modelling notation. In Martin Hepp, Knut Hinkelmann, Dimitris Karagiannis, Rüdiger Klein, and Nenad Stojanovic, editors, *Proceedings of the Workshop on Semantic Business Process and Product Lifecycle Management (SBPM 2007)*, 2007.

[2] Michael Adams. The resource service. In Arthur H. M. Hofstede, Wil M. P. van der Aalst, Michael Adams, and Nick Russell, editors, *Modern Business Process Automation*, pages 261–290. Springer-Verlag Berlin Heidelberg, 2010.

[3] AGG. *The AGG 1.5.0 Development Environment - The User Manual*, 2006.

[4] AGG. AGG Homepage. `http://user.cs.tu-berlin.de/~gragra/agg`, 2011.

[5] J. Stuart Aitken, Bonnie L. Webber, and Jonathan B.L. Bard. Part-of relations in anatomy ontologies: A proposal for RDFS and OWL formalisations. In *Pacific Symposium on Biocomputing*, pages 166–177. World Scientific, 2004.

[6] Dean Allemang and James Hendler. *Semantic Web for the Working Ontologist: Effective Modeling in RDFS and OWL*. Morgan Kaufmann, 2008.

[7] Thomas Allweyer. *BPMN 2.0: Business Process Model and Notation*. Books on Demand GmbH, 2 edition, 2009.

[8] Kerstin Altmanninger, Wieland Schwinger, and Gabriele Kotsis. Semantics for accurate conflict detection in SMoVer: Specification, detec-

tion and presentation by example. *International Journal of Enterprise Information Systems (IJEIS)*, 6(1):68–84, 2010.

[9] Grigoris Antoniou and Frank van Harmelen. Web ontology language: OWL. In Steffen Staab and Rudi Studer, editors, *Handbook on Ontologies*, pages 67–92. Springer-Verlag, 2004.

[10] Patrizia Asirelli, Maurice H. ter Beek, Stefania Gnesi, and Alessandro Fantechi. A deontic logical framework for modelling product families. In David Benavides, Don S. Batory, and Paul Grünbacher, editors, *4th International Workshop on Variability Modelling of Software-intensive Systems (VaMoS'10)*, volume 37 of *ICB-Research Report*, pages 37–44. Universität Duisburg-Essen, 2010.

[11] Ahmed Awad, Alexander Grosskopf, Andreas Meyer, and Mathias Weske. Enabling resource assignment constraints in BPMN. Technical Report BPT Technical Report 04-2009, Hasso Plattner Institute, Potsdam, Germany, 2009.

[12] Roswitha Bardohl, Hartmut Ehrig, Juan de Lara, and Gabriele Taentzer. Integrating meta-modelling aspects with graph transformation for efficient visual language definition and model manipulation. In *Proc. Fundamental Approaches to Software Engineering (FASE'04)*, volume 2984 of *Lecture Notes in Computer Science*, pages 214–228. Springer Berlin / Heidelberg, 2004.

[13] Egon Börger. Approaches to modeling business processes: A critical analysis of BPMN, Workflow Patterns and YAWL. *Software and Systems Modeling*, pages 1–14, 2011.

[14] Egon Börger and Ove Sörensen. BPMN core modeling concepts: Inheritance-based execution semantics. In D. W. Embley and B. Thalheim, editors, *Handbook of Conceptual Modeling: Theory, Practice and Research Challenges*, chapter 9. Springer-Verlag, 2011.

[15] Alex Borgida and Ronald J. Brachman. Conceptual modeling with description logics. In Franz Baader, Diego Calvanese, Deborah McGuinness, Daniele Nardi, and Peter Patel-Schneider, editors, *The Description Logic Handbook: Theory, Implementation and Applications*, chapter 10, pages 359–381. Cambridge University Press, 2003.

[16] Egon Börger. Modeling workflow patterns from first principles. In Christine Parent, Klaus-Dieter Schewe, Veda Storey, and Bernhard

Thalheim, editors, *Conceptual Modeling - ER 2007*, volume 4801 of *Lecture Notes in Computer Science*, pages 1–20. Springer Berlin / Heidelberg, 2007.

[17] Egon Börger, Ove Sörensen, and Bernhard Thalheim. On defining the behavior of OR-joins in business process models. *Journal of Universal Computer Science*, 15:3–32, 2009.

[18] Jan Broersen and Leendert van der Torre. Ten problems of deontic logic and normative reasoning in computer science. European Summer School of Logic, Language and Information (ESSLLI), August 2010.

[19] Manfred Broy. *Informatik - Eine grundlegende Einführung*, volume 2 - Systemstrukturen und Theoretische Informatik. Springer-Verlag, 2 edition, 1998.

[20] José Carmo and Andrew J. I. Jones. *Deontic Logic*, pages 265–343. Kluwer Academic, Dordrecht, 2002.

[21] Pablo F. Castro and Thomas S. E. Maibaum. A complete and compact propositional deontic logic. In Cliff Jones, Zhiming Liu, and Jim Woodcock, editors, *Theoretical Aspects of Computing - ICTAC 2007*, volume 4711 of *Lecture Notes in Computer Science*, pages 109–123. Springer Berlin / Heidelberg, 2007.

[22] Marco Colombetti. A commitment-based approach to agent speech acts and conversations. In *Proceedings of the Workshop on Agent Languages and Conversation Policies*, pages 21–29, Barcelona, 2000.

[23] Carlo Combi and Mauro Gambini. Flaws in the flow: The weakness of unstructured business process modeling languages dealing with data. In Robert Meersman, Tharam Dillon, and Pilar Herrero, editors, *On the Move to Meaningful Internet Systems: OTM 2009*, volume 5870 of *Lecture Notes in Computer Science*, pages 42–59. Springer Berlin / Heidelberg, 2009.

[24] Juan de Lara, Roswitha Bardohl, Hartmut Ehrig, Karsten Ehrig, Ulrike Prange, and Gabriele Taentzer. Attributed graph transformation with node type inheritance. *Theor. Comput. Sci.*, 376:139–163, May 2007.

[25] Gero Decker and Alistair Barros. Interaction modeling using BPMN. In Arthur ter Hofstede, Boualem Benatallah, and Hye-Young Paik, editors, *Business Process Management Workshops*, volume 4928 of *Lecture*

Notes in Computer Science, pages 208–219. Springer Berlin / Heidelberg, 2008.

[26] Frank Dignum and Hans Weigand. Communication and deontic logic. In Roel Wieringa and Remco Feenstra, editors, *Information Systems, Correctness and Reusability*, pages 242–260. World Scientific, 1995.

[27] Frank Dignum and Hans Weigand. Modelling communication between cooperative systems. In Juhani Iivari, Kalle Lyytinen, and Matti Rossi, editors, *Advanced Information Systems Engineering*, volume 932 of *Lecture Notes in Computer Science*, pages 140–153. Springer Berlin / Heidelberg, 1995.

[28] Remco M. Dijkman, Marlon Dumas, and Chun Ouyang. Ontology development 101: A guide to creating your first ontology. Queensland University of Technology, Faculty of Science and Technology, 2007.

[29] John Dixon and Teresa Jones. Hype cycle for business process management, 2011. Technical Report G00214214, Gartner, July 2011.

[30] Eclipse. BPMN modeler. http://www.eclipse.org/bpmn/, 2011.

[31] Hartmut Ehrig, Karsten Ehrig, Ulrike Prange, and Gabriele Taentzer. *Fundamentals of Algebraic Graph Transformation*. Springer, 2006.

[32] Hartmut Ehrig, Annegret Habel, Hans-Jörg Kreowski, and Francesco Parisi-Presicce. From graph grammars to high level replacement systems. In Hartmut Ehrig, Hans-Jörg Kreowski, and Grzegorz Rozenberg, editors, *Graph Grammars and Their Application to Computer Science*, volume 532 of *Lecture Notes in Computer Science*, pages 269–291. Springer Berlin / Heidelberg, 1991.

[33] Hartmut Ehrig, Annegret Habel, Hans-Jörg Kreowski, and Francesco Parisi-Presicce. Parallelism and concurrency in high-level replacement systems. *Mathematical Structures in Computer Science*, 1:361–404, 1991.

[34] Hartmut Ehrig, Michael Pfender, and Hans Jürgen Schneider. Graph-grammars: An algebraic approach. In *Proceedings of FOCS 1973*, pages 167–180. IEEE, 1973.

[35] Thomas Eiter, Viviana Mascardi, and V.S. Subrahmanian. Error-tolerant agents. In Antonis Kakas and Fariba Sadri, editors, *Computational Logic: Logic Programming and Beyond*, volume 2407 of *Lecture*

Notes in Computer Science, pages 83–104. Springer Berlin / Heidelberg, 2002.

[36] Albert Fleischmann, Werner Schmidt, Christian Stary, Stefan Obermeier, and Egon Börger. *Subjektorientiertes Prozessmanagement - Mitarbeiter einbinden, Motivation und Prozessakzeptanz steigern.* Carl Hanser Verlag München, 2011.

[37] Dagfinn Føllesdal and Risto Hilpinen. Deontic logic: An introduction. In Risto Hilpinen, editor, *Deontic Logic: Introductory and Systematic Readings*, pages 1–35. Dordrecht: Reidel, 1971.

[38] Robert France and Bernhard Rumpe. Model-driven development of complex software: A research roadmap. In *2007 Future of Software Engineering*, FOSE '07, pages 37–54, Washington, DC, USA, 2007. IEEE Computer Society.

[39] Chiara Francescomarino, Chiara Ghidini, Marco Rospocher, Luciano Serafini, and Paolo Tonella. Reasoning on semantically annotated processes. In *Proc. of the 6th Int. Conference on Service-Oriented Computing*, ICSOC '08, pages 132–146. Springer Berlin / Heidelberg, 2008.

[40] Jakob Freund, Bernd Rücker, and Thomas Henninger. *Praxishandbuch BPMN.* Carl Hanser Verlag München Wien, 2010.

[41] Denis Gagné and André Trudel. Time-BPMN. In *Proceedings of the 2009 IEEE Conference on Commerce and Enterprise Computing*, CEC '09, pages 361–367, Washington, USA, 2009. IEEE Computer Society.

[42] Verena Geist, Christine Natschläger, and Dirk Draheim. Integrated framework for seamless modeling of business and technical aspects in process-oriented enterprise applications. *Int. Journal of Software Engineering and Knowledge Engineering (IJSEKE)*, to appear, 2012.

[43] Andrew Gemino and Yair Wand. Complexity and clarity in conceptual modeling: Comparison of mandatory and optional properties. *Data & Knowledge Engineering*, 55:301–326, 2005.

[44] Chiara Ghidini, Marco Rospocher, and Luciano Serafini. A formalisation of BPMN in description logics. Technical Report TR 2008-06-004, Fondazione Bruno Kessler, Data & Knowledge Management, 2008.

[45] Aditya Ghose and George Koliadis. Auditing business process compliance. In Bernd Krämer, Kwei-Jay Lin, and Priya Narasimhan, editors,

Service-Oriented Computing (ICSOC), volume 4749 of Lecture Notes in Computer Science, pages 169–180. Springer Berlin / Heidelberg, 2007.

[46] Stijn Goedertier and Jan Vanthienen. Designing compliant business processes with obligations and permissions. In Johann Eder and Schahram Dustdar, editors, Business Process Management Workshops, volume 4103 of Lecture Notes in Computer Science, pages 5–14. Springer Berlin / Heidelberg, 2006.

[47] Stijn Goedertier and Jan Vanthienen. Declarative process modeling with business vocabulary and business rules. In Robert Meersman, Zahir Tari, and Pilar Herrero, editors, On the Move to Meaningful Internet Systems 2007: OTM 2007 Workshops, volume 4805 of Lecture Notes in Computer Science, pages 603–612. Springer-Verlag, 2007.

[48] Gerhard Goos and Wolf Zimmermann. Vorlesungen über Informatik - Grundlagen und funktionales Programmieren, volume 1. Springer-Verlag, 4 edition, 2006.

[49] Guido Governatori and Zoran Milosevic. A formal analysis of a business contract language. International Journal of Cooperative Information Systems, 15(4):659–685, 2006.

[50] Davide Grossi, Lambèr Royakkers, and Frank Dignum. Organizational structure and responsibility: An analysis in a dynamic logic of organized collective agency. Artif. Intell. Law, 15:223–249, January 2007.

[51] Jörg Hansen. The Paradoxes of Deontic Logic: Alive and Kicking. Theoria: A Swedish Journal of Philosophy, 72(3):221–232, 2006.

[52] Jörg Hansen, Gabriella Pigozzi, and Leendert van der Torre. Ten philosophical problems in deontic logic. In G. Boella, L. W. N. van der Torre, and H. Verhagen, editors, Normative Multi-agent Systems, volume 07122. Dagstuhl Seminar Proceedings, Internationales Begegnungs- und Forschungszentrum für Informatik (IBFI), Schloss Dagstuhl, 2007.

[53] William H. Hanson. Semantics of deontic logic. Logique et Analyse, 8:177–190, 1965.

[54] John Hebeler, Matthew Fisher, Ryan Blace, and Andrew Perez-Lopez. Semantic Web Programming. Wiley Publishing, 2009.

[55] Risto Hilpinen. Deontic logic. In Lou Goble, editor, The Blackwell Guide to Philosophical Logic, chapter 8, pages 159–182. Blackwell Publishers, 2001.

[56] Jörg Hohwiller, Diethelm Schlegel, Gunter Grieser, and Yvette Hoek-stra. Integration of BPM and BRM. In Remco Dijkman, Jörg Hof-stetter, Jana Koehler, Wil van der Aalst, John Mylopoulos, Michael Rosemann, Michael J. Shaw, and Clemens Szyperski, editors, *Business Process Model and Notation*, volume 95 of *Lecture Notes in Business Information Processing*, pages 136–141. Springer Berlin Heidelberg, 2011.

[57] John Horty. *Agency and Deontic Logic*. Oxford University Press, New York, 2001.

[58] Marta Indulska, Jan Recker, Michael Rosemann, and Peter Green. Business process modeling: Current issues and future challenges. In Pascal van Eck, Jaap Gordijn, and Roel Wieringa, editors, *Advanced Information Systems Engineering*, volume 5565 of *Lecture Notes in Computer Science*, pages 501–514. Springer Berlin / Heidelberg, 2009.

[59] Bartek Kiepuszewski, Arthur ter Hofstede, and Christoph Bussler. On structured workflow modelling. In Benkt Wangler and Lars Bergman, editors, *Advanced Information Systems Engineering*, volume 1789 of *Lecture Notes in Computer Science*, pages 431–445. Springer Berlin / Heidelberg, 2000.

[60] Jan Willem Klop and Roel de Vrijer. *Term rewriting systems*, chapter First-order term rewriting systems, pages 24–59. Cambridge University Press, 2003.

[61] Vladimir Kolovski, Bijan Parsia, and Yarden Katz. Implementing OWL defaults. In *Workshop on OWL: Experiences and Directions (OWLED)*, 2006.

[62] Birgit Korherr and Beate List. Extending the EPC and the BPMN with business process goals and performance measures. In *9th International Conference on Enterprise Information Systems, ICEIS 2007, Revised Selected Papers*, pages 287–294, Funchal, Madeira, June 2007.

[63] Felix Kossak. Discussion: Inheritance of Deonic BPMN. Memo, May 2011.

[64] Markus Krötzsch, Frantisek Simancik, and Ian Horrocks. A description logic primer. Technical report, Department of Computer Science, University of Oxford, 2012.

[65] Matthias Kunze, Alexander Luebbe, Matthias Weidlich, and Mathias Weske. Towards understanding process modeling – the case of the BPM

academic initiative. In Remco Dijkman, Jörg Hofstetter, Jana Koehler, Wil van der Aalst, John Mylopoulos, Michael Rosemann, Michael J. Shaw, and Clemens Szyperski, editors, *Business Process Model and Notation*, volume 95 of *Lecture Notes in Business Information Processing*, pages 44–58. Springer Berlin Heidelberg, 2011.

[66] Leen Lambers, Hartmut Ehrig, Annegret Habel, Fernando Orejas, and Ulrike Golas. Local confluence for rules with nested application conditions based on a new critical pair notion. Technical Report 2010-7, Technische Universität Berlin, 2010.

[67] Leen Lambers, Hartmut Ehrig, Ulrike Prange, and Fernando Orejas. Embedding and confluence of graph transformations with negative application conditions. In *Proc. of the 4th International Conference on Graph Transformations (ICGT'08)*, 2008.

[68] David Lewis. Semantic analyses for dyadic deontic logic. In Sören Stenlund, editor, *Logical Theory and Semantic Analysis: Essays Dedicated to Stig Kanger on His Fiftieth Birthday*, pages 1–14. Reidel Publishing Company, 1974.

[69] Barbara H. Liskov and Jeannette M. Wing. A behavioral notion of subtyping. *ACM Trans. Program. Lang. Syst.*, 16:1811–1841, November 1994.

[70] Rong Liu and Akhil Kumar. An analysis and taxonomy of unstructured workflows. In Wil van der Aalst, Boualem Benatallah, Fabio Casati, and Francisco Curbera, editors, *Business Process Management*, volume 3649 of *Lecture Notes in Computer Science*, pages 268–284. Springer Berlin / Heidelberg, 2005.

[71] Clark & Parsia LLC. Pellet. `http://clarkparsia.com/pellet`, November 2011. Visited: Nov. 2011.

[72] Gert-Jan C. Lokhorst and Lou Goble. Mally's deontic logic. *Grazer philosophische Studien*, 67:37–57, 2004.

[73] Michael Löwe. *Extended Algebraic Graph Transformation*. PhD thesis, TU Berlin, 1990.

[74] Michael Löwe and Martin Beyer. AGG – an implementation of algebraic graph rewriting. In *Rewriting Techniques and Applications*, 1993.

[75] Matteo Magnani and Danilo Montesi. BPMN: How much does it cost? An incremental approach. In Gustavo Alonso, Peter Dadam, and Michael Rosemann, editors, *Business Process Management*, volume 4714 of *Lecture Notes in Computer Science*, pages 80–87. Springer Berlin / Heidelberg, 2007.

[76] Matteo Magnani and Danilo Montesi. BPDMN: A conservative extension of BPMN with enhanced data representation capabilities. *CoRR*, abs/0907.1978, 2009.

[77] Steffen Mazanek and Mark Minas. Business process models as a showcase for syntax-based assistance in diagram editors. In Andy Schürr and Bran Selic, editors, *Model Driven Engineering Languages and Systems*, volume 5795 of *Lecture Notes in Computer Science*, pages 322–336. Springer Berlin / Heidelberg, 2009.

[78] Thomas J. McCabe. McCabe metrics. `http://www.mccabe.com/iq_research_metrics.htm`, July 2011.

[79] Paul McNamara. Deontic logic. In Dov Gabbay and John Woods, editors, *Handbook of the History of Logic*, volume 7, pages 197–288. Elsevier Press, 2006.

[80] Joachim Melcher, Jan Mendling, Hajo A. Reijers, and Detlef Seese. On measuring the understandability of process models. In *Business Process Management Workshops*, volume 43 of *Lecture Notes in Business Information Processing*, pages 465–476. Springer Berlin Heidelberg, 2010.

[81] Jan Mendling, Gustaf Neumann, and Markus Nüttgens. Towards workflow pattern support of event-driven process chains (EPC). In *Second GI-Workshop of XML for Business Process Management (XML4BPM 2005)*, volume 145, pages 23–28, Karlsruhe, Germany, March 2005. CEUR Workshop Proceedings.

[82] John-Jules Meyer. Dynamic logic for reasoning about actions and agents. In Jack Minker, editor, *Logic-based Artificial Intelligence*, chapter 13, pages 281–311. Kluwer Academic Publishers, Norwell, MA, USA, 2000.

[83] John-Jules Meyer, Roel Wieringa, and Frank Dignum. The role of deontic logic in the specification of information languages. Report UU-CS-1996-55, Utrecht University: Information and Computing Sciences, December 1996.

[84] John-Jules Ch. Meyer. A different approach to deontic logic: Deontic logic views as a variant of dynamic logic. *Notre Dame Journal of Formal Logic*, 29(1):109–136, 1988.

[85] Milan Milanović, Dragan Gašević, Gerd Wagner, and Marek Hatala. Rule-enhanced business process modeling language for service choreographies. In Andy Schürr and Bran Selic, editors, *Model Driven Engineering Languages and Systems*, volume 5795 of *Lecture Notes in Computer Science*, pages 337–341. Springer Berlin / Heidelberg, 2009.

[86] Daniel Minoli. *Enterprise Architecture A to Z: Frameworks, Business Process Modeling, SOA, and Infrastructure Technology*. Auerbach Publishers Inc., 2008.

[87] Ugo Montanari, Marco Pistore, and Francesca Rossi. *Handbook of Graph Grammars and Computing by Graph Transformation*, volume 3, chapter Systems via Graph Transformations, pages 189–268. World Scientific Publishing Co. Pte. Ltd., 1999.

[88] Daniele Nardi and Ronald J. Brachman. An introduction to description logics. In Franz Baader, Diego Calvanese, Deborah McGuinness, Daniele Nardi, and Peter Patel-Schneider, editors, *The Description Logic Handbook: Theory, Implementation and Applications*, chapter 1, pages 5–44. Cambridge University Press, 2003.

[89] Christine Natschläger. Deontic BPMN. In Abdelkader Hameurlain, Stephen Liddle, Klaus-Dieter Schewe, and Xiaofang Zhou, editors, *Database and Expert Systems Applications*, volume 6861 of *Lecture Notes in Computer Science*, pages 264–278. Springer Berlin / Heidelberg, 2011.

[90] Christine Natschläger. Towards a BPMN 2.0 ontology. In *3rd International Workshop on the Business Process Model and Notation*, 2011.

[91] Christine Natschläger, Christa Illibauer, and Verena Geist. Decomposition and reusability in BPMN. In *22nd European Japanese Conference on Information Modelling and Knowledge Bases (EJC)*. to appear, 2012.

[92] Christine Natschläger, Christa Illibauer, Verena Geist, and Dagmar Auer. Identifying issues in modeling and model integration - a case study. Technical Report SCCH-TR-0948, Software Competence Center Hagenberg GmbH, June 2010.

[93] Christine Natschläger, Felix Kossak, and Klaus-Dieter Schewe. BPMN to Deontic BPMN: A trusted model transformation. *International Journal on Software and Systems Modeling*, submitted, 2012.

[94] Christine Natschläger and Klaus-Dieter Schewe. A flattening approach for attributed type graphs with inheritance in algebraic graph transformation. In Andrew Fish and Leen Lambers, editors, *Local Proceedings of GT-VMT (2012)*, pages 160–173. Electronic Communications of the EASST, 2012.

[95] Natalya Noy and Deborah McGuinness. Ontology development 101: A guide to creating your first ontology. Technical Report KSL-01-05 and SMI-2001-0880, Stanford Knowledge Systems Laboratory and Stanford Medical Informatics, 2001.

[96] OASIS. Web services business process execution language (WSBPEL) v. 2.0. http://www.oasis-open.org/committees/tc_home.php?wg_abbrev=wsbpel, April 2007.

[97] Bernd Oestereich. *Developing Software with UML: Object-Oriented Analysis and Design in Practice*. Pearson Education Ltd, 2 edition, 2002.

[98] OMG. Semantics of business vocabulary and business rules (SBVR), v1.0. http://www.omg.org/spec/SBVR/1.0, January 2008.

[99] OMG. Business process model and notation (BPMN) 2.0. http://www.omg.org/spec/BPMN/2.0, January 2011.

[100] OMG. Issues for mailing list of the business process model and notation 2.1 revision task force. http://www.omg.org/issues/bpmn2-rtf.html, November 2011. Visited: Nov. 2011.

[101] OMG. OMG Unified Modeling Language (OMG UML), Superstructure. http://www.omg.org/spec/UML/2.4.1/Superstructure/PDF/, August 2011. Version 2.4.1.

[102] Vineet Padmanabhan, Guido Governatori, Shazia Wasim Sadiq, Robert Colomb, and Antonino Rotolo. Process modelling: The deontic way. In *Proceedings of the 3rd Asia-Pacific conference on Conceptual Modelling - Volume 53*, APCCM '06, pages 75–84, Darlinghurst, Australia, 2006. Australian Computer Society, Inc.

[103] Jean-Claude Raoult. On graph rewritings. *Theoretical Computer Science*, 32:1–24, 1984.

[104] Lennart Åqvist. *Deontic Logic*, pages 147–264. Kluwer Academic, Dordrecht, 2002.

[105] Jan Recker. BPMN modeling - who, where, how and why. *BPTrends*, 5:1–8, 2008.

[106] Jan Recker, Marta Indulska, Michael Rosemann, and Peter Green. How good is BPMN really? Insights from theory and practice. In Jan Ljungberg and Magnus Andersson, editors, *14th European Conference on Information Systems*, Goeteborg, Sweden, 2006.

[107] Leila Ribeiro and Fernando Dotti. Linear-ordered graph grammars: Applications to distributed systems design. In Pierpaolo Degano, Rocco De Nicola, and José Meseguer, editors, *Concurrency, Graphs and Models*, volume 5065 of *Lecture Notes in Computer Science*, pages 133–150. Springer Berlin / Heidelberg, 2008.

[108] Alfonso Rodríguez, Eduardo Fernández-Medina, and Mario Piattini. A BPMN extension for the modeling of security requirements in business processes. *IEICE - Transactions on Information and Systems*, E90-D:745–752, March 2007.

[109] Nick Russell, Arthur H.M. ter Hofstede, David Edmond, and Wil M.P. van der Aalst. Workflow Resource Patterns. BETA Working Paper Series WP 127, Eindhoven University of Technology, Eindhoven, 2004.

[110] Nick Russell, Arthur H.M. ter Hofstede, Wil M.P. van der Aalst, and Natalya Mulyar. Workflow Control-Flow Patterns: A Revised View. Technical report, BPMcenter.org, 2006.

[111] Shazia Sadiq, Guido Governatori, and Kioumars Namiri. Modeling control objectives for business process compliance. In Gustavo Alonso, Peter Dadam, and Michael Rosemann, editors, *Business Process Management*, volume 4714 of *Lecture Notes in Computer Science*, pages 149–164. Springer Berlin / Heidelberg, 2007.

[112] August-Wilhelm Scheer. *ARIS – Business Process Frameworks*. Springer Berlin / Heidelberg, 3 edition, 1999.

[113] August-Wilhelm Scheer. *ARIS – Business Process Modeling*. Springer Berlin / Heidelberg, 3 edition, 2000.

[114] August-Wilhelm Scheer, Oliver Thomas, and Otmar Adam. Process modeling using event-driven process chains. In Marlon Dumas, Wil M.P. van der Aalst, and Arthur H.M. ter Hofstede, editors, *Process-Aware Information Systems: Bridging People and Software through Process Technology*, chapter 6, pages 119–146. John Wiley & Sons, Inc., 2005.

[115] Klaus-Dieter Schewe and Bernhard Thalheim. The co-design approach to web information systems development. *International Journal of Web Information Systems (IJWIS)*, 1(1):5–14, 2005.

[116] Klaus-Dieter Schewe and Bernhard Thalheim. Conceptual modelling of web information systems. *Data & Knowledge Engineering*, 54(2):147–188, August 2005.

[117] Klaus-Dieter Schewe, Bernhard Thalheim, and Roland Kaschek. A deontic logic for group-oriented web information systems. In Fernand Feltz, Andreas Oberweis, and Benoît Otjacques, editors, *Informationssysteme im E-Business und E-Government (EMISA)*, volume 56 of *LNI*, pages 107–116. GI, 2004.

[118] Bruce Silver. *BPMN Method & Style*. Cody-Cassidy Press, 2009.

[119] Timothy J. Smiley. Relative necessity. *J. Symbolic Logic*, 28:113–134, 1963.

[120] School of Medicine Stanford University. Protégé. `http://protege.stanford.edu`, November 2011. Visited: Nov. 2011.

[121] Gabriele Taentzer. AGG: A tool environment for algebraic graph transformation. In *Applications of Graph Transformations with Industrial Relevance (AGTIVE)*, Lecture Notes in Computer Science, pages 481–488. Springer-Verlag, 2000.

[122] Gabriele Taentzer. AGG: A graph transformation environment for modeling and validation of software. In John Pfaltz, Manfred Nagl, and Boris Böhlen, editors, *In: Applications of Graph Transformations with Industrial Relevance (AGTIVE)*, volume 3062 of *Lecture Notes in Computer Science*, pages 446–453. Springer Berlin / Heidelberg, 2004.

[123] Gabriele Taentzer and Arend Rensink. Ensuring structural constraints in graph-based models with type inheritance. In M. Cerioli, editor, *Fundamental Approaches to Software Engineering*, volume 3442 of *Lecture Notes in Computer Science*, pages 64–79. Springer-Verlag, 2005.

[124] Kaijun Tan, Jason Crampton, and Carl A. Gunter. The consistency of task-based authorization constraints in workflow systems. In *Proceedings of the 17th IEEE workshop on Computer Security Foundations*, pages 155–169, Washington, DC, USA, 2004. IEEE Computer Society.

[125] School of Computer Science University of Manchester. FaCT++. `http://owl.man.ac.uk/factplusplus`, November 2011. Visited: Nov. 2011.

[126] Department of Computer Science University of Oxford. HermiT 1.3.5. `http://hermit-reasoner.com`, November 2011. Visited: Nov. 2011.

[127] Wil M.P. van der Aalst. Workflow verification: Finding control-flow errors using Petri-net-based techniques. In Wil van der Aalst, Jörg Desel, and Andreas Oberweis, editors, *Business Process Management*, volume 1806 of *Lecture Notes in Computer Science*, pages 19–128. Springer Berlin / Heidelberg, 2000.

[128] Wil M.P. van der Aalst and Arthur H.M. ter Hofstede. Workflow patterns homepage. `http://www.workflowpatterns.com`, July 2011.

[129] Wil M.P. van der Aalst, Arthur H.M. ter Hofstede, Bartek Kiepuszewski, and Alistair P. Barros. Workflow patterns. *Distributed and Parallel Databases*, 14:5–51, 2003.

[130] Dániel Varró, Szilvia Varró-Gyapay, Hartmut Ehrig, Ulrike Prange, and Gabriele Taentzer. Termination analysis of model transformations by Petri nets. In Andrea Corradini, Hartmut Ehrig, Ugo Montanari, Leila Ribeiro, and Grzegorz Rozenberg, editors, *Graph Transformations*, volume 4178 of *Lecture Notes in Computer Science*, pages 260–274. Springer Berlin / Heidelberg, 2006.

[131] Georg Henrik von Wright. Deontic logic. *Mind*, 60(237):1–15, 1951.

[132] Georg Henrik von Wright. A note on deontic logic and derived obligation. *Mind*, 65:507–509, 1956.

[133] Georg Henrik von Wright. *Deontic Logic and the Theory of Conditions*, chapter 7, pages 159–177. D.Reidel Publishing Company, 1971.

[134] World Wide Web Consortium (W3C). OWL 2 Web Ontology Language Primer: W3C Recommendation. `http://www.w3.org/2009/pdf/REC-owl2-primer-20091027.pdf`, October 2009.

[135] Hans Weigand, Egon Verharen, and Frank Dignum. Interoperable transactions in business models – a structured approach. In Panos Constantopoulos, John Mylopoulos, and Yannis Vassiliou, editors, *Advanced Information Systems Engineering*, volume 1080 of *Lecture Notes in Computer Science*, pages 193–209. Springer Berlin / Heidelberg, 1996.

[136] Stephen A. White. Process Modeling Notations and Workflow Patterns. www.bptrends.com, March 2004.

[137] Stephen A. White and Derek Miers. *BPMN Modeling and Reference Guide: Understanding and Using BPMN*. Future Strategies Inc., 2008.

[138] Roel Wieringa and John-Jules Meyer. Applications of deontic logic in computer science: A concise overview. In *Deontic Logic in Computer Science: Normative System Specification*, pages 17–40. John Wiley & Sons, 1993.

[139] Petia Wohed, Wil M.P. van der Aalst, Marlon Dumas, Arthur H.M. ter Hofstede, and Nick Russell. On the suitability of BPMN for business process modelling. In Schahram Dustdar, José Luiz Fiadeiro, and Amit P. Sheth, editors, *Business Process Management*, volume 4102 of *Lecture Notes in Computer Science*, pages 161–176. Springer, 2006.

[140] Christian Wolter and Andreas Schaad. Modeling of task-based authorization constraints in BPMN. In Gustavo Alonso, Peter Dadam, and Michael Rosemann, editors, *Business Process Management*, volume 4714 of *Lecture Notes in Computer Science*, pages 64–79. Springer Berlin / Heidelberg, 2007.

[141] Peter Wong and Jeremy Gibbons. A process semantics for BPMN. In Shaoying Liu, Tom Maibaum, and Keijiro Araki, editors, *Formal Methods and Software Engineering*, volume 5256 of *Lecture Notes in Computer Science*, pages 355–374. Springer Berlin / Heidelberg, 2008.

[142] Michael Wooldridge. *An Introduction to MultiAgent Systems*. John Wiley & Sons Ltd, 2 edition, 2009.

[143] John A. Zachman. A framework for information systems architecture. *IBM Systems Journal*, 26(3):267–292, 1987.

[144] Michael zur Muehlen. BPM research forums - process modeling - BPMN XPDL OWL, ontologies. www.bpm-research.com/forum/index.php?showtopic=502, June 2009. Visited: Nov. 2011.

Curriculum Vitae

Personal Information

Name	Christine Natschläger-Carpella
Date of birth	December 31st, 1982
Place of birth	Linz, Austria
Nationality	Austria

Education

2009 - 2012	Doctoral Studies in Technical Sciences, Institute for Application Oriented Knowledge Processing, Johannes Kepler University, Linz
2007 - 2009	Master Studies in Information Engineering & -Management, University of Applied Sciences, Hagenberg
2001 - 2005	Diploma Studies in Softw. Engineering for Medical Purposes, University of Applied Sciences, Hagenberg
1993 - 2001	Secondary School with focus on Natural Sciences, Realgymnasium Peuerbachstrasse, Linz

Professional Experience

2004 -	Industrial Researcher at Software Competence Center Hagenberg GmbH (SCCH), Hagenberg
2003 - 2004	Tutor at University of Applied Sciences, Hagenberg
2001 - 2002	Independent Contractor at MC Marketing GmbH, Linz
2001 - 2001	Independent Contractor at Time4Team GmbH, Linz

Publications

V. Geist, C. Natschläger, and D. Draheim: Integrated Framework for Seamless Modeling of Business and Technical Aspects in Process-Oriented Enterprise Applications. International Journal of Software Engineering and Knowledge Engineering (IJSEKE) (to appear), World Scientific, 2012.

C. Natschläger and K.-D. Schewe: A Flattening Approach for Attributed Type Graphs with Inheritance in Algebraic Graph Transformation. In A. Fish, L. Lambers (editors). Local Proceedings of GT-VMT 2012, pages 160-173, Electronic Communications of the EASST, Tallinn, 2012.

C. Natschläger: Towards a BPMN 2.0 Ontology. In R. Dijkman, J. Hofstetter, J. Koehler (editors). Business Process Model and Notation, Lecture Notes in Business Information Processing, pages 1-15, Springer, Luzern, 2011.

C. Natschläger: Deontic BPMN. In A. Hameurlain, S. Liddle, K.-D. Schewe, and X. Zhou (editors). Database and Expert Systems Applications, Lecture Notes in Computer Science, volume 6861, pages 264-278, Springer, Toulouse, 2011.

C. Natschläger, C. Illibauer, V. Geist, and D. Auer: Identifying Issues in Modeling and Model Integration – A Case Study. Technical Report, SCCH-TR-0948, Software Competence Center Hagenberg GmbH, 2010.

C. Natschläger and T. Kopetzky: Classifying and Resolving Unique Constraint Violations during Synchronization Processes. Proceedings of the 2nd International Symposium in Logistics and Industrial Informatics (LINDI), pages 160-165, eXpress Conference Publishing, Linz, 2009.

C. Natschläger: Objektbasierte Synchronisation in .NET – Betriebswirtschaftliche Analyse und technische Entwicklung einer mobilen Anwendung mit Synchronisation von Datenobjekten in .NET. Master Thesis at the University of Applied Sciences, Hagenberg, 2009.

D. Draheim and C. Natschläger: A Context-Oriented Synchronization Approach. Electronic Proceedings of the 2nd International Workshop in Personalized Access, Profile Management, and Context Awarness: Databases (PersDB 2008) in conjunction with the 34th VLDB confercence, pages 20-27, Auckland, 2008.

C. Natschläger: Design und Implementierung eines Konzeptes zur Synchronisation von mobilen Clients mit .NET-Technologien. Diploma Thesis at the University of Applied Sciences, Hagenberg, 2005.